THE TWO FACES OF MANAGEMENT

THE TWO FACES OF MANAGEMENT

An American Approach to Leadership in Business and Politics

Joseph L. Bower

HOUGHTON MIFFLIN COMPANY · BOSTON

Library of Congress Cataloging in Publication Data

Bower, Joseph L.
  The two faces of management.

  Includes bibliographical references and index.
  1. Industry and state—United States. 2. Business
and politics—United States. 3. Industrial management—
United States. 4. United States—Politics and government—1981-   . I. Title.
HD3616.U46B68   1983   658.4'00973   83-141
ISBN 0-395-33119-6

Printed in the United States of America

V 10 9 8 7 6 5 4 3

For my parents

Contents

Preface   ix

1 The Wisdom of Difference   1

2 Technocratic Management versus Political
   Management   13

3 Technocratic Management Systems at Work   46

4 Political Management Systems at Work   67

5 The President: Top Manager of a Political
   System   86

6 Contact Sport: When Political and Technocratic
   Managers Meet   114

7 Managers and Wizards   166

8 The United States Isn't a Company, It's Not Even
   Japan   197

9 Small May Be Beautiful, but Local Works   218

10 Who Leads?   256

Notes   277

Index   293

Preface

At Harvard University we have a School of Business Administration dating back to 1908 and a Kennedy School of Government born sixty years later. I joined the faculty of the former in 1963, working with the Business Policy course under the leadership of Kenneth R. Andrews and C. Roland Christensen. There I had a chance to study the general management problems of very large corporations. In 1966 I joined a study group at the Littauer Center for Public Administration led by Ernest May and Richard Neustadt that would eventually become a central piece of the faculty of the new Kennedy School of Government. The present dean, Graham Allison, began his thesis from his notes of the group's discussion of the Cuban missile crisis. In that group I learned that there was no real understanding of what general management meant in government. In fact it might mean nothing.

During the 1970s I had substantial opportunity while walking back and forth across "the river" to contemplate the differences between the two schools and their constituencies. Neustadt, Phil Heymann, Mark Moore, and I tried to create a curriculum that would reflect the peculiar tasks of management in the public sector. On the "other side" I worked with those in the Business Policy course and those considering the problems of business, government, and the international economy — especially Bruce R. Scott, George C. Lodge, and John W. Rosenblum. Later we were joined by J. Ronald Fox and Thomas McCraw.

It was quite extraordinary: at the Business School we focused on the international economy, the threat of Japan, and the collapse of U.S. competitiveness. From a company perspective we considered the dilemma of sustainable growth in the turbulent 1970s. At the Kennedy School we worried about how to spend the money needed by the many new domestic agencies created by Lyndon Johnson and enhanced by Richard Nixon. When international issues were considered, they were "foreign policy," primarily military force posture. Trying to understand this gap in perspective, Richard Neustadt and I began a dialogue exploring the differences between public and private management that is still under way.

Somehow the great differences observed cannot be explained in terms of business and government. Too many of the management problems are the same. Instead, the key differences have to do with the most cherished values of those who are involved, not the form of ownership. The realization that they had to do with politics and management, or what I eventually realized were the two faces of modern management, led to this book.

My acknowledgments, therefore, are very numerous. Basically I am indebted to both faculties. Recognizing that I will not mention many who deserve it, let me thank those who read the manuscript and offered comments: Kenneth Andrews, Joseph Auerbach, Joseph Badaracco, C. Roland Christensen, Raymond Corey, John T. Dunlop, J. Ronald Fox, George C. Lodge, Richard E. Neustadt, Robert Reich, Eric Rhenman (of SIAR), Ezra Vogel, Martha Weinberg (of MIT), Frank Weil (of Ginsburg, Feldman, Weil and Bress), and Abraham Zaleznik. John McArthur, Harvard Business School's dean, deserves thanks because he stimulated me to write a book on this subject and supported an extensive program of study of business and government at the Business School. I should also mention Austin Olney, Gerard Van der Leun, Arthur Hepner, and Sarah Flynn at Houghton Mifflin. They have substantially revised my appreciation of the art of editing. Darlene Indorato typed the text and guarded the original of the manuscript. Finally, my wife, Nancy, dealt graciously with the impact of this project on our lives already full with her research and my teaching.

This book, in other words, could not have appeared without the contributions of others. As in management, authorship is shared, but — as in politics — the buck stops here.

THE TWO FACES OF MANAGEMENT

1 The Wisdom of Difference

"BUSINESS AND GOVERNMENT must cooperate."
"We need to establish a better relationship between business and government."
"Government and business require a clearer understanding of national interests."

These pleas are legion in publications as varied as the *New Statesman, Fortune,* the *New York Times,* the *Harvard Business Review, The New Yorker, Business Week,* the *New Republic,* and *Forbes.*

Heads nod in assent, befuddlement, and sleep. Still, what do such slogans mean in our present society? What is "business" and what is "government"? IBM and Joe's Community Store in the south part of Lincoln, Massachusetts, where I live, are both businesses. The latter differs little from the fabled Phoenician merchants or Ming shopkeepers, whereas the former represents the cutting edge of high technology and modern entrepreneurship and management. The United States Congress and the Lincoln Town Meeting are both government legislative bodies. One manages a $3 trillion economy through a network of committees in two houses of elected representatives, while the other, consisting of more than half the eligible citizens gathered in one auditorium, reviews and approves a $3 million budget.

In bureaus of the federal government men and women who are experts or outstanding leaders in their fields work at stable professional careers. Except that they are often (but not always) lower paid than private counterparts, they are indistinguishable from managers and staff in private companies. The National Oceanic and Atmospheric Administration (NOAA) is an example. Thirty thousand–odd men and women work there in a reasonably conventional fashion to provide some of the best meteorological service in the world. Timely and accurate forecasts being worth billions to agriculture, shipping, and air carriers, NOAA gets on fine with business.

Yet in other sectors of government, men and women make utterly outrageous statements about business that they know to be untrue because they also know the immediate consequence of such utterances will be headlines that will increase public awareness of both the speaker and the issue. Agreements solemnly made by an official of the administration can be and are abrogated by a successor who happens to be appointed by another political party. On some days there is no formal authorization to pay the salaries of our federal employees. On November 24, 1981, the "government" was sent home because President Ronald Reagan was fighting with the House of Representatives about the budget.

The consequences of the business/government relationship affect all American citizens and a goodly part of the world. There must be a better diagnosis of the problem than offhand references to two vague abstractions. We must ask ourselves why we can't manage better. It does no good to yearn for a better understanding to just happen, like first love. We must seek it out.

The popular answer is to call for an "industrial policy." As we don't have one, this is the beginning of wisdom. A number of sensible people have demanded changes in our system of government so that this or that agency or institution can lead, guide, plan, or manage a more effective use of the nation's economic resources. Citing the often chaotic structure of government, these voices have called for new, more coordinated restructuring of our traditional institutions.

At the same time, paradoxically, we have elected a president and many sensible legislators who offer a program dedicated to "getting the government off the backs of the people." Rather than a more *effective* government, they envision economic progress through *less* government.

How can it be that sensible people hold such widely differing views of the same phenomenon? The answer, it turns out, lies in a confusion buried deeply in the language we are accustomed to use when discussing public policy. For myriad reasons, we habitually underscore the difference between public and private ownership — and name these two concepts "government" and "business." This is usually false. What we are most often talking about are two different ways of managing affairs. One is political. We use political management to distribute costs and benefits of our society's activities so that we can also enjoy stability and a sense of legitimacy. The other is a very different kind of management, which we can properly call technocratic. We use it in order to achieve a higher degree of efficiency in domains where we are less concerned with equity or freedom.

These two different systems are commonly used in government and business. Much of the confusion in the present debate results from our forgetting why.

In a profound sense, the United States is an unmanaged society. Yet we have political leadership. Our compelling present need is to understand how to use the two different systems of management to improve the performance of the society while preserving the integrity and character of our institutions.

The Basic Dilemma

As we debate the wisdom of various policies proffered as means to improve our domestic and international positions, we confront two fundamental problems. The diagnoses are almost always partial and oversimplified, and the prescriptions are so abstract that they do not relate persuasively with the diagnosed symptoms.

The sickness of the economy is easy to see. So far, the 1980s have been hard times. People are worried by inflation and unemployment. Double-digit interest rates have prevented many new families from buying homes and at the same time reduced the liquidity of most Americans' primary investment. The news from overseas makes things look worse. Forty million people were unemployed in the Western industrialized nations in the winter of 1982. My neighbor who speaks 1960s slang says the economy is a "bummer." Big businesses complain that government has burdened them with its interference, but the automobile, steel, textile, and shoe industries — accounting for 17 percent of 1981 U.S. employment[1] — seek government protection and talk longingly of the nonadversary relationship between business and government in Japan. At the same time anti-Japanese rhetoric mounts.

Politicians of every ideology focus on the economy. Even those who have made a practice of attacking business find that in a weak economy jobs for their constituents must be provided by private firms because the tax revenues to support more government employment are too unpopular. And worse still, for reasons most cannot fathom, the deficit is already so high that more borrowing seems unwise.

At the same time, we have rediscovered that we are not one nation but, regionally speaking, several. The North Central states that traditionally housed heavy industry have become the target of competition in trade from Europe and Japan. High technology has kept employment in New England relatively high, and energy development on top of high tech has kept the Southwest booming. Agriculture kept the Midwest and South strong until two years of high interest rates and subsidized European competition led even the strongest of U.S. sectors to falter. Some measure of regional difference is provided by the voting patterns in presidential elections. West of the Mississippi, Democrats are much harder to find.

Similar divergences can be found in the attitude and behavior of social groupings. Somewhere between 1950 and 1980 the politics of equal opportunity shifted toward the politics of entitlement to equal outcome. Congressional politics that had been developed to compromise regional and industrial differences were now turned to deal with differences in sex, age, physical condition, and national origin. One group after another used the political tactics of the civil rights movement to assert its constitutional right to a piece of the pie. At this moment we can observe the beneficiaries of Social Security, Medicare, and veterans' pensions asserting their rights to indexed benefits that have the potential, as they increase, to bankrupt the U.S. economy.

Ronald Reagan, the president we elected to balance the budget, supports policies that are creating unbelievable deficits. Increased defense spending on top of indexed benefits to the middle class has dwarfed the spending cuts he has managed.

George McGovern, the liberal champion of income support programs, is alleged to have said, "I knew I would lose my 1980 Senate race when two elderly women approached me in a supermarket and told me that I had lost touch with my constituents. When they got to the cash register, they paid with food stamps." One wonders how those ladies are faring today.

None of this is surprising. The greatest transfer of wealth in history is under way from the industrial West and Japan to the oil-rich nations of OPEC. Only industrial enterprise can create the wealth we need to pay for our oil. Everywhere people seek some arrangement of business and government, private and public, that will give us a healthy, productive, competitive economy that provides good jobs and is congruent with society's other needs. Thus the governments of all nations have become concerned with the way in which business is managed.

A serious complication is the relative success that Japan, Taiwan, Hong Kong, Singapore, and Korea have had in developing powerful export-driven economies. Their rapidly growing share of world markets has provided them the earnings to pay for oil. Yet these may be "bicycle" economies, staying upright only as long as they move forward rapidly. The recession in the industrial West has led one nation after another to seek ways to drive out the attractive competition from the East. Threatened by the potential loss of exports needed to pay for the imports they require for survival, some countries have become more aggressive. Trade wars appear imminent.

In principle, the United States ought to be above the battle. Blessed with rich resources of energy and food, possessing strong companies and leading universities, it should be able to compete effectively on the world scene and still provide some assistance for the resource-poor underdeveloped nations.

The reality is that several of our most important industries are in trouble as measured by the share of the U.S. market taken by imports and the staggering losses recorded by the constituent companies. Even General Motors lost money on its automotive operations in 1980 and 1981 ($984 million and $15 million, respectively).

Moreover, business in the United States has been under political attack. The multinational oil companies have been particularly tempting targets, but the 1960s made ITT a dirty word. And during the very years that imports were becoming a concern, various agencies of the government brought suit against major companies such as Ford, Kodak, AT&T, and IBM.

Worse still, in areas where there are major problems with the promise of clear solutions, we seem paralyzed. We cannot develop a coherent energy policy. We need coal, for example, but we cannot agree how it shall be mined or how it shall be transported. Nor can we agree where the deep harbors will be constructed for shipment to coal-hungry Europe. We need good schools, but we cannot agree how to fund them or how to balance the teaching of life science and moral values.

Why is it that the United States has these problems in making plans and implementing decisions on major economic questions? We have capable managers, politicians, and economists. Why is there so little progress?

A Confusion of Means

When we pledge allegiance, it is to the republic of the United States of America, "one nation, indivisible, with liberty and justice for all." A careful consideration of these goals reveals that except for indivisibility, they are tests of the means of government. While this represents a brilliant choice of political philosophy, it also leaves a great deal of room for disagreement about the specifics of national purpose and arrangements for management. Some of the unresolved differences were recognized when the Constitution was written and are not settled today. We still seek free trade in agriculture while trying to protect our weaker manufacturers. The Civil War did not settle the problem.

The problems we face have historical, institutional, and ideological sources. The conflicts and inconsistencies were always present. They were merely hidden by the economic boom of the post–World War II period and the absence of serious competition from the economies of other nations.

The questions about how we will manage our resources are also ancient. For example, recently a jury, no members of which had graduated from high school, heard the trial of the largest private antitrust case in history, *Memorex* v. *International Business Machines Corporation.* The eleven-week trial ended with a hung jury. After a survey, the judge found that the jury had not understood the evidence presented. Consider also that until the Reagan administration dropped the government's thirteen-year-old case against IBM in 1982, the case was being tried by a judge with no technical or economic background whom both sides privately agreed was incompetent. Contrast Japan, where the structure of the computer industry has been monitored and supported by the most talented parts of the government and includes a series of industry-government joint ventures. Why in the United States do we do what we do?

Much of the debate and action concerning industrial policy in the United States has been left to lawyers. Is it sensible today for us to have a modern industry shaped by two teams of lawyers debating whether a company's behavior violates some law drafted to please farmers and small businessmen in the nineteenth century? Lawyers usually know very little about the complexities of the industry, firms, or management, but guided by the belief that truth will emerge from the adversary process, they have plunged ahead. When they have paused to seek conceptual guidance, they have turned to economists who have paid even less heed to industry, firms, and management. In economic journals the debate about firms is often on the order of "If I were a firm, here's how I would behave." On the basis of such opinions we have constructed the economic rationalization for our antitrust laws. Armed with these laws, we attack firms such as IBM, Xerox, and Kodak, firms that lead the United States not only in technology but in important noneconomic areas such as desegregation, worker safety, and broad contribution to the community. If the government seeks these objectives, why does it prosecute the best achievers?

The answer in part is that there is no government, in the sense of a related set of organizations seeking to achieve a common purpose. Instead we have a network of autonomous institutions sharing power in a staggering variety of arrangements. The example of the IBM antitrust cases points in the direction of the appropriate analysis.

Many countries would never think of using the courts to manage industry structure. What can we find out if we focus analysis carefully on the systems we use to manage ourselves, rather than on whether they are owned privately or by the government? In fact, a great deal — for there has been extensive study of different arrangements for management. The means we use to achieve liberty and justice turn out to be awkward mechanisms at best for generating the wealth we seek to support our high national standard of living. The managers who deal with issues of equity and justice are seldom well equipped to administer efficiently and effectively. In the extreme those managing political systems speak of administrators with contempt: "All he or she cares about is the budget." And in turn comes the equally contemptuous reply, "All he or she cares about is the next election." Although we need both kinds of managers to run the country and sometimes even the same institution, technocratic and political managers tend to have different values and language and often approach each other with contempt.

When one pauses to ask one or the other sort of manager whether representative democracy or large-scale bureaucracy might not call for precisely the kind of behavior being critiqued, the answer is almost always "Well, if you put it that way, I suppose so, but . . ." The respondent goes on to a deeper and richer description of the problem in question, usually involving inappropriate behavior in a specific instance.

Two Systems of Management for Two Different Problems

Actually, in discussions with both kinds of managers it is possible to establish the need for organizations that are politically responsive or technocratically effective. The main difficulty is that managers whose principal responsibility is running one sort of institution fail to understand the other sort. Using parochial standards for evaluation, the other fails. Oddly enough, political and technocratic managers think that the job they don't understand is easy. They are encouraged in this belief by media that treat both kinds of management as obvious after the fact and focus on whatever friction develops between the two. Economists further confuse the matter by speaking as if their mathematical models describe accurately the work of both sorts of managers.

The purpose of this book is to help political and technocratic executives by laying out how both systems of management operate, how they work best together, and what changes in approach might be desirable. The categories turn out to be ideal types — most management jobs have both technocratic and political dimensions — but in the first chapters it is useful to emphasize differences in order to comprehend the magnitude of the gap between some of our institutions.

Under this view, there are few villains among the actors. Today, responsible political officials must deal with high-stake interdependent problems, in public view and with very little time. Using the standards of technocratic managers who deal with lower-stake issues, over long periods of time, often in private, the task of the political manager is impossibly difficult.

Not surprisingly, political and technocratic managers go at their problems in somewhat different ways. They think differently. They are trained differently; often their home, background, and experience are different. Unlike much of the rest of the world, whose leaders are schooled together and interrelated socially, our business and government leadership remain strangers and adversaries in a wide range of activities.

In other fields, where there are great differences in background, training, and perspective, we are accustomed to conflict. We understand the problems of the Middle East in these terms, as we do C. P. Snow's "two cultures" of science and politics.

In the field of science policy, we have developed mechanisms for bringing scientists into effective working relationships with politicians. The results are far from perfect, but the National Research Council, the National Academy of Sciences, the National Bureau of Standards, the House Science and Technology Committee, and the office of the president's science adviser all represent institutions designed to help physical and biological scientists contribute to the making of public policy. Don K. Price, a long-time student of U.S. governments, has even found it useful to speak of the "scientific estate."

In economic and public policy it might look as if we have done the same thing by using economists. But unlike physical scientists, economists — with rare exceptions — do not study the workings of the economy; they study economics. Somewhat like conflicting monastic orders, the monetarists and the Keynesians fight their battles within the walls of universities, using relatively crude macroeconomic series as data. Except in their academic politics, where they can be xenophobic, economists tend to represent a dispassionate system of belief that all economic activity can be summarized by quantities and prices, which by simple mathematics can be converted to models that will predict economic behavior. Their assumptions violate most of what we know about industries, firms, and managers, but economists do not usually test their models with observations of firms or consumers. Milton Friedman, for example, argues that theory is better when it doesn't correspond to complex reality.[2] The historian Thomas McCraw has called the fragmented economy about which economists theorize "peripheral," and shown that the giant industrial complexes they attack as imperfectly competitive constitute the "core" of any modern economy.[3]

Once we examine the way our managers of public and private institutions relate to each other, it is easier to see why their conflicts are often unproductive. The politically managed parts of the U.S. federal government, for example, turn out to be very imperfect mechanisms to use for devising a coherent long-term policy for industry. At the same time, using the framework for analysis proposed here, it is apparent that many problems have local boundaries. Within a smaller arena, contesting groups can often resolve their differences after they take the time to agree on the facts. In this process, both managers and politicians have valid and important roles that need to be carried out effectively and responsibly. Difficulties begin to develop when either group fails and the local problem is elevated. Elevation leads inexorably to politicization. To avoid this trap, new kinds of mechanisms have been devised by local managers and politicians to cope with their problems. To the extent that they succeed, the role of federal activity can be better defined.

But these conclusions follow from a careful examination of what it means to manage, and what we seek from politics. It is surprising how much we can learn from analysis of the remarkably different kinds of tasks that face people we casually think of as part of the general class of managers. In turn, these findings imply important changes in the way we observe and encourage the interactions of politicians and management.

2 Technocratic Management versus Political Management

ANYONE WHO HAS PLAYED bridge or tennis with a spouse is aware of the pressures generated by cooperative efforts in competitive settings. The central ingredient in developing a more realistic understanding of the relationship of business to the state is knowing that similar consequences follow from the pervasive use of large organizations to accomplish most of our objectives. Although we talk about policy as if it were only technical and economic issues that mattered, the range of possible outcomes is limited by the capabilities of the groups that pursue them. These capabilities are limited in turn by the effectiveness with which the group has managed to take advantage of individual energies and resources.

Organizations Are Inevitable

Except for a limited set of intellectual and artistic activities, all important achievements are accomplished through organizations. The divisions of American manufacturing corporations may seem reluctant to adopt conservation measures quickly; our school systems seem mired in parochial, outdated practices; and Congress appears paralyzed by its fragmentation. But as the Pulitzer Prize–winning historian Alfred Chandler, Jr., has shown, the allocation of various tasks to separate divisions was the organizational tool that facilitated the effective corporate response to the opportunities for growth in the first half of this century. In the same sense, highly decentralized, local schools have permitted a diversified response to the needs of heterogeneous states and localities. Finally, a committee system of some sort is the only imaginable way that an elected legislature of 435 congressmen and 100 senators can carry out the work of the lawmaking, budgeting, taxing, and oversight that society requires.

If organizations are inevitable, they are also costly. Just as the white line down the street reduces an individual's available driving space by 50 percent, so too do particular organizations constrain how we may use our resources. In the same ways that bricklayers may object to pipe fitters opening a hole in a brick wall, separate U.S. Army, Navy, and Air Force goals and training affect the policy and conduct of war. And in universities, cross-departmental exercises are as hard to plan and implement as joint service programs such as the TFX aircraft. Economics departments fight political science departments as fiercely as the Navy fights the Air Force. Organizations are not lifeless collections of resources. They have direction and impetus independent of their members.

This is not the same point as is often made when historians or journalists offer an "organizational interpretation" of a sequence of events that emphasizes bureaucratic rivalry. Much more important is the idea that organization is not just a tool of policy. Organization is also the mechanism by which policy is developed and implemented. In the jargon of business, not only must structure serve strategy; structure also shapes strategy by molding the perspective of both those who generate options and those who commit resources to a few selected proposals. There has to be a Navy before you get a Navy point of view.

Organizations come into being because individuals want to do something that they cannot accomplish acting alone. They agree to contribute effort cooperatively, discuss their objective, and communicate about their work. It's exactly what happens when a car gets stuck in the mud or snow. People gather to help. They arrange themselves around the car and they rock it together, often warning an inexperienced driver not to spin the wheels.

Most theories of organization are constructed around these basic elements — cooperation, goals, and communication — undoubtedly because Chester Barnard formulated his classic diagnosis of organization management in these terms.[1] In order to understand how to manage or influence organizations, we need to know why organization members contribute effort cooperatively, how goals are chosen, and how information is disseminated and used. This point may seem obvious, but we behave constantly as if it is not true. Serious discussion of economic policy is carried on with a negligible understanding of how the institutions of business and government actually operate. Serious cooks have a better understanding of the physics and chemistry of a soufflé than many policymakers have of the workings of the economy.

In 1981, the Reagan tax cut proposals were put forward on the basis of a quasi-mystical belief in the anticipated response of savings and investment to those changes. It had to be sheer belief because macroeconomic studies of investment are notoriously uncertain. There are as yet no careful studies of how either savings or investment respond to specific government action. A large firm does not invest without plans. What sorts of plans will a firm have drawn up in the face of the economic turmoil of the 1980s? Are these the kinds of investments that the president's advisers are seeking? Does it help the problem of international competitiveness or domestic employment if Standard Oil of California buys AMAX, the great mining firm? Or if U.S. Steel buys Marathon Oil?

Oddly enough, it is not that scholars and practitioners have not studied organizations and management. They have. But they have not linked their understanding to the problems of policy and politics. To do this it is not necessary to survey all organization and management theory. Two very basic notions provide all we need to develop an understanding: what requirements organizations must satisfy in order to function; and how the work of an executive accomplishes those functions through the setting of goals, the design of organization, and administrative activity. These notions help us to see the dramatic differences that exist as different kinds of business and government managers go about their work.

The Foundations of Organizations: Purpose, Careers, and Systems

Three ideas are critical to an understanding of how organizations work:

1. Organizations do not work unless members are willing to contribute effort. There must be inducements. Authority is grounded in the reasons that a member has chosen to contribute. There is an implicit contract.
2. If an organization is to function over long periods of time, its activities must generate the resources to provide inducements in exchange for contribution. As a matter of logic, if the common purpose that draws members together is long term, and if there are no other means for the members' physical and economic support, these inducements have to include life support or the money to acquire it.
3. The only way to measure whether an organization is effective is relative to the common purpose around which it is organized. The appropriateness of that purpose must then be assessed relative to the likelihood of success: is there an opportunity to succeed and does the organization have the required resources? Information must be organized to satisfy the need to measure results relative to purpose.

With these ideas in mind, we can begin to understand how to measure an organization's performance. On a regular basis organizations must generate a surplus; the size of the surplus can be compared with the

cost of inducements. In business this surplus is approximately measured by accounting profit; in a private university, by the level by which tuition and gifts exceed costs; in a voluntary organization, by the level of satisfaction with participation that induces future contributions. Witness the Republican party in Massachusetts, which seldom wins and has few members; it is therefore ineffective.

An effective organization is one that meets enough of the purposes common to the group of members so that they are willing to continue their contributions. An effective organization can be inefficient — for example, it could be argued on the basis of their behavior that a group of tightly unionized public employees is running the Massachusetts Bay Transit Authority for its own convenience at a staggering cost. In such an instance the group may have met its goal of being well paid for doing little. On the other hand, an efficient organization can be ineffective. It may achieve its goal at minimum cost but create no sustaining value. Thus the manufacturers of buggy whips disappeared.

The Work of Executives

The job of an executive in an organization involves managing the evolution of purpose, the recruitment of members, and the balancing of individual inducements with contribution so that the strength of the organization is adequate to its chosen task and the value of its work creates adequate wealth to maintain the organization. Executive responsibility in such circumstances involves a sense of fitness — finding a set of goals and policies that matches needs with resources and that satisfies individual and community standards of behavior. Farmers exploiting migrant labor may be efficient and effective, but on observing the process the community has often decided that the behavior is unacceptable. It may be legal for an organization to fire a worker six months before his pension vests, but many regard the practice as immoral — and their views will be reflected in the behavior of other company employees.

The subtlety of executive work is complicated by the fact that most of it is performed in groups or coalitions. Both informed observation and research show that in every organization there is a group of members whose views count most. This group is the executive core. In most small towns, it is the "town fathers" — a mixture of officials, ex-officials, and strong personalities — who lead in the management of town affairs. In Congress it is the "leadership"; in a company it is some sort of group, possibly including key outside directors; in a class of teen-age boys it is often the best athletes. To succeed, this executive core must maintain its social integrity while striving to achieve its substantive purpose. The goals of an organization are reflected in the social and political processes of this executive core. A chief executive must manage the balance of power within this group so that its goals are compatible with the available organizational resources while not excluding key members.

Lyndon Johnson provided an especially pithy example of this principle. When asked why he put up with the extraordinary nuisance of an elderly, cantankerous J. Edgar Hoover, he said, "Well, it's probably better to have him inside the tent pissing out than outside pissing in."[2]

In popular commentary, this sort of behavior is often described pejoratively as compromise, giving up a higher level of attainment in order to satisfy group pressure. But for a leader, the range of views in the executive core is critical. It tends to define the range of action open to the group. President Johnson apparently concluded that he gave up less accommodating Hoover's presence inside his administration than he would have to pay fighting him. He might have been wrong, but he was not compromising.

Managing the question of who is in the core is related to the question of whose views provide direction for the group. Often there is a considerable range of views, only some of which seem to be expressed. Others might be articulated if latent attitudes can be mobilized. Understanding and modifying the range of executive views constitutes an important part of the top manager's work. If an organization's purpose is defined by the ideas of its key members, then determining which members are key and how conflicts among them are resolved is not merely an organizational process. It is central to the determination of purpose.

Choosing a Goal Imagine a group of hikers setting out on a walk. How do they decide how far to go? Generally some seek more exercise than others. An obvious hypothesis is that the majority with the shortest walk in mind will make the decision. If there is no very strong-minded individual with a very long or very short walk in mind, the laziest majority will have its way.

Or imagine a company with a seven-member executive core debating trade-offs between profit and growth. One executive is ambitious, seeking high levels of both. The financial vice president is more cautious; he would like the growth but will be satisfied with high profit. Still another officer — whose group is participating in a rapidly growing market — wishes to grow rapidly to achieve a high market share even if it means sacrificing profit.

We can think about White House debates over the war in Vietnam during the Johnson administration in the same way. Opinion divided on the wisdom of military or political intervention. In his essay "How Could Vietnam Happen?" James Thomson suggests that those who opposed military escalation were gradually driven out of the executive core.[3] This caused severe problems when politics in the United States and the military situation in Vietnam required a withdrawal.

Often in management, goals for a group seem to come from outside in the form of a law or directive. But even after legislation is passed or a divisional charter is given, there is usually enormous leeway in the establishment of goals for the organization in question. An executive core might select many goals, or sets of objectives. So the key question in management theory becomes "What is a good goal?" Most approaches to organization theory duck this question by accepting the idea that goals are given by someone else. It is assumed that means and ends do not interact. Some commentators, especially Kenneth Andrews, sharpen the general manager's dilemma by noting that his task includes the *development*, as well as the implementation, of objectives. The selection of goals must be managed so that the core believes them to be feasible, moral, and appealing. Goals must attract cooperation and resources. Responsibility includes avoiding a charter doomed to failure. Andrews's concept of "strategy" is an elaborate argument on how to carry out the task of developing good goals.[4] Examples of the concept applied are dramatic in their diversity.

- Between 1955 and 1961 George Romney succeeded in saving American Motors's fortunes by reconceiving an out-of-date automobile as a "compact car" at that moment when a recessionary economy sought an alternative to "gas-guzzling dinosaurs." Romney had inadequate resources to compete with the Big Three — Ford, Chrysler, and General Motors. He could not change styles or bring out a new car. In fact, he had to drop models. By advertising the "compact car" he was able to put a positive face on what he had. The limited sales provided by the market for such a car were all he needed to survive.

- The Boston Symphony Orchestra thrives, despite revenues from concerts and records that are below costs, because its programs and its performance attract an audience that includes a few who are, because of the orchestra's excellence, willing to give from personal wealth to make up the deficit. In this case, the opposite of Romney, the ambitiousness of the goal — to be the best — attracts the resources to make it feasible.

- The Japanese government has managed to grow its economy very successfully by encouraging a cooperative network of banks, manufacturing giants, trading companies, and government agencies to use a highly trained, security-minded labor force to add increasingly competitive value to the raw materials Japan must import to improve her quality of life. Individual and organizational political and social freedom have, relative to the United States and Europe, been sacrificed so as to achieve a more efficient pattern of economic development despite a limited resource base.

- The Digital Equipment Corporation has managed to grow rapidly and prosperously in the face of the awesome market strength of IBM by using distributed data processing technology to serve customers in a way that provides high value while complementing rather than confronting the capability provided by IBM. Digital focused on serving the needs of limited groups of customers that did not require IBM's broad support, and initially satisfied those needs with an approach to technology that IBM would not want to imitate.

The generality of the concept of strategy has given it its enormous usefulness in researching and teaching public and private management. So far in these examples, however, nothing has been said about ownership, sources of power, or the rules and procedures of the executive core. That discussion is deferred to the next two chapters.

It is more interesting here to explore the problem of choosing a good goal. Because for millennia philosophers have unsuccessfully tried to provide a formula for this choice, there should be general agreement that there is none. More intriguing are the ways that have been found to manage the development of goals. Analyzing the efforts of effective and ineffective managers, academics and consultants have found the feasibility and desirability of goals to be approachable through *internal* tests that examine (1) the relative competence of the organization to pursue its objectives and (2) the consistency of policies chosen for that pursuit and *external* tests that examine (3) the value that the environment places on the activities, products, or services of the organization and (4) whether these factors will be able to attract resources in the future.

For example, when Howard Head set about manufacturing and marketing the first metal ski, he produced a standard, Model T-type product that had the effect of substantially improving the performance of the average or beginning skier. In fact, the skis were called "cheaters." The skis were marketed through specialty stores that were staffed with expert skiers who could, in effect, instruct and reassure the novice. Advertising reinforced both the seriousness and the status of the product, while high price provided further evidence of quality — as well as profits that attracted funds for expansion. In this instance (1) the product was simple enough for a small organization to make well and sell effectively; (2) the way it was made, priced, distributed, and advertised was consistent; and (3) large numbers of affluent customers appreciated the product and its price so that (4) future growth was sustainable.

In principle and fact there may be more than one set of feasible goals an organization can pursue. But, given the talents of the executive core, there is usually one strategy that fits the values and talents of that core better than others. At the end of the Second World War, General Motors was one of the country's largest producers of aircraft. Alfred Sloan, Jr., who was chief executive at the time, reported in his memoirs[5] that the executive committee concluded that although there might be a good business in aircraft, (1) it would require a research capability in which GM did not excel, and (2) it would not require the mass production and distribution at which GM did excel. The aircraft businesses were sold and the resources devoted to mass-market automotive businesses.

On the other hand, the set of goals that meets internal tests may not meet external tests. An organization may often want to do things beyond its capability. When the gap between ends and means is not recognized, we see failure. Thus, the Underwood Typewriter Company disappeared after its management and advisers chose to respond to IBM's electric typewriter by producing computers. And Howard Head failed when he tried to market engineered ski wear.

Choosing Core Executives   When a leader recognizes that the ends the core seeks are not consistent with the means available or the demands of the environment, he must alter the configurations of the executive group so that its talents are more realistic. He can do this in several ways.

By adding new people. When Thomas Watson, Jr., became IBM's chief executive officer, he inherited a superb commercial organization, but only an average (for the computer business) research capability. He hired a chief scientist from outside IBM and arranged for him to be situated both high and centrally in the IBM executive group.

By changing the training of people. In his first speech to a large group of management, William Sneath, then the new chief executive officer of Union Carbide, said that he would be the "last CEO of Carbide [who] did not have a wide range of international and product experience." The company proceeded to move people overseas and rotate staff through product management positions.

By changing the dominant coalition within the executive core so as to exploit latent capability. This type of change represents a shift in the balance of power. In a company that has been growing rapidly it may simply represent a newly apparent willingness to heed the cautions of the chief financial officer. In a firm becoming more international it may represent a stream of decisions freeing "Jean-Pierre's people" from policy restrictions imposed by domestic divisions, or building an overseas research facility, or funding a European product line.

To accomplish these shifts a general manager can draw on *personal* administrative skills and whatever administrative tools his organization possesses. Administrative skills are often invisible to those who have not considered the problem. Good managers are often persuasive in face-to-face encounters; they can run a meeting so that it has the outcome they had in mind; they know how to schedule activity so that learning or actions cumulate in desired directions; they know how to draw on the skills of other organization members and know which members have which skills. As well, they are not afraid of power. They can use it when they seek change.

Personal skills such as these have an impact when exercised and may be missed when not possessed by a leader, but they are not active when the leader does not use them. Administrative tools are different.

Choosing Administrative Tools: The Role of Structure and Systems   Life in organizations is substantially affected by a wide range of administrative systems such as agendas, budgets, career planning programs, compensation programs, long-range plans, measurement systems, and formal organization and associated job descriptions. These systems shape the routine of organizational life and the pace at which routine activities are performed. Most of the ways in which an individual member of an organization learns about the work expected of him are through these administrative systems. As such these systems represent powerful sources of managerial influence. They are tools of the general management craft.

But, unlike personal skills, administrative systems will shape behavior whether or not they are in the control of the general manager. Whether ideology or law determines the pattern of these systems, they are still the most persuasive influence on organizational behavior. It is the differences in the way managers behave when they can control these systems and when they cannot that are at the heart of the problems we are exploring.

Consider the case of William Ruckelshaus, appointed in November of 1970 to head the newly organized Environmental Protection Agency — a collection of pieces of other federal organizations assembled by executive order of President Richard M. Nixon to implement the new provisions of the Clean Air and Water Act of 1970. Ruckelshaus was a stranger to this agency, and promptly found himself attacked for "doing too little" by Nixon's rival Edmund Muskie, then chairman of the Senate Subcommittee on Environmental Pollution. Ruckelshaus's budget was also threatened by the very conservative congressman Jamie Whitten of Mississippi, who set the EPA's budget in the agriculture subcommittee of the House Appropriations Committee. With key staff positions unfilled, Ruckelshaus was unsure of the quality of his organization. He was nevertheless expected to take positions within one hundred twenty days of assuming office that would affect the future of the U.S. auto industry, the use of DDT by farmers and states, and the standards of clean air and water in the United States. The whole time he was subject to direct review by the press. Within twenty-eight months, regarded as a great success, he would be serving in another job elsewhere in the government.[6]

Consider one of the men who would tangle with Ruckelshaus's agency. In 1970 Henry Ford II, the chief executive of the Ford Motor Company, had been responsible for Ford since fighting his father's cronies for control of the company in 1948. The budget, personnel, and substantive policies of his company were demonstrably in his control. His task was to manage the evolution of the line of passenger cars and trucks so that in the face of competition from other such companies, Ford would remain economically healthy. In retrospect, he had had almost eight years available in which to respond to the shifts in energy cost and consumer preference he would be facing.

Both Ruckelshaus and Ford are managers, but their work is so different that it is easy to be confused. The power of the purse, the power to hire and fire, the ability to operate out of the corrosive glare of the press, the ability to limit objectives so that they can be achieved, the time to study, organize, and act efficiently: these were attributes of Ford's job but not Ruckelshaus's. The right to set policy for the United States, the right to pick cities and companies and attack them with speeches and suits in exemplary fashion, the right to ignore potential short-term cost to industry in order to establish the credibility and integrity of his agency: those were attributes of Ruckelshaus's job but not Ford's. The differences are not superficial. They separate the two jobs and the world view that goes with them.

Two Kinds of Management Systems

It is common to hear businessmen say, "Without the power of the purse and the power to hire and fire, you can't manage!" For most people who think about, discuss, or practice management, control over administrative tools is the sine qua non of top management. Control of budgets, information, and personnel is key. Without it you may have a system, but it is not managerial. Control over these tools sets the boundary of a corporate managerial system.

In fact, many top managers do not control these tools, yet they think they run a managerial system. And some managers who have the control of administrative tools are not in corporate business. A better phrase than "corporate managerial system" is needed. "Technocratic management system" may do the job despite inappropriate but not especially misleading connotations.

The term *technocratic management* is adopted in this book to describe the type of organization used to achieve efficiency and effectiveness in the production and distribution of goods and services. In principle, if not always in fact, the leadership of a technocratic management system has authority over the contract, the inducements, and the purposes of his organization.

Opposed to technocratic management systems are political ones. The term *political management* is adopted here to describe organizations that respond to the needs of individuals and groups concerned with the distribution of goods and services over which there are common or overlapping claims. The "products" of political systems are usually law and public policy. It is typical in a political management system for several individuals or coalitions to each control separate ingredients of the administrative systems required for effective action. Consequently, members are regularly in a position to bargain over goals and the distribution of benefits to be generated by collective action.

Most of the time we do not bother to make the distinction between these two sorts of management systems. Indeed, talk of "corporate politics" and "government business" suggests that there is no distinction. As usual, everyday language, though imprecise, contains an element of truth. The discussion that follows makes a great deal of the distinctions between two different sorts of management activity — political and technocratic. But these are exaggerated to help with the diagnosis. Once the framework of analysis is understood it can be used much more loosely than the next chapters might suggest. As we define them, both technocratic and political features can be found in most large, complex public and private systems.

Much has been said about the characteristics of technocratic and political systems. Of particular importance are the contrasts to be found in elements of the general management tasks in these systems. The most important differences are in (1) the contract, or the decision to contribute and the nature of inducements; (2) the form of organization; (3) the information systems; and (4) the systems for shaping purpose and allocating resources.

The Contract

In a technocratic organization, the decision to recruit a member is taken with some seriousness. Unless the person does not work out, he or she will be around for a long time. In the civil service and in many large corporations, the contract is for "life." In turn, the technocratic organization expects complete commitment from the member. As the member rises in the hierarchy the demands may become greater, so that family life and individual privacy may seem threatened. Senior managers find it hard to speak as individuals separate from the organization where they manage and to which they are known to be loyal.[7]

In return for the services contributed, compensation — usually money but also a range of perquisites — is provided in proportion to rank, seniority, and contribution. Naturally, these interact. It is rare to find junior members at high rank, and the potential for relatively great contribution is often present at high rank.

Perhaps most interesting in the present context, the surplus generated in successful technocratic activity is sometimes explicitly shared with organization members. Profits are distributed as bonuses; sales representatives are sent on trips south in the winter as rewards for increased productivity. The usual premise is that group effort should be rewarded equally, and individual effort in proportion to contribution.

Some systems utilize extreme rewards or penalties. At Texas Instru-

ments, individuals responsible for successfully managing the intro-
duction of an important new product have been awarded $1 million.[8]
In some companies managers who do not meet their budget are fired.
In others, those who are not promoted are asked to leave (up or out).

The contract in political management systems works in a very
different fashion. To begin, there is no obvious referent organization.
Issues have a life of their own, and an undefined network of individuals and organizations works at influencing policy and the distribution
of resources. The "contract" in a political system relates to the issue
and crosses the apparent boundaries of technocratic organizations.

Consider this example. While serving as acting assistant secretary
of state for security and consular affairs, Philip Heymann conceived
the idea that it would be good if U.S. visa policy was liberalized.
Heymann arrived at the assistant secretary's job in 1964, following the
departure of Abba Schwartz. Schwartz had been driven out by his
subordinate Frances Knight, the bureaucratically and politically powerful head of the Passport Office. It was an era when J. Edgar Hoover
was still powerful at the FBI, and anticommunism was a salient
agenda issue.

In reviewing his responsibilities, Heymann concluded that the regular renewal of visas was an unnecessarily tedious process and not
really useful to internal security. Whereas Americans could cross the
border of almost any ally by showing their passport, residents of even
our closest European allies had to obtain a visa every four years. The
process was time-consuming and involved long lines. The best that the
frequent traveler could obtain was a four-year visa. Heymann could
not see why a free society would want to put up an unnecessary barrier
at its borders.

As he saw his situation, the involved players were his superiors in
the State Department, including the secretary, Dean Rusk; the Justice
Department, including the FBI and the Immigration and Naturalization Service (INS); the consular affairs bureaucracy; the White House
staff; and those members of Congress interested in trade, foreign
affairs, and the communist threat — especially the oversight subcom-

mittee responsible for the budget of the State Department, chaired by Congressman Michael Feighan, an Ohio Democrat.

Almost no one viewed the visa problem the same way Heymann did. Most players saw the easier entry of potentially disloyal foreigners and unregistered aliens, the potential loss of consular jobs, or a bureaucratic flap with Hoover or Knight, with the State Department vulnerable to charges of being "soft on communists." In short, no one had a reason to be positive, and Heymann had limited authority and resources to act.

He was able to have a new policy of an "indefinite visa" approved by (1) getting the proposal studied by his career subordinate so that it would be put forth in a technically sensible fashion, and enlisting that subordinate's commitment by naming the proposal after him; (2) using high-level friends at Justice to neutralize potential objections of Hoover; (3) changing the face of the issue for the White House so that it could be proposed as a protourism move that would be included on a list of steps being taken to improve the balance of payments; (4) exploiting the long-standing relationship of the now committed career subordinate with the key subcommittee chairman so that very conservative gentleman could be informed and reassured that this was a step in favor of efficiency; and (5) informing the secretary of state of the action under way with a memo explaining that certain regulatory language would be changed from one form to another on such and such a date unless the secretary disapproved.

Under these circumstances, what is the organization? To whom was Heymann loyal? It was certainly to his concept of what was right for the country. He was also loyal to a school of thought that believed the country is best served by free trade, market-oriented economics, and due process in its politics.

At the same time, Heymann had personal goals. Among the issues he might have considered, the indefinite visa had the advantage of being compact enough so that if it was handled skillfully, Heymann had a real chance to accomplish a change in policy within his tenure, despite his relatively low-level position. Such an accomplishment would enhance his reputation for effectiveness as well as reinforce his self-esteem. Next time an administration was assembled he might be chosen.

By packaging the proposal so that it served the needs of others in the White House and the bureaucracy, and by succeeding, Heymann strengthened his ability to accomplish other tasks in the future. It is a process quite analogous to deal making on Wall Street, where new syndicates are put together for each project. A successful deal breeds trust in the syndicate organizer. But in Washington, unlike on Wall Street, one can't take one's cash and move. The power that reputation, access, and favors owed provides can only be reinvested in Washington — in either new projects or a new job.

It is critical to note that political management has no hierarchical system in which salary and incentive compensation can be used congruently with structure to manage coherent development and implementation of plans and programs. Heymann and most other political system managers are quasi-independent entrepreneurs, not professional managers who can rely on their organization and their superiors for resources and advancement. The secretary of state is given a chance to veto. But in the context of a very wide range of issues involving his department, he does not lead. This is not to say that he *cannot* make policy. In fact, he may be a very effective player with more resources to draw on than an acting assistant administrator. But it is the same game as Heymann's and not the technocratic one.

The president of the United States — or the mayor or governor who does not understand this process — finds it bedlam, especially if he thinks in terms of the technocratic model of the chief executive that is drawn from private corporations. He often finds the web of power in which he is enmeshed frustrating. How can he give orders, how can he plan, how can he implement policy in the midst of a bazaar of entrepreneurs who are effectively renegotiating their terms of employment with each issue in which they have an interest?

Such independent behavior can only be experienced as disloyal, if not treasonable. The executive's response, predictably, is to seek control — through either wiretapping subordinates suspected of leaking; the careful use of office size, location, and decor such as that described by John Dean; or the forms of psychological persuasion along the lines of those employed by Lyndon Johnson.[9]

Another common response is cronyism. It's all very well to have the best talent in the country in the cabinet; but the best talents are often the most independent. Independent cabinet behavior is interpreted as presidential weakness — see, for example, Richard Neustadt's description of Eisenhower's deference to Treasury Secretary George Humphrey.[10] And in Washington, we are told, the perception of weakness is soon translated into loss of power.[11]

An extended example of cronyism was provided unintentionally by E. Pendleton James, President Reagan's chief personnel officer. He described the criteria used to select high-ranking managers for the new administration as (1) commitment to the policy, philosophy, and objectives of Ronald Reagan, (2) unquestioned integrity, (3) competence, (4) ability to be a team player, (5) toughness, and (6) commitment to change. Noteworthy in their absence from the list are experience in managing any large organization and experience in managing or knowledge of the career people who manage the organizations that they are hired to lead. James noted that President Reagan appointed 3148 new people.

Students of the presidency — or the mayor's office — repeatedly report that elected executives know or learn that they need a group of trustworthy subordinates who must be personally loyal because of family, ancient friendship, or total dependency. Thus we find kitchen cabinets — or, more extreme, the "Georgia White House," a group of young, inexperienced friends and campaign managers for Jimmy Carter — trying to manage the presidency of the United States.

Two other aspects of the contract in political management systems are patronage and the attention Congress and state legislatures pay to the terms that the executive can negotiate with his or her subordinates. Congress has legislated a ceiling on executive branch compensation — generally below where congressional salaries begin. This ceiling has ensured that there is not much leeway for rewarding outstanding performance with salary or bonus. Moreover, through civil service regulation, and through withholding consent on appointments and line item oversight of budgets, Congress has retained or captured for itself much control over the use of compensation as a source of administrative influence. In other words, Congress has wrested much control over the contract away from the putative top management.

Patronage is a related feature of the contract in the political systems. In place of a distribution of profit, a political manager can allocate jobs, dams, post offices, and other "programs." Patronage and the right to distribute it are not just the politician's privilege. The great growth of state and local government has usually been attributed to the lengthening public agenda, but from an administrative perspective one might also see it as evidence of Congress's desire to see money spent locally as employment in the district rather than centrally in accord with some executive branch determination of national policy. This tendency could be expected even where a Congress member could achieve no direct control over the potential patronage inherent in these state and local jobs.

A final aspect of the contract in political systems as opposed to technocratic systems is its duration. In corporate systems a failing employee can usually be fired. But it takes enormous effort to dismiss a political appointee who can fight dismissal through effective use of Congress and the press. The threat of leaving is a credible one. On the other hand, public humiliation, the "broom closet," and calculatedly unattractive assignments can force the resignation of entrenched individuals.

For example, during the revitalization of the Federal Trade Commission under Caspar Weinberger, his assistant, Basil Mezines, is reported to have forced resignations by such tactics as reassigning a lawyer with a prosperous Washington, D.C., real-estate business to Cleveland, and assigning an alcoholic attorney who had not litigated in years to trial work in New York City.[12]

What usually happens is that the cadre of talented individuals who would lead a technocratic system and provide wisdom and continuity rotate in and out of the top management of the political system. It is a rare careerist who waits out the political wars to rise to real managerial power. The exceptions to this generalization are almost always in the more technocratic departments — the military, the foreign service, or the forest service, for example.

Careers

The contrast between the long-term commitment of technocratic institutional life and the temporary "syndicate" quality of political systems is especially visible in the careers of the two groups of managers.

Increasingly, corporate managers are professionals — trained members of a cohort regarded by top management as the key resources of the organization. It is typical for managers of large companies to say, "Our most important asset is our people." Reflecting that attitude is the careful attention to recruitment, and the heavy investment in training throughout the organizational life of the member.

In his opus on management, Peter Drucker calls particular attention to the way in which all great companies invest in management education. He cites General Motors, Mitsui, and Marks & Spencer, but IBM, Xerox, General Electric, Procter & Gamble, Philips Lamp, and others could be added to the list. The goal of each of the systems constructed by these companies is to hire talented people and then prosper by helping them to develop those talents to the utmost. Development is achieved by careful progress through a sequence of increasingly demanding jobs. Beginning with a narrow substantive problem, individuals gradually learn the technical content of their business and how to manage the effort of others working with the substance of the business. Over a sequence of assignments they rise from technical doer to generalist planner, cooperator, and motivator.

Although there is movement from firm to firm, the typical corporate executive enters one company, learns the business, and stays there.[13] At the top, the chief executive works with a set of officers whom he has known for years, whose skills and ideas he has calibrated, and who are personally committed with him to the success of their institution.

The public sector offers a dramatic contrast. Most top jobs go to inexperienced individuals, especially the elective jobs. Hugh Heclo has revealed dramatically how ill prepared many public executives are for their work, and how transitory are the working relationships.[14]

The appointed officials at high levels are almost always making a temporary lateral move. Having established themselves as lawyers, academics, or entrepreneurs, they turn to "public service" to "get some public experience."[15]

Even their nongovernment work is significant. Many government managers are lawyers. They are trained to work as individuals on a project-by-project basis — often in temporary alliances — but always in an adversarial process. Economists and other academics are equally unprepared for management work, focused as they are on substantive issues and verbal debate. Institutional life, except in their own very undermanaged firms and universities, is held in contempt.

These are what one career government official has called "the tourists." Operating from a mixture of personal and public motives, they move through high levels of government as part of nongovernmental careers.

As for elected officials, they typically begin their political careers working in campaign organizations. Eventually they run for office themselves. Achieving success, they often set their sights on higher office. For example, starting with his election as a county commissioner, Paul Tsongas of Massachusetts won six elections in nine years, eventually rising to the United States Senate. Central to a politician's official life is the constant requirement to raise money for the next campaign, and a constitutional system that encourages most legislators to dabble in a variety of fields rather than gain expertise in a few. Instead, their staffs (including many young lawyers) provide the professional substance of our system.

And what of career managers in our political system? In fact — if we focus on top management — there are none.

Organizational Structure

The dramatic difference between technocratic and political top management is also reflected in the structure of the respective organizations. In the technocratic world, the organization itself is the basis of management. Executives work very hard to devise a structure ideally suited to accomplish the key tasks necessary for achievement of the organization's strategy. As the strategy shifts, the organization is fine-tuned or reshaped to meet new needs.

The trick in building an organization is to take maximum advantage of specialized knowledge, skills, and facilities while using teams, task forces, and other formats to achieve whatever coordination is required across functional specialities to get integrated effort. The more highly differentiated the organization, the more effort that is required to achieve integration. An ice cream company provides a simple metaphor. Manufacturing organizations like to produce level quantities of "vanilla and chocolate" day in and day out. Change is planned over long periods. Sales organizations like to have twenty-eight flavors available for their customers "yesterday," regardless of their plan. It is often not easy to integrate the work of manufacturing and sales organizations for this reason.

Generally, once units are built around different tasks, they develop their own goals, values, and time horizons. Organizational design is an art involving the trading of the benefits of specialization with the costs of the administrative effort required to bridge the differences created. Large multinational organizations have units specialized by product (consumer electronics versus home appliances); function (sales, manufacturing, engineering); country and region (Europe, North America, Far East); and time horizon (budget and control versus strategic planning, or division development versus corporate research).

Managers — especially top management — devote a good deal of time and effort to the shaping of the organization. The reason is that together with the reward system, the division of work is the principal way managers learn what is expected of them. A manager responsible for cost, quality, and output of a refinery has a different job from the manager responsible for the profit of the refined products business.

All large technocratic systems have elaborate and specialized organizations. A little bit like the differentiated sails on the clipper ship, they are spread out or reefed as the direction and strength of the weather changes. The key to long-term success is continuity in command and a sense of final destination. It is that sense of purpose that gives meaning to all the administrative work involved in organizational shifts. It is the consistent direction of strategy and structure that gives stability to technocratic systems. Even as direction and mode of operation change, the contracts are secure and careers are developed.

As in history's great armies, it is the supportive character of organizational life as experienced by its members that enables technocratic systems to adapt to new challenges in fundamental ways. The surplus generated by successful change is used to compensate individuals for dealing with the costs involved in learning new jobs and developing new relationships. The profits achieved by shifting resources from a mature business to a growing one are like the loot distributed to troops conquering new territory. The ability to distribute rewards frees technocratic organizations from the base of any single given mission.

In contrast, with exceptions such as Richard J. Daley's Chicago or Kevin White's Boston, American political systems are relatively unstable. Political organization is far more constrained than technocratic in the degree of differentiation and the elaborateness of the hierarchy it supports. Much political organization is temporary, representing an alliance of individuals concerned with a particular issue. When the issue is resolved or the individuals lose interest, the alliance disappears. Much of the Vietnam-inspired antiwar movement dissolved when its younger members were relieved of the threat of the draft. The remainder came apart with peace.

The problem is that the basic inducement to participate is the goal that brought the group together. With no economic surplus to distribute, there is nothing to maintain allegiance as the group's goal becomes obsolete.

More permanent political organizations tend to be based on economic class, religious, or regional variations that are more long-standing. Ward politics of the Tammany variety is the clearest example of this form of organization, but so is the British Labour party. A permanent base permits the construction of a more elaborate organization. Still, the high degree of differentiation necessary for an efficient use of resources remains hard to develop. Political organizations regardless of tenure usually lack economic rewards and career support required to keep specialized units consolidated. Only charismatic leaders can hold such organizations together, and even these find that highly differentiated organizations represent a countercharismatic power base that threatens political purpose. Chairman Mao apparently found it necessary to attack his own bureaucracy with the least differentiated part of the party — the Red Guards.

Information

The fluidity and instability of political systems mean that information to measure cost in relation to performance is hard to develop on a regular basis. The careful accounting of raw materials and the painstaking development of cost allocation systems in order to measure the relation of investment to results that one finds in large business corporations is lacking in political systems. There are, of course, exceptions. U.S. presidential campaign organizations probably put as much effort into budgeting and measurement as most businesses. But usually performance measures are fragmented and tend to be about perceptions. To the extent that political systems are organized around issues, only information that pertains to those issues gets attention. The war on poverty, for example, was a success for Lyndon Johnson to the extent that a long list of legislative goals was achieved. Whether the many bills passed by Congress actually brought about a redistribution of income would only be learned at a later date, but that was somehow irrelevant to the politics. What was important was the momentum of victory.

Measures of performance are also unpopular for less systemic reasons. Since most politics are about the redivision of "the pie," there is a natural tendency to keep the extent of one's self-interest secret. Private goals are cloaked in the language of public purpose. Public cost is seldom discussed. The Rehabilitation Act of 1974, designed to help the handicapped, passed Congress overwhelmingly. It is not clear whether those voting recognized that they were making a $10 billion to $20 billion claim on the public purse, but it is as attractive for Congress to levy a hidden tax as it is to convey a hidden subsidy. Disclosure mobilizes opposition.

Private interest is somehow not legitimate in the public debate. Consequently, we talk as if political action has only public benefits. There is no systematic information describing the private allocation of the pie within the system. For example, because Heymann designed his visa proposal so that it would sail easily through bureaucratic channels, there was no system to record which bureaucrats or legislators would benefit from the acceptance. Since pie division is based on power, politicians jealously guard their power — and constantly refine others' perception of it. As formal meetings are full of obvious cues about who has power, much political business is conducted informally, over drinks or dinner. A senator who might never visit the office of a junior might well grab his arm over a punch bowl. It is for this reason that Washingtonians devote so much time to the social columns. Advised one old hand, "You'll learn more in this town by reading what used to be called 'the women's pages' than the front pages. Read the agate type — who gets invited to state dinners and, what's more important, who doesn't."

In contrast, information in technocratic systems is extensive, systematic, and available to a remarkably wide group. Physical measures are developed to design, manage, and improve operations. Economic yardsticks are available to guide planning and resource allocation, measure managers, and ultimately evaluate the competitive strength of the organization.

Some well-run business corporations actually attempt to tie their long-term strategic plans to operating and capital budgets and then to measure operations against both the short-term operational and long-term strategic yardsticks set up in those budgets. This information provides the basis for incentive compensation systems.

It is not that all or even most technocratic systems develop a sophisticated information system. But it is sensible and legitimate to try. One might say that the technocratic ethic with respect to information is egalitarian. The policy that makes this ethic operational is best embodied in the word *disclosure*. Technocratic systems disclose to their members information that leaders of political systems would withhold if they gathered it at all. On the other hand, technocratic systems operate in virtually complete secrecy with regard to the public. Information developed within the organization is kept private. In contrast, at least in the United States, there is a presumption that information available to a political system should be made public. The Freedom of Information Act has made that presumption the law.

Choosing Purpose and Allocating Resources

In technocratic systems, resource allocation is driven in pursuit of three clear goals: survival, growth, and surplus. The clarity of the goals makes it clear that resources should be invested where they will do the most good for the organization. This implies selectivity. Resources should be moved toward areas of activity that promise the highest returns. Return on investment is a key measure by which otherwise justifiable activities can be compared and ranked in attractiveness. Steel is just as attractive as computers; but 2 percent per annum is not as attractive as 15 percent. Carl Kaysen captured the essence of this aspect of technocratic systems when, in reviewing Alfred Sloan's *My Years with General Motors,* he attributed GM's success to Sloan's focus on making money as opposed to cars.[16]

But the essential aspect of a technocratic management system is not profit. It is selectivity. Profit is merely a marvelously simple tool by which selectivity can be guided. Given a purpose, the test of efficiency implies selectivity. If the environment changes, survival may require the organization to alter its purpose and transfer resources. The organization's life can be distinct from its purpose at any particular time. Thus, as consumer electronics becomes more competitive and as its work force grows older, Sony has moved into life insurance and cosmetics — one to ensure cash flow, the other to provide less physically demanding employment for its organization. Sony is an organization of people, not merely a producer of television sets and hi-fis. Similarly, universities that were built to train preachers or farmers now train engineers, lawyers, and business managers.

Because goals in political systems are often diffuse and vaguely specified — consider "ending poverty" as a goal — it is usually very difficult for political systems to rank goals. If there is no clear way of ordering goals, then selectivity is *not* legitimate. Selectivity implies putting one goal ahead of another and this may mean harming one group at the expense of another. It is very difficult to justify harming one part of the base of a political system in order to help another. The consequence is that often we cannot close obsolete military bases and unnecessary veterans' hospitals or cut pension expenditures that overwhelm our budgets. Instead, we print money and let inflation hide the distribution of harm. Similarly, we have a hard time locating power plants, prisons, halfway houses, or even low-income housing. We all want them in principle but not in our neighborhoods.

Whereas technocratic systems can reallocate surplus to compensate injured organization members, there is little basis for such behavior in political systems. The problem is that the rights and obligations of membership in a political system are defined poorly, if at all. If there are no obligations to membership, it is hard to construct a surplus from which compensation can be paid. Moreover, even in technocratic systems compensation is often paid out of profits expected in the future. Those sensibly aware of the fluidity of politics have no faith that they will be rewarded for their present sacrifice in an uncertain future.

To the extent that local communities or even states are able to regard themselves as permanent organizations capable of technocratic management, it is possible to imagine future-oriented compensation systems being devised and regarded as legitimate. The community that accepts the waste treatment plant could get a "bonus" usable for building swimming pools or libraries.

Legitimacy, however, is not all that is required for selective resource allocation. Access to resources has to be controlled so that their disposal can be managed. In some technocratic systems access can be subjected to extreme control. For example, even in a large, multibusiness, multinational complex such as Textron, cash balances are managed centrally and reviewed daily; expenditures above relatively low limits must be approved at high levels of the company; and hiring of salaried personnel is subject to close scrutiny. Even where control from the center is less direct, detailed information systems render the pattern of resource use highly visible. Managers with the discretion to allocate resources know that they will have to explain why their actions make sense in terms of previously approved strategy and plans.

In contrast, access to resources in political systems is often wide open. The separation of powers and the organization of Congress leave budget control in the hands of many subcommittees as well as the press. Given the confused issue of legitimacy, access to the press is equivalent to access to the power to influence resource allocation. There have possibly been coalitions of some company's division management with finance department officers and the press that somehow maneuvered a larger budget allocation than the corporate center desired, but this is not, as in Washington, a day-to-day occurrence.

Moreover, in our federal system, the national budget is only the most important politically managed resource allocation process. The same diffusion is present in greater or lesser degree at state, county,

Aspects of Managerial Systems

	Technocratic	Political
The Contract	Long-term	Revised from issue to issue
	Loyalty is to the institution.	Loyalty is to self or "country."
	Money for services is in proportion to seniority rank performance.	Psychic rewards and rank are in proportion to power to extract ability to contribute on the issue.
	Surplus is shared or reinvested.	Surplus is spent or returned to the polity.
Careers	Professional	"Tourists"
	Trained member of a cadre	Trained in other professions, members of a party or network
	Rise is from technical doer to generalist planner cooperator leader.	Rise is project-by-project or as advance man to state or federal elected official.
Organization	Contingent on strategy for future	Contingent on personality and current issues
	Highly differentiated by function time horizon primary orientation	Largely undifferentiated, based on constituency and region
	Stable culture	
Information	Extensive and systematic: organized by level and phase of activity, e.g., planning versus control	Fragmented, qualitative, about perceptions Few systems

	Technocratic	Political
Information (cont.)	Generally closed to the public	Gossip and informal networks are key.
		Often open to the public
Strategy Formulation and Resource Allocation	Goals are relatively clear: survival, growth, and surplus.	Goals are diffuse or not operational.
	Selectivity is understood to serve the organization as distinct from its parts.	Selectivity is *not* legitimate.
	Return to organization on investment is a key measure.	
	Budget control can be tight by program.	Budget control can sometimes be tight by line expenditure.

and municipal levels. Political coalitions can choose among a wide range of arenas in which they can fight.

Dr. Blanche Bernstein, reflecting on her experience as deputy commissioner for income maintenance in the New York State Department of Social Services, described her problems in ensuring integrity in the administration of the food stamp program. "The battle as it was fought out involved members of Congress, appointed officials in the Food and Nutrition Service of the Department of Agriculture, state and local officials charged with administering the program, the courts, and the food stamp advocacy groups . . . along with related advocacy groups."[17]

In summary, technocratic and political management systems are very different in the contract they offer members, the typical ensuing career patterns of managers, the way in which they are organized, the type of information available for managers, and the philosophical context and systems for resource allocation. The table on pages 42–43 displays these differences in a fashion that makes the contrasts as dramatic as possible.

Business and Government Use Both Systems

Why do we have two such different management systems? How do we use these very different approaches?

In a technocratic system cooperation is contracted formally, infrequently, and in routine ways. This is what Alfred North Whitehead had in mind when he said that "routine is the God of social organization." It is the premise of routine cooperation that permits us to build complex differentiated organizations that can undertake difficult tasks of development, production, and distribution. A technocratic system is usually measured by tests of organizational outcomes — efficiency and effectiveness.

In a political system cooperation is contracted informally — periodically, if not frequently, in nonroutine ways. It is the premise of responsiveness to all active constituencies that permits us to build democratic systems. It is what we have in mind when we pledge "liberty and justice for all." A political system is usually measured by tests of the organization's process and by the pattern of distribution of benefits consequent upon its activity — accountability and legitimacy.

The two tests, efficiency and accountability, give us important insight into why and how the two systems are used. Efficiency in organization tends to be associated with predictability and repetitive actions. Both permit learning and the ability to generate cost savings. In order to achieve an efficiency-producing routine, we use technocratic systems.

But responsiveness to a set of constituencies that puts changing and unforeseen demands on an organization requires a fluid executive core, one in which the balance of power can change rapidly to reflect shifts in constituencies. A format in which bargains are easily re-shaped and a hierarchy that does not constrain shifts in the locus of power are most congruent with such a requirement. In order to achieve responsiveness to a wide set of constituent values, we use political systems.

This reasoning implies that the weakening of hierarchy and rapid shifts in the locus of power are associated with politicization. Thus, when in the early 1970s Common Cause and the Democratic Study Group led a movement for a change in the procedures by which the Democratic majority organized the House of Representatives, the face of the issue was "managerial reform in pursuit of efficiency." But the consequences were the loss of centrally controlled hierarchy, routine, experience, and predictability. Politicization without consensus among the Democrats meant weakness. Despite a substantial numerical majority, the "reformed" House Democrats could not pass legislation or overcome coherent Republican opposition. Reform had deprived leadership of the ability to focus resources selectively.

We can say, using the language developed above, that "reform" shifted the management approach in the House of Representatives from a somewhat technocratic system, leadership of which had been captured by entrenched southern Democrats, to a more political system, responsive to the newly enfranchised blacks and to urban voters. The technocratic system of the House was not *reformed* in the 1970s; it was *replaced* by a more political one.

The special irony of the shift is that it dispersed power toward wider constituencies at that moment in history when the end of the postwar boom meant that the mood in those constituencies would turn far more conservative in orientation than that of the liberals who led the reform. Politicization of systems has costs as well as benefits.

The more general point illustrated by the example is that technocratic systems and political systems are used in both private and government organizations. The problems of managing the institutions we use to accomplish society's agenda can be best understood if they are sorted out in terms of the technocratic-political distinction.

3 Technocratic Management Systems at Work

WORDS SUCH AS *technocratic* and *political* have an abstract quality until they evoke the same powerful images for everyone using them. Case examples are a good way of fleshing out ideas. IBM is at the top of almost everyone's list of big technocratic organizations. The work of IBM's executives in managing the major innovations involved in the third generation of computers illuminates most of the aspects of a technocratic system at work. In the same spirit, the story of reform in New York's state prisons provides a good example of technocratic management in the public sector. Finally, the tribulations of the Memorex Corporation demonstrate what can happen when a technocratic system is poorly used.

The 360 Story at IBM

Thomas Wise[1] has described "the decision by the management of the International Business Machines Corporation to produce a new family of computers, which it calls the system/360, . . . as the most crucial and portentous — as well as perhaps the riskiest — business judgment of recent times." The series of events in what is now regarded as a classic case of new-product development stretched over perhaps ten years. The tale of the 360 involves the rise and fall of key executives, major restructurings of the corporation, and dramatic competitive moves.

The story can begin with the rise of Thomas J. Watson, Jr., to become chief executive of IBM, for it is he who led the company toward powerful commercial computers. In 1954, T. Vincent Learson was asked by Watson to lead the development of the 702 and 705 computers, IBM's first major entry into the commercial field. In 1959, Learson was rewarded for his success by promotion to group executive responsible for both the General Products line of computers — the famous 1401 — and the Data Systems Division computers, the 7000 series. This was a radical step. For up to that point the two divisions were thought to have had separate charters. Indeed, they competed with each other in overlapping areas of the market. The 1401s were selling very well, and there seemed to be no immediate problem with the 7000. Nevertheless, there was some confusion within the market. Meanwhile, in the development laboratories, a new series of large computers, the 8000 series, was being planned under the leadership of one Fred Brooks. In addition, a large scientifically oriented machine, called Stretch, was also in development.

In the spring of 1961, Stretch was in trouble; its performance was not up to its price. And when Watson cut the price to match performance, it was no longer a profitable product.

As he began to assess his problem, Learson appears to have perceived the necessity of taking advantage of the totality of his resources. IBM was larger than its competition, but its approach to the market did not use IBM resources to provide customers something remarkably matched to IBM's skills. He moved in early 1961. To work on the problem, Learson brought over a young man from the General Products Division, Bob Evans, to become head of Data Systems Planning and Development. May 1961 was a month of funerals. In addition to the killing of Stretch, Evans killed the 8000 project, and Arthur Watson, Tom's brother, killed Scamp, a computer project under way in Great Britain that too closely resembled a machine being proposed for interim purposes by Evans.

This last move was of no small consequence. The British company was part of IBM World Trade, a kingdom under the rule of Arthur Watson. Arthur Watson lived in a royal style, traveling about Europe in his own railway car; his approach to life was quite different from that of his frugal and puritan brother. The decision to kill Scamp and accept the American product was a key step in the integration of World Trade into the parent company.

In this prototypical example of a strategic shift, the change begins with a new leader who perceives the opportunity to achieve more ambitious goals. He proceeded by bringing to IBM's core new talent and energy, people who shared his sense that more was possible, and merging two major groups with potentially complementary resources under one manager who was tough enough to force the integration. Over time, the executive core was reshaped when necessary to achieve movement. There were no public "hearings" but many private ones. Talent and organization were shifted, slowly but inexorably, to provide focus on the ambitious and slowly evolving strategy for a compatible line of computers.

Meanwhile, major development projects representing enormous investments of money (and ego) were canceled — despite public loss of face. Not that public loss of face threatened Watson's power. He had defined the problem early enough, while profits on old products were still improving.

By August 1961, thinking had progressed far enough for there to be support for a single product line that would cover both the Data Systems and General Products divisions. Evans asked Brooks, his adversary from the 8000, to head the so-called NPL ("new product line") project. Watson and Learson spent several months discussing the project with the divisions. Eventually, dissatisfied with the pace of discussion, Learson founded a special committee called SPREAD (Systems Programming, Research, Engineering and Development) in October 1961 to plan the project. Chairing the committee was John Haanstra, a vice president of General Products, and included were Evans, Brooks, and the designer of the Scamp computer. After thirty more days with little progress, Haanstra was removed and promoted to president of the General Products Division; Evans was made head of the committee. In January 1962, Brooks presented the SPREAD committee's report to top management. It proposed a single, compatible family of computers.

This was a critical moment in the project. Up to the time when a single family of computers was proposed, future strategy was still unclear. Learson had drafted some of the development talent of the old separate divisions into a combined army. But after a commitment to compatibility was made, all activity could be measured to see if it was focused on the corporate target.

The later history of the project would see Arthur Watson and Emanuel Piori, the vice president of research, going to San Jose — a major IBM development center — to stop independent development of a low-power machine. That work and many of the engineers were then transferred to Germany. At another point, the Corporate Management Committee was abolished so that a single individual, Learson, could be responsible for the marketing of the 360 series.

Consistently during the project's development, the executive core worked together to keep resources focused on the chosen strategic target. Resources were denied the managers who would not serve the corporate goal. Power was concentrated in Learson's hands so that he could direct the multiple forces of the extensive administrative apparatus toward the corporate goal.

Also significant was that at a critical juncture in the development of the project, Thomas Watson, Jr., held a meeting in his Stowe, Vermont, ski lodge with eight top executives and Brooks. There, this relatively nontechnical group discussed the critical issues surrounding the programming of the new and highly ambitious series of computers. Major risks were analyzed and top management committed themselves to a hybrid form of circuits that would insure IBM against the newer, fully integrated circuits.

Often in the administrative history of critical events, we find key decisions delegated to "experts" because of their technical content. In this instance, however, the core gave themselves the time and the occasion to understand the issues. Interestingly, their decision had the effect of hedging the risks these generalists did not understand, while accepting commercial risks that they did.

An equally important problem was that of producing components. Until 1960, IBM had been primarily an assembler of components made by others. But at that time, Albert L. Williams, the president of the company, convinced Thomas Watson, Jr., that a component manufacturing division would be appropriate. It was a happy decision, for as the 360 series developed and integrated circuits became an obvious dimension of the project, it became clear that too much proprietary information would be given to a vendor if components were to be purchased from outside the company. Thus, as part of the 360 project, the IBM board authorized a new plant to manufacture hybrid integrated circuits, a first step toward a major technology of the 1970s.

On reviewing the entire story of the 360, historian Richard Neustadt remarked, "For the rich, the birds sing." Clearly, the decision to enter component manufacturing proved fortunate. But a more profound point can be made: given the courage to look ahead, IBM's management had sufficient administrative influence to get its organization to sing more or less in unison.

From a managerial perspective, what is most amazing about this story is that a successful company chose to make its product line obsolete. It chose to do this by a revolutionary concept — a product line that demanded extreme integration of effort — and was able to implement its choices despite the necessity for reorganizing, several times, the effort of proud and successful engineers and managers. It is as if General Motors had decided to downsize its product line and move to a modern engine in the late 1960s and did this by substantially changing the shape of the car divisions so that Chevrolet was no longer a major brand name in the market. Unfortunately for the U.S. balance of payments and the energy problem, General Motors was not as radical or entrepreneurial a company as IBM.

From a human aspect, what is most amazing is that key managers who had invested totally in one or another of the canceled projects did not quit. The reason seems to be that after considering the options most persuaded themselves that there was no better way to use their talent.

To understand why they might reach that conclusion, consider these excerpts from a brochure in which IBM describes itself to its employees.

About Your Company[2]

IBM Principles
An organization, like an individual, must build on a bedrock of sound beliefs if it is to succeed. The organization must stand by these beliefs in its actions and decisions. The beliefs that guide IBM are expressed as IBM Principles.

- *Respect for the Individual*
  Our basic belief is respect for the individual, for his or her rights and dignity.
- *Service to the Customer*
  We are dedicated to giving our customers the best possible service.
- *Excellence as a Way of Life*
  We want IBM to be known for its excellence. We believe that every task, in every part of the business, should be performed in a superior manner and to the best of our ability.
- *Effective Management Leadership*
  Our success depends on intelligent and aggressive management which is sensitive to the need for making an enthusiastic partner of every individual in the organization.
- *Obligations to Stockholders*
  We should provide our stockholders an attractive return on invested capital and exploit opportunities for continuing profitable growth.
- *Fair Deal for the Supplier*
  We want to deal fairly and impartially with suppliers of goods and services.

The pamphlet goes on to describe corporate citizenship and the history of IBM. Eventually, what we have called the contract is described quite explicitly. Excerpts are revealing:

Your Security

For over a quarter century, no IBMer has lost an hour's time in layoffs, despite recessions and major product shifts. We are proud of that record. Today, a great deal of effort is being expended to continue this tradition, if at all possible. This includes retraining, reassigning, and even relocating people when necessary, to match them with alternative jobs in which they can succeed.

Your Advancement

Your advancement will be based upon your job performance plus management evaluation of your ability to accept more responsibility. To help you take full advantage of the opportunities within IBM, the company provides a broad variety of educational and training programs . . .

Job Training

Your training and continuing education begin as soon as you start your first assignment at IBM . . .

Your Performance

Performance evaluations are held twice during the first year of employment and annually thereafter. At the beginning of the evaluation period, your manager will record your key responsibilities and discuss them with you so that you fully understand what will be expected during the forthcoming appraisal period . . .

Your Pay

IBM's pay policies have enabled the company to attract and retain above average employees. Although in your job you may be part of a group, it is you and your individual performance that count in IBM.

The following will give you a general understanding of IBM's pay practices. Additional information may be obtained from your manager.

Pay Objective

IBM's pay policies recognize the skill level of each position and each employee's sustained performance in his job. We maintain an average level of pay that is higher than the composite average level of pay for similar skill levels in leading local or national companies with which IBM competes for employees.

The contract is clear. IBM's commitment is to its members. In return it expects equal loyalty, involvement, and desire for company success. Associated with this pattern are some very unusual personnel practices managed by a strong personnel department reinforced by top management. Early in the consolidation of Data Products and General Systems, Evans, the killer of the 8000, found himself in the position of informing Brooks, the designer of the 8000, that Brooks had been awarded a bonus. He is quoted as remarking, "I assure you I had nothing to do with it." In fact, it is the function of the corporate personnel group to help top management oversee compensation in order to prevent the intense rivalry of IBM executives from becoming excessively divisive.

At another moment in the 360 project, two major programs were being proposed as a way of dealing with a problem. Following the choice of the second approach, the manager of the first proposal was assigned to implement the program. The idea and its proponent could be distinguished. The manager did not "lose"; the proposal that he was responsible for developing was judged inferior to another. But the manager was rewarded for his performance.

IBM's goals and policies are, therefore, the collective responsibility of the management. Competition — *contention* is the IBM word — is seen as a useful device for revealing problems and motivating high-quality analysis. The end, however, is the common good.

Change at New York State's Prisons

Consider a two-year period in the career of Benjamin Ward, a new department manager in the New York State Department of Correctional Services. Just a hundred miles upriver from IBM's Armonk headquarters, the Albany offices of the New York prison system's management are a different world.[3]

In February 1975, Ward was appointed the first black commissioner of the New York State Department of Correctional Services, a department beset with controversy and national attention caused by the Attica uprising of 1971. Ward's appointment was one of the first Governor Hugh Carey had made. Carey was as concerned about the management of the prison system as that of any agency in the state bureaucracy. One reason was that former governor Nelson Rockefeller, only a few months before, had been grilled about his handling of the Attica uprising during congressional hearings on his nomination as vice president. Carey understood that incidents like Attica could become a serious political liability and had picked Ward, in part, because of the favorable publicity Ward had received as New York City's deputy commissioner of police during several tense hostage incidents. More important, Governor Carey hoped that an opportunity now existed to improve the management of a previously unresponsive department.

Ward's reputation as a tough manager was earned in New York City. Working his way up through the ranks of the thirty-thousand-person New York City Police Department, he had risen to the post of deputy police commissioner. In 1973 Mayor John Lindsay had appointed him commissioner of the Traffic Department, where he demonstrated his ability to manage effectively an agency in which he was not an expert. Ward, a lawyer, had instituted several important reforms despite the dominance of traffic engineers. Prior to his appointment by Governor Carey, Ward had never worked in a prison system.

Like Watson, Carey knew he had a strategic problem. In choosing a "manager" rather than a "prison expert" it is possible that he knew the expert's solution to be economically infeasible, and hence strategically unsound. Strategy, for technocrats as well as politicians, is the art of the possible.

In 1974 the New York State Department of Correctional Services was responsible for both the custody and the parole supervision of approximately sixteen thousand men and women housed in its eighteen institutions; 72 percent of this inmate population was black,

Spanish-speaking, or of another minority, but more than 85 percent of the department's nine thousand employees were white. Most of the department's facilities were located in the rural areas of the state. The department maintained security and discipline within its institutions, provided guidance and counseling to inmates, assisted inmates in upgrading their vocational and educational skills, and generally tried to help inmates and parolees in finding employment and adjusting to release.

After the Attica uprising in 1971, the department's budget had increased annually at a rate of about 20 percent, largely to cover "mandated" cost factors such as inflation and union contracts. By the time he became commissioner, although his department's revenues had increased moderately, Ward knew he could not expect this increase to continue unchanged, because the state's fiscal outlook was troublesome. It was clear in February 1975 that any fight Ward might wage for increases in his budget would be conducted amid a climate of statewide belt tightening. The future would also likely be a period in which the prison population would increase as a result of new mandatory-sentencing laws. For example, the Rockefeller administration had enacted a much-publicized law requiring life sentences for drug pushers.

Ward faced three basic strategic alternatives: rehabilitation, warehousing, or diversification.

Adherents of rehabilitation believed that prisons should be used to improve the lot of prisoners. Some reforms that might be considered were "co-ed" prisons, conjugal visits for prisoners, and more minority guards.

Another group argued that prisons as then structured were fundamentally warehouses that lacked the resources for rehabilitation. What was necessary was to recognize this and attempt to run them in as humane a fashion as possible: that is, provide good food, good health services, and decent living quarters.

The premise on which diversification was based was that a prisoner who leaves a maximum-security prison in a rural community and goes directly back to his urban home experiences a type of culture shock that can damage any efforts he has made toward rehabilitation. It followed that a prisoner should not experience either a maximum- or a minimum-security prison, but instead should move through a diversified system of institutions, beginning, perhaps, in a "humane warehouse." Then, if he wished to avail himself of rehabilitation programs and if he was able to maintain a good record, he might be transferred to increasingly smaller and less security-conscious institutions with different types of programs.

When he considered what policy would be appropriate, Ward faced real problems. Diversification would require new institutions closer to New York City as well as an excellent data base describing the prisoners; new institutions required money and data required time. Rehabilitation that involved training and practice at useful work was generally opposed by unions, which viewed the programs as cheap labor. Humane warehousing required a capacity that would be taxed by the increasing population.

Ward had available to him a number of studies commissioned after the Attica uprising. These provided blueprints for a renovation of the system, but they all required large budget increases.

When his appointment was confirmed, Ward discovered further problems. First, some upstate/downstate disagreements surfaced regarding the handling or "coddling" of the prisoners. With an upstate-dominated legislature controlling his budget, this could become a serious issue. Second, his appointment was officially opposed by the guards' union, which believed in a very firm attitude toward prisoners and was concerned that Ward would be too soft.

He also discovered that the prison system consisted of a series of fiefdoms. Each institution was separate from the others, with little coordination. More troublesome, the commissioner had been virtually prohibited from firing the tenured superintendents.

Here a classic difference between public and private institutions is apparent. Unlike IBM's Learson when he took on his job, Ward had limited ability to move key executives.

Ward soon learned that despite substantial differences among the institutions, the system did not have a classification procedure for assigning prisoners to any one of them. In fact, there was no information system describing the prisoners in a way that would permit managing a diversified system.

This is not an unusual situation for a new manager. Despite the obvious desirability of having information as a basis for management, many institutions — private as well as public — fail to collect necessary data.

Finally, Ward discovered that there was a Ku Klux Klan chapter among the prison guards.

His response was a strategy that distinguished short-term needs from long-term objectives. In the short run, faced with limited resources, data, and prospects for cooperation, he aimed to make each institution operate as humanely as possible so that each inmate could expect essential services such as good food and good health care. Ward noted that "food can be very important to the functioning of a prison. A couple of days' bad food or a staff person who doesn't organize the line well so that the first inmates take big portions and the last ones have nothing left, . . . well, after two such days you have riots. You can't let that happen." From Ward's perspective, the best way to overcome the many obstacles was to begin by unifying and strengthening his executive staff and by making the superintendents more accountable as a result of new legislation regarding hiring and firing as well as informal actions he might be able to take.

In the long run, Ward sought to adapt the system to a strategy of diversification by creating a strong centralized system of classification and by opening as many community-based facilities as possible.

Although Ward promised his executive staff there would be no immediate firings, he made a number of personnel changes. First, he created a new deputy commissioner's position, which he filled with a black lawyer from New York City. To this deputy, Ward gave the tasks of handling inmate grievances and supervising the in-house inspector general. He also asked the deputy commissioner to investigate the Ku Klux Klan chapter among the guards.

Second, Ward hired a young ex-priest to work in program services, but soon promoted him to a new position, associate commissioner. A former aide to Mayor Lindsay, the new man also had very close ties to Governor Carey's staff.

Ward began by acknowledging the importance of previous contracts, but in order to deal with broader problems, he brought in outsiders to help him. In a sense Ward used the black lawyer the same way Learson used Evans, but unlike Learson, he did not know the existing organization well enough to draw from inside the system.

These two high-level appointments provided Ward with useful political advice.

Then, when the deputy commissioner for parole resigned over a complete conflict in views, Ward transferred the deputy for programs into the vacant slot. Into the vacant programs position, Ward promoted a middle manager from the critical security department, a Chicano who had considerable experience at the institutional level. Finally, the most powerful of the deputies, the one in charge of security to whom all superintendents reported, was kept on, but Ward promoted a young black man who had been in program services to be the deputy's assistant. In this way, the deputy for security was backed by individuals who would be sympathetic to Ward.

Perhaps most important, Ward was able to get Governor Carey to introduce legislation that would empower Ward to fire a prison superintendent for cause. He then introduced a system of performance measures so that he would have a basis for measuring the effectiveness of prison superintendents.

Once the opportunities to change organization and careers existed, Ward moved to align structure and people with his strategy.

It is interesting to compare Ward to Learson. On the face of it, there is no comparison. Learson did not have to worry about civil service. He had the massive resources of IBM to fund his endeavors. The technology of producing computers and their components was simple compared to prisoner rehabilitation. But from a managerial perspective, there is a remarkable similarity. Learson's basic problem was that IBM was not taking advantage of its resources in a way that would best exploit the opportunities provided by the market and best protect it from threatening competitors. Ward really had the same problem. He had to devise a strategy that took account of his resources, which happened to be very limited. The threat was that if he did not meet the prisoners' minimum needs, they would riot. Second, if he did not meet the guards' needs for security, they would pose political problems. At the same time that Ward resolved his short-term difficulty, he had to devise plans that in the long term would improve the prison situation. There was, however, no point in acting precipitately, since the resources required, both physical and financial, would take time to accumulate.

In making their moves, both Learson and Ward faced organizational and personnel problems. Each relied on the power of his boss to make key moves that opened up the managerial situation and made it more tractable. Each made personnel moves that strengthened his hand by bringing near him individuals of skill whom he trusted. In this sense Ward's problem was very difficult. But it is understandable in terms of a technocratic managerial system. If Ward held his job for ten years, we could even expect results comparable to those at IBM. But well before Governor Carey left office, Ward took another job in August 1978.

Is It Live or Is It Memorex?

It helps in appreciating technocratic management at work to consider examples of failure as well as success. The case of Memorex is particularly interesting because the company's mismanagement was documented in the trial of an unsuccessful antitrust suit against IBM. Rather than being injured by IBM, Memorex was judged to have self-destructed.

Memorex started out with brilliant success. In 1961 three managers from Ampex left with the blessing of their employer — to set up a company that would be a "second supplier" of high-quality computer tape for IBM's tape storage units. With IBM unable to meet all its customers' needs, and Memorex able to produce a good product at a lower price, the company flourished.

The success of this venture led Memorex to try to repeat the feat, this time with discs for computer disc storage. The difference was that the talent to design and build the product was not available inside Memorex. The eventually successful answer was "raid IBM," that is, hire engineers from IBM who know how to make the product.

Aside from the ethics of the approach, it was initially successful and led Memorex eventually to repeat the move, this time in "disc drives," the machines that accessed the information stored on discs.

The company had created three problems for itself, however, that would later grow to damaging proportions and be aggravated as still other products were developed after raids on engineering groups at IBM and Control Data. To begin, the raided engineers were not always able to produce immediately. Delays in a fast-moving industry meant that development costs were high and new products would be competitive for only a short life. Second, the new engineers were often unable to keep up with product improvements offered by IBM and other manufacturers. Finally — and this was extremely destructive — Memorex got into the habit of using enormous incentive bonuses to capture and motivate the raided as well as those of its own employees working on the new products. Memorex engineers and scientists working on existing products such as the original computer tape were not able to obtain such incentives. Performance of existing groups fell behind, and product quality deteriorated in some instances. Employee surveys revealed declining morale both because of the poor performance and because management was perceived as disloyal.

Almost like a family in which some of the children were well treated and others not, at Memorex the way in which "goodies" were distributed literally blew things apart. Consider these comments from letters written to the chief executive:

The Memorex tape division is conspicuous by its absence from consideration as a separate profit center with the same type of management incentive that has been provided for the Disc Pack, Peripheral Systems and postulated European operations. I believe that, whereas Memorex is striving to produce creative environments in its new subsidiaries, it is in fact successfully striving to produce exactly the opposite in its parent corporation. It is obviously stifling the ambitions, aspirations and vitality of its Santa Clara people and encouraging and forcing them to consider possibilities other than long-term Memorex employment.

Our company operates as four independent companies under one roof. This is an impossible situation. The comments made regarding personal contests, secretiveness, petty jealousies, and exaggerations are indeed factual. The condition is prevalent at Memorex today and has been commented upon quite frequently. I personally find that old wounds are continually being reopened . . . but only to the benefit of our competitors. There is simply not enough energy available to fight our competitors and our associates too![4]

If there are natural laws in these matters, they had been broken by the way in which incentives were used to attract outsiders rather than reward insiders. The notion of what was an acceptable contract had been violated.

The problem got worse. In order to fund its rapid growth, Memorex had relied on the stock market. The product success in the new technology was well reported to investors eager to participate in this high-tech opportunity. But when products were delayed, when development costs overran budgets, when competitors introduced superior products, and finally when frustrated salespeople and engineers quit, profits deteriorated. Memorex turned to creative accounting to retain stock market interest until the Securities and Exchange Commission intervened. Funds quickly dried up.

The constituency of private and institutional investors also has a "contract" with a corporation. Although the risk is acknowledged that entrepreneurial high flyers may not work out, the risk that the audited information provided by companies on the New York Stock Exchange is not accurate is *not* considered an accepted part of the game. It happens, but then the contract with external sources of support is broken.

A final difficulty developed as Memorex growth outpaced the skills of its managers, the organizational design and capability, and the information systems available for planning and measuring performance. Rivalries among different raided groups, unfair division of the pie, competitive pressures, unrealistic goals, and deteriorating products put pressures on the organization that its inexperienced managers could not deal with.

Eventually the banks that had loaned Memorex money intervened and removed the top management.

Organizational failures are the most complex. To begin, the pattern of growth was poorly thought through, so that resources were diffused over excessively ambitious goals. This made it extremely important for key resources to be used selectively. Technically, the type of organization structure used to manage the diverse product line was poor. But most important, the absence of generally accepted priorities and due process in resource allocation meant that in contrast to IBM, different groups inside Memorex were rivals for corporate largess rather than competitors for places on the team. The comment of one executive captures the nastiness of the spirit:

> I believe that the primary source of difficulty within the management group in the Company lies within the President's office and in part because of his qualitative, non-factual judgement of certain people, in some cases highly unfavorable, and in part because of his opportunistic nature and aversion to true planning. I do not believe that any successful management team can be developed until these matters are openly aired, [and] the problems of secrecy, lack of forthrightness, lack of time, and apparent lack of interest in developing a truly participative performance-based management are resolved.[5]

This returns us to fundamentals. According to the Scriptures, Joseph's brothers threw him in a pit and sold him to traders because of the lack of perceived equity in the way Jacob treated them.[6] In contrast, loyalty among the Rothschild brothers provided the basis for a banking dynasty.

General Considerations

These case histories from large organizations illustrate basic aspects of technocratic systems everywhere. For example, in the 1980s in the northeastern United States, local school systems are plagued with problems that can be clearly understood in terms of the variables we have highlighted.[7]

Contract: Both in collective bargaining agreements and in the fabric of our belief, faculty are responsible for curriculum. Independence in this function is often manifested by giving a lifetime contract, or tenure, as soon as a teacher is deemed qualified.

Careers: Because we value education highly, teaching has become a profession with entry requirements and other normal accoutrements of a guild. Advancement in role is limited, however, since one early achieves tenure and can only "rise" by ceasing to be a teacher — that is, becoming an administrator, a department chairman, or a principal.

Organizations: Over the years, teachers concerned with lack of equity in the way they were measured and compensated bargained — explicitly or implicitly — for the right to measure themselves or be measured by peers.

Information: Because teachers grade students, it is very hard to know when the teacher fails. A class with low grades is a "bad class." Objective measures of teaching quality are desperately difficult to obtain — and although both students and teachers almost always agree on "who the good teachers are," it is hard to use such knowledge systematically.

Rewards: Because measures are poor, it is hard to allocate compensation equitably unless everyone gets the same amount. Seniority can be measured, however, and can be plausibly related to competence, so compensation is often related to seniority — especially since those who bargain usually represent those with seniority.

For reasons that are probably historical, teachers are often paid low salaries relative to other trades. This is often justified on the grounds that while their income stream is low, it is also secure once tenure is achieved. Many parents, however, act as if schools are organized baby sitters. Such parents presumably compare teachers' salaries with alternative ways of keeping their children out of the house.

Strategy and Resource Allocation: Because, after primary school, teachers teach subjects rather than students, schools are usually assemblages of teachers of subject matter in which strategy — an idiosyncratic way of accomplishing a comprehensive end — is somehow taken for granted. The teachers who want a better school know they can achieve it with more variety and/or a better ratio of teachers to students — that is, more teachers. Since resources are limited, concepts of acceptable teacher-student ratios have emerged.

Under these circumstances, the responses of schools to the post–World War II baby boom can be understood if not acclaimed. More students meant more schools and more teachers. Since the economy was booming, high-paying jobs were available in nonteaching professions and businesses — in contrast, for example, to the Great Depression, when teaching was one of the best jobs available. On the average, with obvious exceptions, the expanding public schools drew into their teaching ranks those who could not get jobs elsewhere. In the late 1960s the cadre of teachers was also joined by a group seeking draft deferments.

In response to a growth in the number of school-age children, schools were built or expanded and more teachers were hired and given tenure who had been recruited from a lower stratum of the pool of college-trained people. This was going on at a time when demographic data revealed that the birthrate had already declined, and the classrooms would be empty and the teachers underutilized within ten years. In the language of business, long-life capital investments were made to meet short-term peak capacity needs.

What the diagnosis reveals, however, is that it would have been very hard to avoid the problem since (1) the executive core was a principal — usually a former teacher — with no training or incentive to look way ahead; (2) if he or she did, the immediate problem would have been a conflict with teachers who had a very well developed — which is to say rigid — concept of how teaching ought to be carried out; and (3) those teachers had equally rigid views of how capacity ought to be provided — that is, by tenured professionals.

Today, as our schools cut back to respond to fewer students and falling budgets, they are left with the senior tenured faculty. Often administrators cannot hire new young faculty because all the slots are filled with the tenured. An equally disagreeable problem is presented by coincidence. Capacity is reflected in tenured bodies, so to a considerable degree the curriculum reflects the capabilities of teachers hired in a different era. Although a growing school can alter its offering by hiring in specific areas that it values, such as mathematics, science, or computer skills, a shrinking school's curriculum is shaped by who it is permitted by contract to fire.

Lest this be seen as an attack on management of the public schools, the Carnegie Council has estimated that one third of the private universities that were operating in 1980 will be closed by the year 2000.[8] It is inevitable that they will face similar problems. Until recently, the formula for recruiting, organizing, or choosing goals for education systems almost never provided for the need to respond to a changing environment.

We can understand the problem of the U.S. automobile industry in a similar way. Great as it was, General Motors was organized to gather information and plan around certain assumptions — especially the existence of cheap energy and strong but imitative competition. When by coincidence the energy crisis and small high-performance Japanese cars eliminated both conditions at the same moment, GM's past recruiting, its career system, its organization, its measures, and its strategy proved as serious a barrier to change as that experienced by a school system or university.

But, and the qualification is critical to our later argument, where and when top managements have awakened to the problem, and where they have had the freedom *and* the skill to use the sources of managerial influence available in a technocratic system, they have responded with programs that can restore the health of their organizations. By health we mean the means to generate the surplus necessary to achieve sustainable independence. How and when organizations can heal themselves is of central importance to this discussion. The appropriate conditions are discussed in chapter 10.

4 Political Management Systems at Work

ORGANIZATIONS ADMINISTERED with technocratic managerial systems are not inherently well managed. But they can be well managed in the sense that over sustained periods of time, resources can be focused on a set of limited objectives even though, as a consequence, individuals and subunits may lose out. Technocratic managements are valued because — or, rather, when — they are effective.

Organizations managed with political systems are effective producers of goods and services or efficient only by accident. Their virtue lies elsewhere. Again, case studies are a useful way of illustrating the point. The problems facing the managers in the U.S. Office of Management and Budget who chose, in 1978, to rationalize the way in which the United States managed immigration and the control of smuggling provide a sharp contrast to the powerful evolution of strategy and structure at IBM. The approach of politicians to Chrysler is also instructive when compared with New York's prisons.

A Loosely Woven Fish Net to Catch Aliens and Smugglers[1]

"The border is leaking like a sieve and nobody gives a damn," a border patrol agent told the *New York Times,* referring to the flow of illegal immigrants crossing the Mexican border. "We will catch a few, but nobody will care one way or the other."[2]

In the late 1970s, border management was more than a problem of illegal aliens and drugs. Millions of legitimate travelers passed through points of entry into the United States, and $130 billion worth of goods and services passed under the eyes of customs inspectors. The so-called border management problem was that much of the flow was illegal.

By 1978, the flood of illegal aliens and illicit drugs across the United States–Mexico border had assumed enormous proportions. Estimates of illegal aliens in the United States ranged up to twelve million, and while the federal government was apprehending increasing numbers of illegal aliens, it believed that for each one caught at least two others got through. Similarly, a huge flow of illicit drugs from Mexico, especially heroin, posed another knotty problem: in 1976, 89 percent of the heroin (and 75 percent of the marijuana) coming into the United States was believed to originate in Mexico, but it was estimated that only 6 percent of the Mexican heroin was seized at the border.

As of 1978, eight agencies representing seven cabinet departments had a physical presence in border operations and enforced more than four hundred federal laws and regulations involving entry and departure of people and goods. This fragmentation was the source of the problem that led President Jimmy Carter's reorganization team to invest effort in the border management problem.

The principal agencies involved in border law enforcement were the U.S. Customs Service in the Department of the Treasury and the Immigration and Naturalization Service (INS) in the Department of Justice. A number of other agencies also participated in border operations:

• The Drug Enforcement Administration (DEA) in the Department of Justice, as the federal agency charged with responsibility for investigation pertaining to narcotics and dangerous drug violators.

- The U.S. Coast Guard (USCG) in the Department of Transportation, with its law enforcement responsibilities on the high seas and U.S. waters.
- The Federal Aviation Administration (FAA), also in the Department of Transportation, which in relation to border control mainly supported air interdiction.
- The Department of State, with its function of visa issuance.

A last group of agencies involved in border law enforcement performed support activities:

- The Animal and Plant Inspection Service of the Department of Agriculture.
- The Center for Disease Control in the Public Health Service of the Department of Health, Education and Welfare.
- The Fish and Wildlife Service in the Department of the Interior.

Obviously, we are seeing a very different system of organization from that of IBM. If border management is the issue, no single agency is organized to address it. Moreover, the organizations that do address the problem are parts of autonomous larger units that each have different strategies, structures, career systems, and technical skills. These administrative systems have influence despite the fact that they are not managed toward any selective set of goals. No wonder someone thought about reorganization.

In 1978, the Customs Service was responsible for two principal tasks: patrolling the borders of the United States on land, sea, and air to enforce the laws covering cargo and passengers, and the investigation of currency violation, Neutrality Act violations, and other similar international economic activity.

The Immigration and Naturalization Service was responsible for administering and enforcing the immigration and nationality laws of the United States. It employed about ten thousand people and had a budget of $267 million. INS had two basic functions: first, to ensure that persons entering or remaining in the United States were entitled to do so under law; second, to provide services such as processing applications and petitions for permanent residence, naturalization, and other benefits under the immigration and nationality laws.

Three factors seemed to inhibit efficient border management: a duplication of effort by the U.S. Customs Service and INS, the neglected area of air and sea enforcement, and the role of the Drug Enforcement Administration in relation to the Customs Service and INS. It was universally agreed that something had to be done. In fact, various reorganizations had been proposed since 1967.

In 1977, after President Carter took office, an interdepartmental task force studied the problem. In August the president followed up with policy proposals aimed at the status and treatment of aliens within the United States.

What is the presidency? What is the White House? These questions receive extended treatment in chapter 5. But in the context of this case, how is the president to be regarded? Is he the head of a technocratic system that manages the border? Clearly not.

What, then, is an interdepartmental task force? Is it like the ad hoc groups used by Watson and Learson to manage the system/360 development? The form looks the same. But the chairman of the task force and the person in the executive branch to whom he reports do not control the careers, the budgets, or very much of the information available to the task force members. They have independent bases for operation.

At the same time, Richard Williams, assistant director of Peter Bourne's White House Office of Drug Abuse Policy (ODAP), set up a team to study and propose a reorganization of border management. Williams had worked on a 1974 Office of Management and Budget border study. The report of the ODAP team reached the White House reorganization project in September 1977.

During 1977 the staff of the President's Reorganization Project (PRP) had several proposals to deal with, including reorganization of the Executive Office of the President; creation of a separate Department of Education, a Disaster Relief Agency, and a Department of Natural Resources; as well as civil service reform and the creation of a Border Management Agency. By the end of 1978, President Carter had already established an Energy Department and an International Communication Agency, realized civil service reform, and reorganized his Executive Office.

This tells us something about the presidency. Compared to IBM's taking ten years to think through, plan, and develop a compatible line of computers, President Carter took two years to establish an Energy Department and an International Communication Agency, as well as reform the procedures of the entire federal civil service. Border management might have been a serious issue, or set of issues, but it could not compete with some of the other problems requiring the president's attention.

In deciding to work on a specific reorganization, "we used four criteria," said Harrison Wellford, director of the PRP: "(1) need for reform in a particular area, (2) a preference to move into program areas which are historically linked to huge budget requests and are in need of reevaluation, (3) how much of the president's time is this reorganization proposal going to take, and (4) the issue of timing and the impact on electoral politics.

"Now, as far as the reorganization proposal to create a Border Management Service, President Carter definitely was interested in it, due to his interest in Latin American affairs and his human rights concern, in this case related to illegal aliens. Relatively speaking, however, for President Carter, the Border Management Agency was not a top priority such as the creation of an Energy Department or civil service reform. In relation to border management there was also the presence of the Hispanic groups that had to be considered, especially in California, which was an important issue for Carter's administration in electoral terms."

Nine months after the Presidential Reorganization Project team had received the ODAP proposal and had done further study and analysis of it, the PRP made its recommendations, which James McIntyre, director of the Office of Management and Budget, presented in July 1978 to President Carter. The plan had three parts:

1. It created a U.S. Border Management Service in the Department of the Treasury.
2. It transferred the visa *policy* function from the State Department to the Department of Justice.
3. It shifted the administrative and enforcement responsibilities related to explosives, bombings, arson, and firearms from the Treasury to Justice.

Doris Meissner, deputy associate attorney general in the Justice Department, gave the following perspective on the three-part reorganization proposal:

> The PRP had to put together some kind of package. There is a split jurisdiction and a lot of competition and overlap between the FBI and Bureau of Alcohol, Tobacco and Firearms. You see, this border reorganization was part of a project on law enforcement reorganization. The only reason that it came out early was because Peter Bourne's office [ODAP], over in the White House, had started on the drug side and so, in order for the PRP to keep its bureaucratic control over all reorganizations, it had to move forward much more quickly with the border than with some of its other stuff. But the firearms business kind of got thrown into this pot just because they (PRP) were going to have to give something back to the Justice Department if they were going to take something away.

Consider the terrain Meissner describes here. A number of organizations — the FBI, the Justice Department, the Bureau of Alchol, Tobacco and Firearms, the White House Office of Drug Abuse Policy, and the President's Reorganization Project — are involved as players. The words she uses suggest a surprising lack of hierarchy among them.

The visa side really has to do with the House Judiciary Committee chairman, Mr. Rodino: he was not too keen on losing part of INS to Treasury, which would then no longer report under his committee. So then he wanted both the BATF (from the Treasury Department) and the visa function of the State Department to come to Justice. Also, being from New Jersey, he has always been interested in the Italians and the Europeans and has been very aggravated for years by the fact that he hasn't been able to get at the State Department in those areas.

A new voice is included here, that of Congressman Peter Rodino and the House Judiciary Committee. The committee had remarkable power over a number of issues affecting border management, but no direct control over the moves President Carter or Congress might make.

Finally, border management reform was entangled in a seamless web of other political issues salient to President Carter. First, he had under study substantive changes in the immigration laws involving employer sanctions and amnesty for those already in the United States that would have completely changed the mission of the INS. These proposals had little support from outside constituencies.

Second was the union situation. The problem was that Treasury and INS employees were organized by different unions, the National Treasury Employees Union and the American Federation of Government Employees, respectively. Harrison Wellford commented that the AFGE originally supported the proposal but later switched its position and fought it. The AFGE's opposition was quite critical, for the Carter administration depended upon its support for civil service reform. As a consequence, it was decided to delay the border management proposal while civil service reform was fought out and then passed in Congress. The delay in the passage of the civil service reform from a scheduled February 1978 to an actual August 1978 might well have cost the border management proposal key momentum. It was also important for President Carter to have the support of the AFGE on the Panama Canal Treaty, since the AFGE represented the Panama Canal workers. The AFGE lobbied intensively on Capitol Hill via grassroots efforts, and members from more than three hundred congressional districts sent letters to their representatives.

Third, Hispanic groups were also important to the proposal. They were involved both directly through concern over immigration and indirectly because the head of INS, Lionel Castillo, was the highest ranking Mexican-American in the Carter administration. The votes of Mexican-Americans would be critical to congressional elections. For example, in November 1978, Congressman Jack Brooks (D–Texas), who chaired the committee that would have to approve any reorganization proposal, was up for reelection. But President Carter was counting on the Hispanic vote.

The point is clear. A vaguely definable issue — border management — is enmeshed in a web that seems to involve everything from civil service reform to the Panama Canal and the reelection of the president. There is no definable hierarchy to deal with the problem and everyone with an interest gets to play. The system is designed to give each of them a voice.

Chrysler in Crisis

An example of a similar political management system at work, involving the market sector, is provided by the handling of the Chrysler Corporation as it began to experience difficulties between 1978 and 1980. Chrysler is an example of an increasingly observable phenomenon: a private company that no longer can compete with other technocratically managed companies shifts to a political management system in order to avoid conventional bankruptcy. The British and Italian economies are replete with such companies. Chrysler is one of the most dramatic examples in the United States.

In the early 1960s Chrysler came under the direction of Lynn Townsend, a flamboyant Michigan M.B.A. with ten years of experience at Touche Ross & Company, Chrysler's independent auditors.

Townsend believed that the automobile industry was evolving into a worldwide integrated structure. Whereas before competitors designed and manufactured products for specific markets from regional bases, the future seemed to be in the "world car" concept. Townsend embarked on a strategy of international expansion in the early 1960s but found, much to his chagrin, that General Motors and Ford had already skimmed the prime opportunities. Chrysler was forced to settle for marginal acquisitions. Domestically, Townsend attempted to match Ford's and GM's moves, but he found the company strapped for cash because of its ambitious expansion plans.

By 1970, hoping to revive the company's profits, Townsend ignored the threat of Ford's downsized Pinto and GM's Vega, and instead chose to invest $350 million to redesign the higher-margin, full-sized Chrysler cars. The new styles were introduced right before the oil embargo in 1974, and the sales Townsend had anticipated never materialized. The chairman responded with a draconian cost-cutting program designed to reduce Chrysler's overhead and break-even volumes. The company laid off and fired thousands of designers, engineers, and younger managers. Product programs and quality suffered as a result. In 1976 thousands of Volarés and Aspens were recalled because of defects. New product introductions until recently were consistently six to eight months behind schedule because of manufacturing snafus.

Removed by his board, Lynn Townsend was succeeded by John Riccardo. Chrysler was a battered version of its former self. Losses in 1974 of $52.1 million grew to a staggering $260 million in 1975. The company's market share had eroded from a high of 16.2 percent in 1969 to 11.7 percent by 1975.

Townsend's failure set the stage for Chrysler's transformation from a technocratic system to a political one.

Riccardo took stock of the company's situation and decided a fresh product strategy was required. Riccardo concluded that the company should retrench in its home market and compete actively in the downsized, fuel-efficient segment against Ford and GM. To do that,

Chrysler's old factories, mostly concentrated around Detroit, would have to be modernized. Since Chrysler was the low-volume producer of the Big Three, Riccardo recognized that the fixed costs of meeting government standards for fuel efficiency, emissions, and safety would fall disproportionately on his company. The company would have to map out a new plan if it was to remain a viable competitor.

> By the end of 1976, the Rescue Plan was ready. For four years, starting with its 1979-model cars, Chrysler was to bring out all new models — first the standards, then the intermediates, then compacts, and finally trucks and vans. While each new line was being made ready for production, the plant that was to produce it would be gutted and refitted . . . The company couldn't move ahead, however, until the government had set those emissions, safety, and fuel economy standards. When those numbers finally came down and Chrysler put a price tag on its program, management was shocked to discover that the tab, estimated earlier at $5.5 billion, had risen to $7.5 billion. That squashed Chrysler's hope of financing its plan internally.[3]

Chrysler expected that of the $7.5 billion needed, $3.6 billion would be design costs, product development, and introduction costs. Of the remaining $3.9 billion, depreciation of new tools and machines was expected to cover $2.6 billion. The remaining $1.3 billion would have to be funded externally. Chrysler had posted losses during the previous two years, so the prospect of raising the needed capital looked dismal at best. To deal with the problem Riccardo went into high gear. The company began a systematic process of paring down its balance sheet and lobbying Congress and federal regulators for some form of relief.

Riccardo discovered that he had inherited an enterprise that could not succeed in the conventional market economy. His problem was to restructure Chrysler so that it could take part in the political process. Like the State Department's Philip Heymann, he had to change the "face of the issue," in this instance from "a failed automobile manufacturer" to "the catastrophic consequences of bankruptcy, especially hundreds of thousands of lost jobs."

The profitable tank-manufacturing activity aside, what followed was a dramatic liquidation of all but the essential domestic auto manufacturing capability of the company. The overseas subsidiaries were sold. Chrysler was particularly ingenious in extracting $370 million from the British government just after Parliament had received a major Department of Industry study recommending the end of automotive bailouts. Equally ingenious was a $230 million deal with the French automaker Peugeot-Citroën. (No deal of this sort would have been approved without the tacit acceptance of the French government.)

By the time Chrysler went to the traditional source of funds, Wall Street, for support, it had to pay 6 percent over the prime rate for money and, in addition, offer warrants as part of the package. A careful reading of the prospectus of June 1978 shows the consolidated Chrysler companies in debt over $10 billion, requiring $7.5 billion to remodel, and holding as principal assets the Chrysler finance company and a realty company that held the paper of the weaker dealerships. It would take twelve more months before the political system began to grasp the existence of a serious problem.

Public awareness of Chrysler's impending problems surfaced in 1976. The task force of the House Committee on Banking, Currency and Housing reported, "The continuation of federally mandated requirements which require large capital outlays by the industry places a greater proportionate cost burden on Chrysler and American Motors, thus making their competitive position more difficult."

Later, in November 1978, the Department of Transportation's National Highway Traffic Safety Administration (NHTSA) commissioned a study to investigate corporate strategies of American automotive manufacturers. Anticipating a recession, the report concluded that Chrysler would not be able to survive as a full-line manufacturer. "Federal regulations," the study projected, "will penalize the smaller automobile companies by applying equally difficult standards to unequal companies . . . The regulatory framework will contribute to a considerably greater degree of relative industry concentration."

A second report, commissioned after the first was rejected as biased toward the companies, concluded that profit performance would be poor, cash flow problems would restrict necessary spending in new product development, and the effect would be a weakened competitive posture, but not necessarily failure. As a final caveat, it stated that economic cycles could make Chrysler's slim profits disappear, perhaps triggering a Defense Department–inspired bailout of the firm.[4]

The basic problem was that the information collected did not relate to a political issue. In 1978, the debate over autos still turned on the issues of safety and environmental regulation. It was clean air and the health of workers that was being contested, not the health of Chrysler. In that context, Chrysler's economic problems were perceived as obstructionism or irrelevant.

In December 1978, a third report to the Department of Transportation concluded that Chrysler faced a "severe" financial burden in meeting mandated fuel-economy standards. The DOT's Transportation Systems Center in Cambridge, Massachusetts, reported, "Chrysler is in a period of serious financial problems, which has every indication of extending five to eight years in the future." The center projected a "worst-case" scenario of a complete shutdown and bankruptcy with the following effects:

- Loss of 292,000 to 345,000 jobs.
- Loss of $30 billion of commercial production, or 1.5 percent of GNP.
- Increase of $1.5 billion per year in welfare costs.
- Increase in the balance-of-trade deficit by $1.5 billion per year.
- Loss of $500 million per year in income taxes.
- Increase in Detroit unemployment from 8.7 percent to 16 to 19 percent.
- Additional minority unemployment of 38,000 (principally blacks in Detroit).

The report was kept confidential until September 1979, when Senator Thomas Eagleton, Democrat of Missouri, released it four days before Chrysler officially submitted its first bailout plan (fourteen months after the gloomy prospectus). When asked why the DOT report was kept secret so long, the associate director of the NHTSA replied, "We did not feel it appropriate for the government to be the first to publicize Chrysler's difficult financial situation." Perhaps more to the point, no federal agency — except perhaps the Department of Labor, but certainly not the National Highway Traffic Safety Administration — had a charter that involved concern for the health of a particular private company.

Against a backdrop of slumping sales, lean cash accounts, high gas prices, and gloomy pronouncements of recessions, Riccardo planned his moves, the first of which was the arrival in 1978 of Lee Iacocca, who had recently been dismissed by Ford. With Iacocca installed in the president's office, Riccardo concentrated all efforts on the painful process of selling divisions to raise cash and lobbying government agencies for regulatory relief. During late 1978 and early 1979 he petitioned the White House, Commissioner Barbara Blum of the Environmental Protection Agency, Senator Edmund Muskie of Maine (chairman of the Senate Budget Committee and of the Subcommittee on Environmental Pollution of the Committee on Public Works), Congressman Henry Waxman of California (chairman of the Health and the Environment Subcommittee of the House Committee on Interstate and Foreign Commerce), and Joan Claybrook (head of the NHTSA), among others. Rebuffed on all sides with little sympathy for his cause, Riccardo fired his financial advisers, commissioned another report, and hired the lobbying services of Patton, Boggs and Blow. (Firm member Thomas Boggs is the son of the late senator Hale Boggs and a friend of Louisiana senator Russell Long, chairman of the Senate Finance Committee.)

As Chrysler transformed itself to use a political managerial system, its personnel had to change. With Iacocca to run internal operations, Riccardo could concentrate on forming political and economic coalitions. The Boggs lobbying firm was more useful than an investment bank.

On May 15, 1979, GM and Chrysler announced a joint research and development program to develop transaxles and more fuel-efficient engines. Though initially hesitant about the deal, the Justice Department later found the agreement to be acceptable and ruled out any antitrust action against the pair.

During the following two months, Riccardo met frequently with Douglas Fraser, head of the powerful United Auto Workers, and the two Michigan senators, Donald Riegle, Jr., and Carl Levin. On June 2, Fraser, in a speech to the rank and file, proposed an aid package for Chrysler be funded by $1 billion in new equity investment from the Treasury. He urged the membership to consider accepting profit-sharing bonuses in lieu of some of the wage increases planned in the September UAW contract negotiations. Meanwhile, Riegle and Levin were emphasizing their concern about a Chrysler failure to President Jimmy Carter and chief domestic affairs adviser Stuart Eizenstat. The senators cornered the president during a limousine ride from downtown Detroit, where Carter had just delivered a speech on urban policy, and urged him to draft a Chrysler aid plan.

This drama on the precipice of bankruptcy played itself out through the election-year spring of 1980 until May 11, when Congress voted to guarantee a portion of Chrysler's debt.

From the fall of 1979 to the spring of 1980 it was possible to observe the efforts of a political coalition in a struggle to keep Chrysler alive. Working for Chrysler were the United Auto Workers, the professional management of the company, and the representatives of both of these constituencies in the House of Representatives and the Senate. Other interest groups were involved as well, such as associations of dealers and auto suppliers. Perhaps most interesting, however, was the unpublicized role of the banks holding Chrysler's debt. Because by 1980 employment had been reduced to about as far as it might be expected to drop, even in a bankruptcy reorganization, some were claiming that the rescue was really a bailout of banks holding large sums of bad loans.

General Considerations

It is dramatically clear that by 1979 Chrysler could not be well understood as a technocratically managed system operating in the market economy. In fact, the situation at Chrysler was not easy to distinguish from the border management problem in the President's Reorganization Project. The managers faced the same dilemma. Their goal could not be achieved without the cooperation of a large number of players, each of whom sat outside the traditional boundaries of their organizations. Consequently, the approach to the problem was piecemeal and reflected a short political time horizon. It was more important to the problem that Chrysler was the largest employer of blacks in Detroit than that Chrysler once held 16 percent of the U.S. automotive market. Congressmen deeply committed to a free enterprise system voted against their principles in order to provide federal guarantees for Chrysler because enormous constituent pressure made it difficult to do otherwise.

Interestingly, under these circumstances the role of Chrysler's chief executive was not so much to present Chrysler as economically sound as it was to show the company in dire economic distress but otherwise "deserving." It was important to strip Chrysler of those assets or characteristics that might appear to the uninitiated to be an excuse for not providing the bailout. In effect, when Riccardo came to Capitol Hill to beg for support, he had to come in sackcloth and ashes.

In fact, the behavior of Chrysler is even more remarkable. The plan circulating in support of the request for federal guarantees struck most industry analysts as hopelessly optimistic. More interesting perhaps, as Senator William Proxmire pointed out, the plan called for the federal government to support Chrysler in competition with other domestic manufacturers. The effect of supporting Chrysler would be to exacerbate the problems of the Ford Motor Company.

Border management and Chrysler exemplify the political management system at work. It is clear that there are measures of success available. The market system provided dramatic evidence that

Chrysler had failed. Lynn Townsend moved overseas too late, and in 1974 and 1977 Chrysler brought out the wrong models at the wrong times. The border of the United States is still leaking like a sieve. There are millions of illegal aliens and billions of dollars' worth of illegal drugs. Yet the evidence is also clear that the political managers are only able to move slowly if at all to correct the situation. Indeed, they may not even care what the long-run consequences of their actions are likely to be.

Given the limited resources available to deal with either the border problems or Chrysler, the central fact is that some kind of selectivity in the application of such resources must be exercised if either problem is to be resolved. The situations of all the interested players cannot be improved or even maintained.

In the end, viewed technocratically, a central piece of the Chrysler problem is the relatively high wages paid to auto workers. The wage level is not justified by higher productivity than can be obtained in Japan or Germany at lower wage levels. On this basis, U.S. capacity is uncompetitive. The conclusion of the market is that some U.S. manufacturing capability should move aside to make room for the Japanese and the Germans. A second piece of the problem is related to the low price of gasoline in the United States. As long as Congress insisted upon subsidizing the price of gasoline, it was not surprising that American manufacturers built cars designed to exploit that American premise. The decision made by Chrysler and Ford to go with relatively large cars can be directly related to an explicit choice of the political managers. In both wages and gasoline prices, neither unions nor drivers wanted to give up their positions. The political system reflected their views successfully.

Turning to the question of border management, we find that southwestern manufacturers do not wish to see the problem solved; the government of Mexico, a potentially large source of energy for the United States, does not wish to see the problem solved; the Mexican-American community has mixed feelings about the problem; the government unions involved do not wish to see the problem solved at the expense of their voting power and clout; and the Congress members involved do not wish to see their personal control over important areas of the U.S. policy diluted. Under these circumstances, with no one willing to give, it is difficult to see where there is a solution. By political measures, maintenance of the status quo is a success.

In contrast, a critical feature of the technocratic system is that managers, even the manager of a correction system, are in a position to make choices that match goals to the limited resources available. Both Ward in New York State and Learson and Watson at IBM were trying to adjust the product/service mix of their organizations to the resources available. IBM succeeded by reducing its offering to a single compatible line of products. Ward succeeded by postponing the reform agenda until the level of security and comfort in his system were adequate, until he had the information required to diversify his system, and until he had the resources to build the facilities needed to implement a diversified system.

Both top managers of IBM saw the competitive problem over a long term. We do not have a record of Watson's views, but Learson apparently conceived the situation in terms of rapidly evolving technology and capable competitors. The need was to move as rapidly as possible to serve customers with data processing systems.

The strategies of both of these managers reflects their setting. Over time they focused more of IBM's resources on the emerging sense of what IBM was going to have to do in order to maintain or improve its competitive position as the leading supplier of data processing equipment. In this learning process they could reorganize, hire, rearrange, study, and debate — all in private — from 1959 or 1960 to 1967, until it was appropriate to announce publicly the outcome of the process.[5]

Finally, at every step along the way, the company was free to adjust the way in which men and women were assigned and compensated in order to reflect the evolving sense of corporate strategy. Although bureaucratic tendencies and individual selfishness constantly affected attitudes, management had access to sources of influence that could be directed to such difficulties if it had the will to do so.

The presence or absence of the focusing of effort in order to do a limited number of things well is a theme that appears again and again when we study technocratic systems and compare them with political systems. Leaders using political systems are constantly searching for a definition of purpose that can mobilize a temporary coalition of legislative and bureaucratic players. If a way can be found to phrase a policy objective so that managers at different points in the system can support it publicly, then it may be possible to pass legislation or appropriate money. On the other hand, both legislation and appropriation may be irrelevant to the achievement of outcomes. The pattern of expenditure is much more likely to reflect the divergent stakes of the players than the needs of the corporate organization, in this case, the country.

Thus, in 1979, with some ten million unregistered aliens in the country, with a flood of drugs estimated at a value greater than that year's total deficit in the balance of payments, and with customs inspection an important potential nontariff barrier, a team of middle-level White House bureaucrats made the opening moves in a complex policy and reorganization game. They did not even take into account the needs of the key players. For example, though it was low on the list of priorities, the president was considering a major shift in long-term policy that would provide an amnesty for aliens presently in the country and soften policy toward employers. Nevertheless, they treated the reorganization in total isolation from other substantive issues, such as U.S. policy toward Mexico and its natural gas. They also ignored legislative politics that were totally intertwined with the issues. Key House and Senate subcommittees were distinctly uninvolved in either the president's effort or the President's Reorganization Project proposal. In the end, the final proposal that died was a complex patchwork designed to meet the bureaucratic and political stakes of each of the involved players but failed even to do that.

Fortunately, two of the involved departments were able to cooperate in the implementation of one sensible proposal. Today when American citizens arrive at most ports they can walk past immigration and check both passport and baggage at customs. Called one-stop shopping, this step forward was the result of cooperation between middle-level managers in the Immigration and Naturalization Service and the Customs Service. No legislation was required. The source of this innovation, cooperation between two technocratic organizations, is a theme that is to be explored in later chapters.

5 The President: Top Manager of a Political System

OBSERVERS OF THE U.S. POLITICAL PROCESS are usually baffled. They watch a Chrysler crisis or a budget battle play out and they marvel. Foreign businessmen, especially Europeans and Japanese, want to know why there isn't more coherence, why there isn't a plan, why the president doesn't manage. Because they have in mind the more technocratic systems in their companies or centralized parliamentary democracies, they expect to see the head of the executive branch behaving in a more directive fashion — as the brain, if not the body, of the government.

Understanding of the U.S. political system is increased in important ways by focusing on the presidency to see what it is and what it is not. The demands of the office are extraordinary, literally killing. Without the power of the purse, with limited ability to hire and fire, the president is held accountable for one Chrysler crisis or border management affair after another. Some insight into what this means for a manager is provided by W. Ross Ashby's discussion of the brain as an adaptive executive.

Ashby asks what kind of function is appropriate for a system like the brain that must respond to a wide range of stimuli and learn. How can the brain's designer "specify the 'correct properties' for each part if correctness depends not on the behavior of each part, but on its relations to the other parts?"[1] The answer involves the ability to map the environment in terms of the system's ability to respond.

When a system can impose its mapping on the environment, it can dominate that environment. Ashby's law of requisite variety asserts: "Only variety in one system can force down the variety due to another system: only variety can destroy variety."

Ashby's "law of requisite variety" applied to organizational life yields the following propositions:

1. For there to be a high probability of success, an organization must be able to more than match the variety of stimuli it receives from the environment with which it interacts. It has a program for every contingency.

2. If it cannot match its environment's variety, it can only adopt a responsive mode, in which segments of the organization try to prepare to respond after the fact to the more critical moves in the environment.

What about the president? Can he or his office match the variety of environment for which he is in some way responsible? To ask the question is to anticipate the answer and hence the focus of organization appropriate to the presidency — a response mode. Nevertheless, the effort of a full answer is rewarding.

The president is responsible for the security of the nation as well as its material and spiritual well-being. Military strength is obviously important, but economic health is also important. Americans have come to expect an improving quality of life.

The relationship among military, spiritual, and economic health poses an important difficulty for the president. It is, in fact, a sharp dilemma on which Presidents Johnson, Nixon, Ford, Carter, and Reagan have occasionally impaled themselves: the reality of the present and future world situation is one in which the United States will consume resources and production at a rate that either guarantees our population *looking* fat while others starve, or worse, guarantees that we *become* fat by depriving others of the resources they need to survive. The conventional analysis in the 1950s and early 1960s was that science and technology would protect us from that political and moral dilemma. But this has not come to pass. The dilemma remains squarely facing the president. Human rights on a global basis simply will not square with U.S. (or European, or Japanese) economic aspirations.

Interestingly, the president faces the same problem when he looks at the domestic economy. Economic theory suggests that one should think about an economy in terms of the allocation of resources and the distribution of income. Government is active on both sides of this equation. It reallocates resources and redistributes income through inflation, regulation, taxation, and transfers. Increasingly important, it is an employer of a significant portion of the population.

Note that in the "good old days," when economic growth and relative military strength were taken for granted, these problems were less important. The pie was getting bigger, and that meant that politicians did not have to worry too much about the size of the individual slices. Even if one's proportionate share was declining, the size was still likely to increase. In fact, some parts of the population never had a larger piece of the pie. And in the period from 1965 through 1975, when the material situation of most did improve, significant numbers thought their situation was unsatisfactory.[2]

The politics of the 1970s and 1980s reflect a recognition by the baby-boom parents and their children that the economy is a system whose growth and health cannot be taken for granted. For those maturing after World War II, the business cycle was equivalent to the colds or diseases one got and recovered from while growing from childhood to adulthood. The present stagnation and the prospect of future limited growth are political shocks equivalent to the recognition that one is individually vulnerable to serious debilitating disease. The implication that the material gain of one person comes at the material loss of another is astounding to a society brought up to believe that it was classless. The myth of social and economic mobility has obscured the fact that we are a socially and economically stratified society. The prospect of a loss of this mobility is more than individually shattering. It is political dynamite.

This complex of social, political, economic, and ideological problems faces the leadership of the United States at least for the next decade. The problems are both endemic in the world situation and systemic, in the sense that in cases such as border management, the causes and effects of individual parts are highly interdependent. No matter who is president or what his party, the problems will remain. The only question is how well the president helps our nation, and perhaps others, to cope with them.

Yet the political process ensures that the specific issues that make up the problems arrive at the door of the president in highly variegated and fragmented fashion. There is the problem of apartheid in South Africa; there is the question of shoe imports from Italy and Korea; there is the question of hide exports and leather imports to and from South America; there is the problem of steel and the closing of mills; there is the problem of an Arab-Israeli conflict; there are problems of shipyard closings, failing railroads, and mass transit that cannot be built; and there are problems of racial violence. The list, of course, is nearly endless. What makes the task of the president quite horrifying is that each of the demands, each of the claims for resources and time represented by one of these issues is, in fact, entangled in another one. If sufficient environmental and safety regulations are imposed to raise the performance of an industry to a level that seems socially acceptable, it is at least conceivable that the economic burden or the uncertainty posed by such intervention will paralyze its management to the point that the industry is seriously vulnerable to imports.

The way in which the steel industry deteriorated provides a painful example. The industry has been the bête noire of one administration after another since well before the Second World War. Until 1980, no one in the government took seriously the proposition that the goal of intervention ought to be a healthy, efficient steel industry. It was taken for granted that the individual managements of the firms would take care of that problem. This was the position of various administrations despite the fact, obvious to investors, that the industry had been noticeably laggard in adopting new technology and was generally doing a poor job at maintaining its competitiveness. Somehow or other, we were always sure that the adversary clash of ideas and special interests in the marketplace, in the courts, and at the polls would ensure through some invisible process that everything would work out. This faith, like that in reincarnation, has not yet been rewarded. In the libertarian era of 1982 and 1983 we found the government risking trade war with Europe to protect the *industry* from imports at the same time that the companies in the industry were diversifying and liquidating.

As the president of the United States considers the array of problems such as a declining steel industry, he must do so in a world populated by a number of other nations operating on substantially different assumptions and playing by different rules. Most other nations never believed that the the world was inevitably bountiful. They did not think that the prosperity of their neighbors would inevitably enhance their own well-being. As business historian Alfred Chandler, Jr., has shown, family and the government are substantially more important institutions in other parts of the world and business is a much more recent and less legitimate participant in the governing scheme of things. While it vastly exaggerates the point to suggest that other nations are "managed," Switzerland is probably the only nation left, other than the United States, that believes in a predominantly free market system. The rest of the governments have systematically tried to influence their economies in order to generate the wealth desired by the population. Firms are subordinate to this process.[3] With almost no exceptions, the most managed parts of other nations' economies are those involved in international trade. For this vast economic world of trading partners, the U.S. market is the cornucopia of riches — more than two hundred million people whose consumption expenditures are supported by government policy, often at the expense of U.S. manufacturers.

As the president begins to study these problems, he discovers that the managers of this foreign economic activity have prepared for, studied, and worked at their problems for years. They are sophisticated players, often the elite of their nation, and the nature of the game is clear to them. It is economic war.

Speaking of free trade under the British empire, Sir Edmund Dell notes that "international trade was, as Clausewitz might have put it, the prosecution of power politics by other means."[4]

The contrast exists in military policy as well. Our notion of military rotation, together with the ebb and flow of political administrations, brings relative newcomers to a conflict to which opponents have devoted the better part of their lives. Moreover, it is alleged that U.S. military thinkers are not as instinctively aware of the importance of economic activity to their strategic position as are their foreign counterparts. Since military and economic war interrelate, we are at a further disadvantage.

Perhaps the most dramatic example of the divergence of viewpoint was provided by President Carter's dismissal of half his cabinet members during the summer of 1979. Naturally, U.S. allies throughout the world were concerned. Imagine their consternation when Carter said in effect: "Don't worry, our position with respect to the rest of the world will be stable. I have kept Brown, Vance, and Brzezinski. I have merely fired the secretaries of the treasury, commerce, health, education and welfare, transportation, and housing and urban development." To Carter the economy was a domestic issue, and judging by his organization of the White House, it has been for President Reagan as well.

A Managerial View

The answer to Ashby's question is clear. The "variety" facing the president is overwhelming. A technocratic manager looking at the problems just described would be impressed by the range of issues, the vast importance of several, the extent to which they were intertangled, and the long periods of time over which they developed and played out. Numerous decisions would have impact for decades to come. He would, in turn, be concerned with the limited resources, physical and financial but also managerial, that he was to bring to bear on these problems. He would know that strategy is a matter of focus: the application of massive resources to limited objectives. Instinctively, then, his attention would be directed to the problem of how to limit the agenda, how to find a set of more limited manageable goals that might be addressed successfully.

Setting priorities would imply claims for the time and resources available. Some projects could be funded and others could not. Since issues were inevitably crossing departmental lines and since it would be inevitable that units would compete, a technocratic manager would be concerned with establishing a climate of cooperation. His experience would tell him that in complex issues, how policy was carried out was often at least as important as what he thought the policy was, and he would thus be deeply concerned with the plans for implementation. Finally, because the extraordinary uncertainties enveloping the questions before him gave him no sure course of action, he would be interested in taking just that minimum risk which was necessary to avoid paralysis. Then he would want to gather information and focus resources so that as problems were discovered over time, the negative consequences of chosen alternatives could be avoided or minimized. As time passed and the chosen programs worked themselves out or failed, he would be concerned that his organization learned appropriate lessons and altered goals.

The way in which a sophisticated technocratically managed system might organize itself to accomplish a set of demanding tasks is exemplified by the history of the Texas Instruments Corporation.[5]

A System for Managing Growth

Led by Pat Haggerty and then Mark Shepard, this manufacturer of instruments and electronic devices grew and profited for twenty-five years at a rate that put it among the leaders of American companies. What makes it especially useful as an example is that TI executives wrote and thought extensively about how they were managing to reach their ambitious objectives.

Texas Instruments has tried to use recruiting, organization, budgeting, planning, and reward to obtain cooperative behavior in both formulating and implementing its objectives. The philosophy on which the company's approach was founded seems to have been to hire talented engineers and give them demanding goals, but in the context of job assignments and business units that could not succeed unless there was cooperation among individuals and units.

As a general rule, it seems that the higher one rose in the TI organization, the more one depended on the efforts of those in other parts of the organization. Marketing groups in one division sold products made in several others. In turn, a development team might draw talent from two or three departments to design a system to be sold by still another division.

Instead of designing small profit centers so that a manager can "run his own little business," TI broke itself down into seventy-seven "product-customer centers" dependent on each other in various ways for success. TI's key administrative tool designed to link these units was its "objectives, strategies, and tactics" (OST) system.

The OST system was designed to weave the smaller operating units of TI into a corporatewide team pursuing short- and long-term objectives explicitly. The comments of one of the planning officers give the flavor of the system:

> Our corporate objective states the economic purposes, the reasons for the existence of the organization. It also states, in broad terms, our product, market, and technical goals. The corporate objective is supported by a set of business *objectives.* Each of these is expressed in terms of (1) a business charter which establishes the boundaries of the business, (2) an appraisal of the potential opportunities we perceive in the business, (3) a study of the technical and market trends, and (4) the overall competitive structure of industry serving this business.
>
> We attempt to look at ourselves in a mirror and critique the overall

objective. We expect the objective to be challenging enough, even *shocking* enough, to force a radical rethinking of the strategies and tactics. At the next level in the goal structure is the strategy statement. The strategy statement describes, in detail, the environment of the business opportunity to be pursued in support of the objective. Normally, there will be several strategies supporting each objective. For example, if we had an objective to achieve certain goals in the automobile market, we might have one strategy involving automobile electronics, one involving material applications, and perhaps another for safety systems. The strategy looks ahead over a number of years, normally from five to ten, and intermediate checkpoints are defined along the way, providing milestones against which to judge a process. Next in the goal hierarchy is the tactical action program, or TAP. The TAP is a detailed action plan of the steps necessary to reach the major long-range checkpoints defined by the strategies. It is normally short-term, covering six to eighteen months' effort. As we progress downward through the OST system, plans are formulated at an increasing level in detail. Below the tactic level, each TAP is broken down into individual work packages, which we manage by means of standard program management techniques.

What we have with OST is a system that gives us a method of planning review and control, which cuts across the operating structure, groups, divisions, and product-customer centers. It provides a mechanism for assembling capabilities and challenging efforts to achieve results that could not be achieved by any one organizational element.

What is unusual in this description is the attempt to have organizational elements cooperating across subunit lines as a matter of course. To make the system work, TI devised a two-hat concept of management in which a manager might be held responsible for the short-term performance of one of the product-customer centers at the same time that he may have been wearing the hat of a TAP manager or a strategy manager. Rather than allow the long term to be a result, the outcome of year-to-year incremental moves, TI tried to harness the energy of its subunits to corporate objectives through an explicit long-term-oriented planning and budgeting system. The second hat makes accountability visible and performance measurable.

To drive this system, and to keep a balance between individual and team/corporate performance, a compensation system was devised that measured performance against short-term and long-term goals, but also compared and ranked performance of managers across all divisions. Finally, although huge bonuses were occasionally paid to reward outstanding management accomplishment, a major part of incentive compensation was tied to corporate achievement of long-term profit objectives.

To further help knit the system together, two top management committees with overlapping membership met frequently, one to discuss operations, the other — the OST committee — meeting for a full day to consider, or reexamine, at least one business objective.

The resource allocation process was also interesting. With business objectives chosen by the OST committee, strategies were evaluated and chosen. The tactics were then grouped into logical, stand-alone "decision packages," which were ranked according to priority by the strategy managers. Based on the guidelines for strategic funding of business objectives and individual strategies, a cutoff line was chosen and packages above the line were given tentative approval. Those falling below the line were not discarded, but remained in a "creative backlog."

In late December of every year, at the end of the planning process, there was a formalization of the results of the planning activity. About five hundred managers attended some part of a three-day conference. Each operating group was allocated a part of the agenda, and in the course of the conference, each PCC manager, each division manager, and each objective manager would speak briefly to the group. The purpose of such a conference was primarily communication. Another advantage was that each manager made a public commitment to what he proposed to achieve during the year, in front of the audience, whose resources he — and not they — was using.

A reader unfamiliar with managing in large organizations may not sense how unusual were these TI systems, and how extraordinarily different they were from anything in our federal government.[6] To the extent that the system succeeded:

1. Short-term and long-term problems were separated. (They are mixed together in the U.S. budget.)

2. Interdependence of issues was recognized. (The committee system of Congress cuts issues apart. The counterpart of a TAP manager might have to testify before a dozen committees, or, like Philip Heymann on the subject of visas, none.)

3. Compensation was carefully managed to reflect individual and team performance. (In order to be equitable and cost-conscious, the salaries of the top one thousand federal managers are more or less the same.)

4. The OST committee devoted at least eighteen full days a year to long-term objectives. (The White House and cabinet agendas are crowded with short-term items such as auto imports, the Soviet pipeline, or war in Lebanon.)

5. The members of the OST committee had long-term experience and substantive knowledge of the company and its problems. (Top federal executives are almost all "tourists.")

6. There was open competition for resources. Five hundred managers met across the entire company. (The federal resource allocation process is a year-long war, fought out in the hearing rooms and back rooms of Congress, and in the White House, as well as in homes and restaurants of the capital. And the five hundred top managers of the government never meet. They may gather at the inauguration or funeral of a president.)

At Texas Instruments the top management drove its organization toward *shocking* objectives, objectives that required stretching. But resources were not committed until careful planning progress suggested that implementation of the subobjectives (the TAPs) would provide a successful program.

And what would a shocking objective be? Well, some time during the late 1960s or early 1970s, TI decided to bring out an electronic watch that would sell for less than ten dollars. TI has brought us equally inexpensive calculators. They then took a dramatic position in the toy business based upon the use of those calculators. The company has also entered the business of minicomputers. But consider that agenda and the one facing the presidency of the United States. If such sophisticated organization is appropriate to meet limited objectives, what should the presidency be like?

The Federal Process

The activities of the federal government are spread out in a complicated network of competing but interdependent executive, legislative, and judicial units — what Lee Fritchler calls a badly woven fishing net.[7] There is no OST committee of top managers. From a technocratic perspective, the key people in this process are usually the careerists who work for the politically appointed assistant secretaries, deputy assistants, and assistant directors. In their role as staff, they must brief a succession of outsider bosses on the true shape of the underlying strategic problem facing that department or agency. As legislation and policy are formulated, they must try to speak to the realities of implementation. Often, the bosses have never worked in a large organization.

The programs they manage are paid for in large part by income taxation of one kind or another (user taxes represent less than 10 percent of the government's revenues). But the choice of activities is made by the committee and subcommittee structure of Congress negotiating with other committees and the executive agencies and departments. In turn, especially in the more recent, more inexperienced Congresses, authority devolves to staff. In this, Congress is not different from a corporation. Texas Instruments, too, must depend on staff work.

But Congress has no OST process to link this year's programs to the long term, nor any obvious way to link or compare broad program categories. David Stockman's comment to William Greider is telling.

This master of the budget confessed, "None of us really understands what's going on with all these numbers. You've got so many different budgets out and so many different base lines and such complexity now in the interactive parts of the budget between policy action and the economic environment . . ."[8] In fact, it is hard to imagine a constitutionally acceptable approach to technocratic management of resource allocation in the federal system. There is too much variety. The technocratically managed pieces of the government cannot justify selectivity. And the political superiors to whom the careerists report have other kinds of responsibilities.

Here, in fact, the role of political managers is dramatically clear. Integration and risk taking are done in the U.S. government despite the "vacuum" of technocratic top management. The functions are performed in a political process by coalitions of active players from their positions of influence in the staffs, the Congress, and the operating agencies. The critical nature of this coalition building and operating process is what lends so much influence in the policymaking process to relatively low-level actors. High-level appointees who do not plug into the process do not make policy. They may take policy positions, but that is a different matter.

Consider the food stamp program. Beginning as an Eisenhower administration experiment, it has slowly been transformed from an agricultural subsidy masquerading as a welfare payment to a close substitute for a negative income tax. Powerfully rooted in the House Agriculture, Rural Development and Related Agencies Subcommittee of the Appropriations Committee, it has received careful attention from a wide variety of the most talented experts in the field of income transfers. At the same time, "welfare reform" — defining and planning a comprehensive program of income support that includes food stamps but also school lunches, Aid to Families with Dependent Children, Medicaid, and housing subsidies — has defied successive administrations.

A program like food stamps can be grown from a few thousand to twenty million recipients. Its purposes and procedures can be changed. It can be cut back. But the broad issue of which it is a part — the support of the weak and poor — involves too many parts of the "badly woven fishing net" to permit the development of a concrete, explicit program to meet long-term objectives.

What we have in the federal process is a network of technocratically managed organizations. Each of these is charged with an independent agenda and competes for the various powers of the government in order to alter the allocation of resources and the distribution of income. Each must do this while preserving or enhancing the peaceful and just order of our society as viewed in each particular organization. What we know is that:

1. Costs to states, cities, or citizens of resources misallocated in the political process are long term. (Lyndon Johnson's inflationary financing of the Vietnam War really hurts in the early 1980s as we try to cure the consequences.) As well, these costs are seldom, if ever, borne by those responsible. From the perspective of the political systems' managers, the tangible costs are political and short term. They are imperfectly, if at all, linked with performance of the technocratic organization to which players may belong.

2. In order to protect itself from this short-term political process, the federal system operates as best it can through the technocratic subunits that are focused narrowly on specific legislated constituencies.

3. Managers within the technocratic system sometimes perceive problems cutting across their departments and form coalitions to change the system's performance — for example, "one-stop shopping" by Customs and the INS at ports of entry.

4. Finally, the process is really vastly more complicated than pictured because much of what the "consumers" of the process experience is delivered by the state and local governments.

It is evident that in any sense remotely close to common usage, the president cannot *manage* the federal system. In four years, or even eight, he can have only a marginal effect on the prevailing system. And in this respect he is no different from a businessman. The chief executive of General Electric or du Pont does not have hands-on management of those companies. He can only influence the way the operating managers do their work. Consider how Reginald Jones describes his work at General Electric:

> Right from the start of our new planning system in 1972, the vice chairmen and I tried to review each plan in great detail. This effort took untold hours and placed a tremendous burden on the Corporate Executive Office. After a while, I began to realize that no matter how hard we would work, we could not achieve the necessary in-depth understanding of the forty-odd business unit plans. Somehow, the review burden had to be carried on more shoulders.[9]

Creating a sector structure that grouped business units into massive, multibillion-dollar aggregates was Jones's way of spreading the review load. The sector was defined as a new level of management that represented a macrobusiness or industry area. Unlike the interdependent groups at Texas Instruments, these were stand-alone business segments, each one larger than TI.

> I had a personal road map of the future and knew when I wanted to retire. Time was moving on, and I could see a need to put the key candidates for my job under a spotlight for the Board to review. The Sector executives' positions would provide the visibility.
>   The men were assigned to Sectors with businesses different from their past experience. I did this not only to broaden these individuals, but also to leaven the businesses by introducing new bosses who had different perspectives.[10]

Jones's words capture the spirit of a company president, but they also remind us that the task of a leader in a large technocratic organization — careful planning and resource allocation — is enormous. After a lifetime at GE and a decade in top management, overseeing all the business units at GE was *too* much for Jones *and* his three vice chairmen. His task was to spread the load in a way that would also help him manage the job of broadening — *leavening* is his word — and choosing among the four or five men who might succeed him. And he had the power to move organization structure and executives to meet the need he defined. Management at such a level and on such a scale may seem very abstract; it has been called meta-management. It is part of what top managers of large organizations must do with whatever power they have.

The president of the United States has four or eight years to work on unaccountable, intractable problems. It may be that he can comprehend the whole of our country in only an abstract sense. If that is true, he must bring to his job a philosophy or a theory of how the country operates that fits closely with reality and then manage by exception on a priority basis.

If one accepts this view of the problem, then one will recognize that the president must have an organizing framework or set of themes. This framework, like a good theory, must only abstract, not oversimplify. It must then be expressed to the nation in a consistent and comprehensive way. Where there is an opportunity to use the limited resources of his office to influence the outcome of the federal process on a specific issue, he may wish to intervene politically. Ronald Reagan has given us examples of this on a limited number of occasions, including the decision to sell AWACS to Saudi Arabia and the budget battles. His intervention to destroy the air traffic controllers' union seems to have been a case where a very small investment let him win a clean, visible victory consistent with his organizing political themes.

Following this theory, Jimmy Carter should never have taken off his sweater. His greatest mistake was in thinking it was possible to produce an integrated energy plan. In reality, and as Carter discovered too late, he could have moved only on isolated issues that fit his view of the problem, while avoiding harmful losses. If, for example, he had recognized how key the price of gasoline was to be, he might have taken a lower profile on other issues.

On another level, the president must also express aspirations and set goals for the private sector, as well as be directly responsible for the conduct of foreign and military relations, for trade policy, for the U.S. monetary agenda, and for a seemingly endless list of operating activities. Clearly, the U.S. president does not have the luxury of being only a systems designer.

On still another level, one also exemplified by the energy problem, we should recognize that the presidency is not able to manage system-wide programs, even under wartime conditions. Realizing this, the president should always be asking, "To what organizations and what managers and leaders am I going to delegate this problem? Is it possible to phrase the charge to them so that their response will be consistent with my basic objectives?"

In short, the presidency must be organized so that it can get problems into the hands of technocratic management. In turn, the president's job is to provide the political premises on which the technocracy should act and to select the immediate staff for the White House and cabinet that will help him in that political process.

In the language used to analyze organizations, these two functions correspond to (1) the building and managing of organizational relationships around organizational purpose, and (2) the recruiting and training of people. Both are meta-management issues. The two activities are unquestionably powers of the "corporate" office. But to fulfill both functions in a political system requires that the president first construct and thereafter maintain his political power base, for the president's source of influence is not administrative systems but political power.

Indeed, the record suggests that most presidents about whom there is good information concerning their approach to management thought they were trying to delegate operations and build political power. More often than not, their failures lay in the consequences of action taken to deal with distracting issues that forced themselves upon them. Lyndon Johnson surely did not seek out Vietnam. Pleiku was not his planning. Nor, for that matter, was the 1973 Yom Kippur War Nixon's. The necessity to respond to these events weakened both administrations' management agendas. Battles are dramatic examples of this problem of distraction, but scandals in the White House staff and Japanese trade successes can pose immediate political problems that must be well handled.

The underlying dilemma is that today's global political-economic problem has no politically attractive solution. If everyone wants more than he has and the pie is growing slowly, if at all, then day after day, the sally of some nation or interest group is likely to arrive at the White House. If the president is to be able to function, he must understand which "buck" stops at his desk and which must be deflected or delegated. With everyone's claims (even the claims of terrorists) achieving press attention, and with most claims constituting a crisis, crisis management becomes a day-to-day demand on the White House.

What makes this aspect of the president's problem extremely difficult — especially in contrast to the job of the technocratic manager — is that seemingly devastating consequences can follow from relatively unimportant issues, hundreds of which pass through the White House and only two or three of which turn out to be key.

The consequences of letting the shah of Iran into the United States provided major time-consuming problems for President Carter for fifteen months. The substantive equivalent of this issue — as opposed to its political or media counterpart — could be relegated to the back burner of a technocratic agenda.

The president, in order to manage, requires an ability to examine issues, evaluate their significance, and devise a way of getting them out of the White House. He must also have a way of tracking and following up on how they are being handled.

In managing the presidency, this last requirement may be the most demanding, if least important, of the tasks we have described. But because the flow of traffic is there; because it is where the action is; because mishandling the flow can be serious; because it is work that politicians do well; because the president's judgment is probably finer and broader in such matters than any of his subordinates'; and finally, because sometimes this activity is hard to distinguish from the administrative aspects of political leadership and meta-management, the president may have a tendency to devote too much of his time to these matters.

Although strategy is a long-term phenomenon, strategic outcomes are a sum of daily details, only some of which are significant because of their impact or precedent-setting qualities. Successful meta-management involves attention to interpersonal and institutional relationships that also turn on detail. Both the detailed aspects of a strategy (those TAPs at Texas Instruments) and the detail of administrative systems design require attention, but someone else has to provide it. Distinguishing among interpersonal, strategic, and institutional details of management activities and providing the different sorts of help that they require would seem to be the core of the problem of organizing the presidency for the 1980s.

Organizing the White House

From a managerial perspective, the kind of organization available to help the president do his work is highly extraordinary. To begin with, the staff is made up of amateurs. It is rare for the White House staff to contain even one high-ranking professional manager.

Kennedy and Johnson brought young, brilliant academics into the White House to complement the usual number of lawyers. The record of those years is cursed by the entanglement of Vietnam and the inflationary financing of the war. Without trying to assess the record of these two administrations, we can see that there is surely a consensus that their weakness lay in limited administrative skills and an associated tendency to underestimate how hard it would be to implement policy and programs.

Nixon's White House staff, no more experienced than Kennedy's, tended to be drawn from the campaign organization. Ford, Carter, and Reagan followed variants of this recipe: one part lawyers, one part campaign workers, and one part academics. This newly recruited collection of unseasoned but enthusiastic advisers and analysts has to help the president relate to two extremely complex groupings of organizations, the cabinet and the Congress. The cabinet is especially perplexing.

There is a tendency for Americans, as well as others, to think about the cabinet as if it represented the power of the dominant political coalition sitting over the administrative apparatus of the civil service. The image is of "sectors" at GE, a set of corporate group vice presidents promoted from within, skillful and knowledgeable. While there may be rivalries among them, if they can agree on a line of action, their agreement commits their party and their departments. In the extreme, one might imagine that if the staff work were good enough, they could debate and argue upon a coherent national program that traded off economic, social, and political costs — a sort of giant Texas Instruments, called USA, Inc.

An American cabinet is, instead, an utterly different phenomenon. Sitting together in one room, it has very little meaning. There is no collective responsibility. The cabinet cannot commit to anything if to commit means to deliver results. Cabinet secretaries are unelected individuals serving as heads of executive departments. They are chosen for the task because their previous background in law, business, government, or academia bears some relationship to the substantive work of their departments. Even assuming what is rarely true, that their background is pertinent to the actual work of the job, it remains true that:

1. The cabinet secretary has no inherent political power linked to his party.
2. The secretary is dependent on his or her bureaucracy for effectiveness and on the press for perceived effectiveness.
3. The budget of his or her department is controlled by several differ-

ent congressional committees, as well as by the Office of Management and Budget, which reports to the president.

4. After the president, the most powerful politicians are the congressmen and senators who control the budget and the tax-raising powers of the government — not the cabinet officers. These people, the chairmen of the House Appropriations Committee and its seventeen standing subcommittees, the chairman of the House Ways and Means Committee, and the chairman of the Senate Finance Committee, usually have tenures in government far longer than the cabinet or the president.

5. Since the budget of his or her department is made up of a number of separate authorizations, each cabinet secretary will also have to get the approval of whichever committees — Senate and House — have responsibility for oversight of the department's programs. In 1977, the secretary of health, education and welfare received funds from more than forty committees.

6. In case the secretary forgets where power lies, all major appointees must be approved by the Senate.

The cabinet, in short, is a group of appointed amateur administrators who are less powerful than the person who appointed them, the people who control their budget, and the people who help make policy in their departments. They have few interests in common except the favor of the president, for which they fight. A cabinet position is anything but a coherent seat of political power.

More extreme is the position of independent agencies. Consider this interchange. Senator Vance Hartke of Indiana is questioning Caspar Weinberger before the confirmation of his 1970 appointment as chairman of the Federal Trade Commission.

SENATOR HARTKE: Do you look upon this position in the Federal Trade Commission as primarily responsible to the Congress or primarily responsible to the president, or to both?

MR. WEINBERGER: It is difficult for me to say at this time whether the Federal Trade Commission should be regarded as a creature of Congress or a creature of the president, or both. I have difficulty in answering that.

I do feel that it was created by the Congress with the president's approval in 1914, and that this should certainly be in the background of anybody's mind administering it. The Congress has passed certain acts directing the commission to do certain things, and the president has signed those. And those obviously should be followed.

SENATOR HARTKE: Let me make it perfectly clear to you that under the Constitution and under the law which created it, the responsibility is only to the Congress, and not to the president, in any regard whatsoever.

MR. WEINBERGER: The reporting responsibilities?

SENATOR HARTKE: No; the direct authority. This is not in regard to the president, but in regard to the presidency — that this is an arm of the Congress, and it is not an arm of the administrative branch of the government. It doesn't mean that you cannot take recommendations from the president, but they really, in the totality of the scene, can only have the same weight that any other individual, probably in the government, can render.[11]

The president of the United States and his advisers must always remember that much technocratic authority and power is in the hands of Congress. As a consequence, it is impossible to manage from the top down any coherent cascade of national objectives, strategies, and programs.

Equally important to the present discussion is the important role of the states and municipalities in the U.S. system. Much of the implementation of federal policy is left to the states. In fact, much of the federal budget that is not committed to (1) interest on the federal debt, (2) Social Security, (3) other pensions, and (4) defense and foreign policy is spent through grants to states and localities. Evidence of this phenomenon is provided by employment figures. While the federal budget has climbed 620 percent in twenty years, federal employment has stayed nearly constant. It is the state and local government apparatus that has more than doubled. And it is these technocratic and political organizations, far removed from the president, that deliver the services we experience.

It is hard to imagine a more peculiar administrative arrangement. But it is this apparatus of departments and states that the president must attempt to influence in order to develop and implement policy.

The memoirs of former members of the White House staff are often sagas of frustration. Good ideas were sidetracked. Cabinet secretaries were "captured by their departments," "lacked energy or vision," or "weren't team players." Because staffer expertise was often greater than that of the president in the particular sphere for which they were responsible, they sought to manage the president — for the nation's well-being.

This is not a rare occurrence in technocratically managed systems. Especially at high levels, many managers think they can do their bosses' jobs better than they are being done. Their successful management of their own departments provides measurable outcomes to prove their worth. But at the same time that they can assert themselves based on results — "track record" — and not good intentions, they work in a system that gives extensive power to their bosses through the administrative systems. The good manager who lobbies for his boss's job today is often gone tomorrow.

During 1979, while there was a battle for succession to the chief executive's job in progress at General Electric, Thomas A. Vanderslice, one of the four or five men clearly under consideration, was written about in a flattering way in *Fortune*. Not too long afterward, Vanderslice found himself in a new job at another company. Cabinet members are more independent than group vice presidents. Through their access to Congress and the press — if they realize they have it and are deft enough to use it well — they can operate significantly free of presidential checks and balances.

A choice example of this distance is provided by the experience of William Ruckelshaus, the first administrator of the Environmental Protection Agency. An agency administrator is only a close cousin to a cabinet secretary, but Ruckelshaus's comments on the advantages and disadvantages to provoking White House disapproval illustrate the relationship to the presidency quite well:

> I felt that to a certain extent the desires of the White House and my feelings that we needed public support [for environmental legislation] were antagonistic. From time to time to get whacked by the White House probably wasn't a bad thing — in order to gain more public support to do something about the issue. I didn't consciously go out and try to antagonize them into slamming at me. But when it did happen, as it did occasionally, I didn't feel that it had hurt the ability of the agency to move forward.[12]

On the other hand, he added,

> Every time I was pitted against the White House it was, in my opinion, a very bad thing. I know that from the point of view of some environmental organizations, if they believe that, it might enhance me somewhat in their eyes. In fact, what happens is that it makes the White House mad. So when you go over there and you are talking about budget items or which direction we ought to go in, the really important policies we are dealing with, they are *already* mad at you. They think you are out there stimulating that publicity.[13]

Despite their administrative independence, there is often little technocratic significance to what cabinet members can do quickly. The civil service, the overlap of responsibility, the states and the cities all lie between them and an early response to policy decisions. In this regard, they are merely the lowest hierarchical rung of the presidency. They are tourists in a land of career specialists. Having made a substantial sacrifice in income and family life to take on the honor of cabinet service, they discover that youngsters half their age have more access to the president and that they must spend all their time negotiating with people outside their organizations in order to get anything done.

The natural response of "rational" managers to this set of problems is to reorganize. In one "border management case" after another, lines are redrawn and activities regrouped so that there can be more effectiveness and efficiency. Always the model is a logical managerial cascade descending from the chief executive as president. The goal is to give the president technocratic management powers over his "subordinate" organization. Richard Nixon put the aspiration well: "A president whose programs are carefully coordinated, whose information system keeps him adequately informed and whose organizational assignments are plainly set out, can delegate authority with security and confidence."[14]

This is the wrong tack. For positive and negative reasons, the president should not be tied to his departments. The positive reason lies in the separation of powers. To give the president executive powers in a technocratic sense would require stripping the powers of the purse from Congress, especially the House of Representatives, an unlikely event. The negative reason is the reverse side of that constitutional coin. Without the power of the purse, the president can expect regularly to see highly imperfect correspondence between his intent and the acts of his appointees. If he accepts technocratic managerial responsibility, then he will constantly be vulnerable to specific — even quantifiable — measures against which he is likely to fail. He will fail because the public agenda will inevitably be out of control; programs will contradict each other; and key programs will lack resources and management to succeed. Why become tied to such costly activity? This brings us back to the political problems of the president.

While he does not want to be committed by others and while he may recognize the diversity of views and the contradictions in behavior of his departments, the president does not want "his" shop to contribute to the problem by speaking in discordant voices. It is his administration and conflict within the cabinet is news, an open sore that the media will pick at so long as it is visible.

At a minimum, the administration must have the appearance of coherence. Even better, if there is to be a chance of working the departments and agencies into a coherent pattern, the White House staff needs to be coordinated. It is the sequence of speeches, dinners, dispersal of patronage, legislative initiatives, and appointments to the executive branch that give the evidence of the president's intentions. All these need to be shaped to a consistent pattern. In this sense the president is an actor on a brilliantly lit stage; inconsistent behavior of any sort confuses the message to the audience.

The problem, of course, is that very few outstanding men and women give up time from serious careers in order to disappear into the shade of a president. Those who do — many of whom are young, ambitious, and idealistic people who want to help the country, or for whom the job is not an economic sacrifice — are the ones who find it hardest to be silent when their counsel is rejected. Glory is hard coin in Washington, and most succumb to the temptation to pursue it. They have come to serve the president, not to work in a smooth bureaucracy. They have energy and ideals that make them excellent warriors in the cavalry charge. They are the ones who find it hard to believe there may be just cause when a perfectly valid program to which they have devoted a significant portion of their working lives is traded for something else the president wants more. In response, the urge to "leak" becomes almost irresistible.

It is not the purpose of this book to resolve the problems of the presidency. Others far more qualified have devoted their lives to the subject. My impression is that the diagnoses of Hugh Heclo, Stephen Hess, and Richard Neustadt, for example, are not inconsistent with mine. They, too, see the president burdened by severe and inconsistent political demands. They also see a fragmented bureaucracy. The importance of a diagnosis of the presidency for present purposes is that it reveals, in the extreme, the awkwardness of political apparatus for technocratic management.

An organization built to receive and respond to incoming demands and attacks from all parts of American society, as well as foreign governments, cannot — except in periods of crisis such as the Cuban missile crisis or the negotiation of the Camp David agreement between Israel and Egypt — devote large blocks of quiet time to the study and discussion of a few issues. There is too much variety to prepare for it in advance. The staffs with the time, training, and experience to develop and program strategy to deal with substantive problems sit in the departments and agencies, as well as in Congress and in business corporations. The White House cannot hope to match this vast analytic capability. Nor can it hope to manage it. What it *may* be able to do is lead by providing a widely accepted interpretation of the changing national environment and how the voters wish to respond to that change. It may also be able to bring together the capable and the interested so that a consensus may be developed. By emphasizing some activities and deemphasizing others, an administrative "program" may be created even where there is none.

For it is also true that as a consequence of the great "variety" (in Ashby's sense) produced by the fragmentation of the federal system, there is a vacuum of comprehensive plans at the top or — more correctly, in our system — at the center. The president's themes, his philosophical statement of where we should be headed, can shape the bottom-up flow of program activity through the ideas of his appointees, through winning the battles he chooses to fight, and through his ability to speak to the people as the president. In that eye of the hurricane, the president's political powers are great. As long as he does not trap himself by confusing his success with that of one or another technocratic program, he may continue to succeed even when objective results seem poor. After all, Franklin Delano Roosevelt won by a landslide in the depression year of 1936.

This sort of balancing act is hard to deliver from a group. It takes incredible restraint for an individual to invest a talented life in the politically "possible" when the limitations of our Constitution are so great. Political managers see fewer tangible results as a consequence of most of their efforts than the egos of most managers require for sustenance. Yet, the logic of organizational analysis suggests that politics is the only successful approach under the circumstance.

The conclusion to which one is drawn by this logic is unhappy for those who seek answers in a strong, technocratically managed central government. Unless we are to revise the constitutional arrangements, the imperative derived from a managerial analysis is simple and direct: "Do less." In order to succeed, the president must use his powers only where they are most effective. That will usually be in the areas where technocratic organizations are committed but in conflict. It clearly means that the president may lead best from a position of participant referee. It may also mean that he cannot pursue a program independent of his party.

6 Contact Sport: When Political and Technocratic Managers Meet

THE USUAL RESULT of a technocrat confronting a politician is a news conference, a court case, and a substantive stalemate. Public policy seldom moves forward as a result. This was acceptable as long as the United States was so rich and strong, relative to our allies and competitors, that a crippled performance did not matter. But today the awkwardness of this single relationship between politicians and managers of business and government technocracies is acutely painful.

The emphasis on political versus technocratic in this diagnosis is fundamental. The disease is not well understood in the usual terms of business versus government. When government has chosen to use technocratic managerial systems to carry out its objectives, company employees dealing with the government can expect to be facing counterparts who are similar organizational bureaucrats. As in business, some will be competent, some not, but unless it is a very badly run agency, most members will respect competence.[1] There will be continuity in staffing — sometimes less than desirable, sometimes more, but the principles will be understood and valued. The talent and long-term perspective of the agency will permit technical knowledge to be applied where it is relevant. As long as an issue under consideration is within the purview of the technocratic managerial system, it is possible for a company to organize in relatively normal ways to do business with the government.

Where government has chosen to use political systems, the reverse is true. A company, or an agency, can expect to be facing counterparts in the government with almost totally different capabilities and stakes. Both individuals and organizations are likely to reflect totally different experience and values. The people in the political system may often appear incompetent from a business perspective, because the skills of political actors are not technical and the actors are often superficially informed as to everything *not* involving the pattern of stakes and consequences. The elected officials *and* their staffs may appear untrustworthy as a consequence, since the knowledge, skills, rules, and procedures they hold dear are politically oriented. Indeed, how often do businessmen say with scorn, "All he or she wants to do is get elected." As if that were not the constitutional imperative.

In fact, businessmen understand power and its uses, but they are unaccustomed and may be temperamentally unsuited to the fluid and somewhat brutal uses to which power is put in government. As one entrant into government remarked, "I thought it was like football, with time outs when someone was hurt; but it's more like rugby and you're lucky if you can drag the wounded off the field."

The businessman engaging the political world may also conclude that there is little, if any, continuity in staffing. In fact, in many political systems there is virtually no continuity. The tenure of political appointees is short. About half the top political appointees stay in their jobs less than two years. The superior/subordinate relationships are also short; roughly two thirds are less than two years.[2] Richard Neustadt has argued that the problem has been particularly noticeable in the last decade, since (1) Congress has "reformed" and lost much of the continuity provided by the seniority system and (2) "anti-Washington" administrations have brought into government people who do not know how the federal political systems work or how the managerial systems of business and labor work. Under these circumstances, business not only faces lack of continuity — it faces ignorance.

In this situation, it is not possible to expect routine operations between a company and political systems. In contrast to the sort of extensive discussion that might lead to consensus over a well-understood policy, there tends to be bargaining over specifics, some particular rule or appropriation. Often the meeting will take the form of a confrontation. The deadline imposed by a legislative agenda will be short. Only power of the sort possessed by some corporate chief executive officers will have any influence. And despite the specificity of the issue, almost always the so-called decision-making process will reflect the compromising of conflicting views held by different powerful interests. In this compromising process, power and negotiating skill may be more important than substantive knowledge or administrative coherence over time. And having half the baby can seem like a reasonable solution.

In order to rise above such outcomes — or simply to survive them — a technocratically managed organization must develop a new set of skills. The leaders must be articulate exponents of their organization's position even to the extent of defending proposals in public under hostile questioning by expert staff. This requires short-cutting the normal chain of command.

Because at the same time that a battle rages in the political arena an organization may have several routine transactions under way on a technocrat-to-technocrat basis, the organizational requirements are awesome. A company president may be fighting the secretary of the treasury over monetary and tax policy at the same time that a division of the company may be working closely with the Customs Service on a trade matter. It may often be true that the apparatus set up within the organization to work over the long term on a cooperative technical basis will come into conflict with the strike force set up to bargain in the political system. Like the proverbial blind men experiencing the parts of an elephant, different units of a company or agency may have very different perceptions of what is needed managerially in order to deal with an issue effectively. Unless great care is taken, the political battle engaging top management can spread through the company. Whether it does depends in part on how the senior managers relate to one another. Many top managers handle themselves badly in the politicized world of congressional hearings and press conferences. New kinds of people with different backgrounds and skills (people who can "speak the foreign language"), new kinds of information, and a flexible organizational format reaching right to the chief executive officer are all required.

When technocrats and politicians try to work together the awkwardness can be comical. As they approach a problem to discuss objectives they have different perceptions of reality. The technocratic executives have a sense of the large organizations behind them, competent but fallible. They know how much time it takes to get even simple plans carried out. They are aware of the web of commitments to individual members of their organization that is embodied in a particular strategy. But they also have a sense of how, if there is enough quiet for the right conversations to take place, the organization can be used constructively to work on problems. There is a system for doing these things.

The political manager will see the issue in the context of many others that require his time and that of his staff at a particular moment, especially the two or three issues he really cares about. He will also be aware of the political environment, what issues are of concern and which are "off the screen" for the time being. If he or his aides have the time to think about the problem, then in all likelihood it will be a crisis. In the busy schedule of political managers, noncrises are almost always distractions. When he does examine the issue — keep a plant open, or alter a piece of tax legislation, or get an increased appropriation for an agency regional office — then it will be measured according to how it will be viewed by the web of his political allies and opponents, and, equally important, how it will play in the media. Until there is widespread awareness of a problem, there may be little he can do even if, like Chrysler in 1978, disaster can be seen just ahead.

So, in 1978 and 1979, when Chrysler's John Riccardo went from office to office with his tale of woe, he was likely to have been obsessed with the nightmarish financial and competitive situation of his company. He would have seen the problem in terms of work that had to be done and loans to be paid in order to survive, the consequence of failure, and the things that agencies or legislators could do to help. But for most politicians, Riccardo represented Goliath — the auto industry, or pollution, or oil imports, or mismanagement, or a bad precedent, or a threat to Ford. And what he sought was a special privilege for an undeserving, greedy tycoon, or a bailout for banks that made bad loans.

That Chrysler is alive today is a tribute to the staying power of Riccardo and the skills of Iacocca. Interestingly, now that survival is a real possibility, the press has begun to discuss Iacocca's political possibilities, focusing on his success in Washington and on television.

But there remains a long list of sick industries with very weak companies. The U.S. auto industry is a problem that is likely to get worse as South Korea and other "new Japans" build modern capacity to utilize their skilled inexpensive labor. The U.S. steel industry is still liquidating behind a growing protective barrier. The small domestic banks are wobbling as international depositors seek stability in whichever major banks seem least threatened by the problems of Mexico, Poland, and Brazil.

Like the border management problem, these industrial policy dilemmas cut across the fragmented U.S. federal system. There is much discussion, but the lack of coherence is reflected even in the organization of the Reagan cabinet, where there are separate councils for economic policy and trade and commerce competing for the action with the Trade Policy Committee and the Office of the U.S. Trade Representative.

It has become common to read in newspapers and magazines pleas from businessmen, academics, and even government administrators for cooperation between business and government. Often these are set forth in articles that contrast the way our system works with the way Japan purportedly works. But what exactly is it that we are asking for? Do we really expect organizations such as IBM to cooperate with organizations such as the President's Reorganization Project or the Office of Drug Abuse Policy?

More realistically, do we expect there to be some part of government with which IBM is going to cooperate on a regular basis? And do we really expect that companies or labor unions will cease to have such differences in stakes and perspective — from one another and from unions and companies in other parts of the country — that they will not seek support from their industry or regional representatives in Congress?

Certainly businessmen have sought to have constructive relationships with regulators and policymakers. The oil industry, for example, has a sixty-year history of long-standing relationships between the major producers and the State Department, the "independents" and the Department of the Interior, and both groups of companies and cabinet departments with key congressmen and senators. Until the world demand for energy began to exceed supply, there was even a fair degree of satisfaction with the results of the relationships. But the record of the last decade is dismal, and especially so in certain industries whose problems have roots in a series of poor decisions taken over the last thirty years rather than in the end of cheap energy in the 1970s. Those who have examined the way companies, bureaucrats, and politicians have worked on these problems find something more complicated going on that is leading to unintended decline.

Federal, state, and local governments have always been involved with business managers as customers, bankers, and regulators. When researchers and participants review the recent record of this activity, what do they find? Some firms seek to avoid the government as a customer. A wide range of regulations makes the selling process distinctly unpleasant. Others enjoy the process as specialists. On the other side of the market, government purchasers are often dissatisfied with their suppliers. Quality or cost is deemed unsatisfactory. Perhaps worst of all, there are numerous areas of activity, especially regionally decentralized ones such as road building, where graft frequently contaminates the relationship.

Government as a banker is often a maker of bad loans or investments. Except in special circumstances, governments rush in where private lenders fear to tread, only to discover that public purpose alone is an inadequate justification for the commitment. The underlying problems that keep private capital out do not disappear with the arrival of government money. Urban renewal, Amtrak, Conrail, and Chrysler are manifestations of government's awkwardness as a banker. Government is asked in to support the technocratically weak.

Government is also a wasteful provider of incentives. The subsidized development of water for irrigation has left us committed to a series of water-intensive crops such as cotton, or soybeans in areas where the aquifer is now destroyed from overuse. We continue to develop southwestern cities despite the already recognized water shortage. We protected our least advanced industries, such as shoe making, and, in the 1970s, attacked leaders like IBM that we helped to develop in the 1950s and 1960s. Through highways and guaranteed mortgages, we induced the migration of industry and middle-class families to the suburbs and thereby lost the tax base to support our cities.

Finally, government regulation is especially fragmented and uncomfortable. In the early phases of most reform efforts, the rule-making process is so hostile that there is virtually no chance the expertise of the affected businesses can be brought to bear on public purpose. Later, it is typical for a cooperative relationship to become entrenched at about the time the public need for regulation has passed. Until this ossified stage, both sides of the relationship reflect distrust.[3]

Why? Is it given that until the actors are moribund, the relationship between U.S. companies and U.S. agencies must be like Catholics and Protestants in Northern Ireland? The answer has already been sketched out. Yes, it is given. In the U.S. constitutional setting it is highly likely that the relationship between a technocratic management system and a political management system will be unsatisfactory — adversarial, nasty, and dysfunctional.

The breakdown develops for three basic reasons that correspond to the core aspects of an organization:

1. It is very difficult to develop common purpose.
2. It is equally hard to build an organization and relationships that provide for adequate communication and problem solving.
3. It is virtually impossible to develop a balance of incentives that keeps coalition members focused on purpose.

Managers of technocratic systems believe *purpose* to be a problem of focus, *structure* to be a question of hierarchy, and *contract* to be defined by managed incentives. Managers of political systems believe purpose is a game of fair division, structure a version of cavalry charge, and contract a problem for skillful bargaining.

The Problem of Purpose: Focus versus Fair Division

We saw in chapter 2 that the essential problem facing the leadership of any technocratic managerial system is to develop a strategy with which resources can be focused on selected objectives. The art of strategy involves appropriately allocating large resources to limited objectives. Risk is thereby reduced, and the higher probability of success makes for a stable organization.

The story of the IBM 360 series is a record of one management's efforts to accomplish this sort of concentration. It wasn't easy. Managers of successful current activity fought the diversion of their resources to a new program. International groups sought to preserve their identity. But recourse to the argument of the greater corporate good was both legitimate and successful. IBM World Trade accepted that the corporation would be better off if Scamp was not produced and if British capability was integrated into an overall design.

Managers engaged in such an activity are not blessed with superhuman skills. They are not brighter than their government counterparts. But they do enjoy a technocratic system that is designed to facilitate focus.

The Problem of Structure: Hierarchy versus the Cavalry Charge

In chapter 4 the management of IBM and the border management project were contrasted. The different units and managers involved in the border management issues were doing their job, as were their superiors. There was, however, no particular presumption that the pieces ought to fit together. Nor did the players have any experience managing systems that did fit together. In fact, they had little experience in managing at policy levels. In contrast, they did have experience bargaining in a world where it is important that the division of the pie be fair.

Technocratic systems such as IBM are encouraged to try to solve problems.[4] The premise is that coordinated effort is necessary to solve problems and, more important, to gain the commitment of those responsible for implementing decisions. Again and again in the IBM 360 story we see Learson and Watson using their power to bring together those with conflicting organizational stakes but potentially complementary talent. Though there are losers along the way, there is an implicit assumption that cooperation will yield a larger surplus that can be divided later. Fair division comes after focus succeeds. Losers will be compensated either with promotions such as John Haanstra's or the "golden handshake" that sometimes follows. Control of resources is imperfect but feasible. It may take time, but eventually top management can deny subunits access to resources.

In contrast, managers of political systems regard problems as opportunities for independent entrepreneurial action. Those with charters charge out on the field to see if they can make something out of it that will help their constituencies.[5]

Studies are often performed, but with a technocratic vacuum at the government's center, they seldom provide a basis for action. Information can be used only to color problems or even hide them. Most task forces are not devices to focus and resolve conflict. They are used to paralyze the system, slow down the pace at which one unit may be galloping forward, and restore the fair-share equilibrium. (And when technocratic managers use the same devices they are behaving politically.)

Perhaps the most dramatic example of this process in action was the TFX. In that instance the hard-charging, powerful, and skillful Robert McNamara, head of the apparently hierarchical Department of Defense, failed even to dent the resistance of the Navy to his desire for the Navy and Air Force to use a common tactical fighter plane. One admiral quoted in the *Congressional Record* said that "the damn plane would never fly off a carrier," and it has not.

The very technocratic process that McNamara thought of himself as mastering was used to block his efforts. Unlike Arthur Watson, he could not send the equivalent of IBM's entire San Jose laboratory to Germany. He could arrange for an occasional admiral to become an ambassador to a small country, but he could not command the cooperation of the Navy. With a defense of institutional values clearly in view, Navy management could easily wait out even a seven-year secretary of defense. There was simply no incentive to cooperate with a short-term manager who, rightly or wrongly, was trying to assert that he and a group of young, bright civilian quantitative analysts could do a better job of defining the defense interests of the nation than professionals who were devoting their careers to the task.

The Problem of Incentives: Managed versus Bargained

In a fundamental sense, the issues of purpose and structure resolve themselves into problems of incentive. It is hard to build a structure, gather information, or measure performance if there is no common goal. In fact, simple logic suggests that structure should be shaped wherever possible to serve purpose. There is no best way of organizing independent of purpose.

The most basic ideas of effective organization turn on the ability to use incentives so as to focus the effort of members of an organization on a common definition of what ought to be done that is emerging as the leaders learn. Take any group; let the members volunteer, organize, and succeed. Over time as they grow, differences will emerge. Founding members of the organization will see value in preserving the form of the subunits they built even while a changing environment requires altering the organizational format. At the same time, managers age. Their goals and material needs change. Cooperation becomes increasingly less natural except around the preservation of the status quo. It takes energy and skill to keep the group focused on ambitious objectives. In his classic analysis of leadership, Philip Selznick describes this conflict-managing function:

> Internal interest groups form naturally in large-scale organizations, since the total enterprise is, in one sense, a polity composed of a number of suborganizations. The struggle among competing interests always has a high claim on the attention of leadership. This is so because the direction of the enterprise as a whole *may be seriously influenced by changes in the internal balance of power.* In exercising control, leadership has a dual task. It must *win the consent of constituent units, in order to maximize voluntary cooperation,* and, therefore, must permit emergent interest blocs a wide degree of representation. At the same time, in order to hold the helm, it must see that *a balance of power appropriate* to the fulfillment of key commitments will be maintained. [*Emphasis added*][6]

Ironically, the political world of fair share denies a manager of an organization the ability to generate or use the funds internally that he could use to buy a focused compromise. Most immediately, it is not legal to pay off discontented power holders with cash. The political system is biased against such managerial fair share. Instead of an imperfect and constantly evolving resolution of conflict, it creates a management world of winners and losers, ins and outs, in which you are either for something or against it. Celebrity status and the distinction of patronage are the fruits earned by apparent victors. Losers wait and grind their teeth.

Consider the early actions of the Reagan administration from a managerial perspective. What can it mean that, faced with the responsibility for running a 2.7-million-person organization, they fired the entire top of the civil service, whether or not they held political jobs? They even fired the long-experienced White House secretaries who might be presumed by a manager to be helpful during a transition, not to mention the auditors (the inspectors general) who are presumed to be high above politics. What lessons are learned by potential government managers?

What, then, are technocratic managers to think of an organization that strips itself of top management and then hires newcomers who will require six months to a year to learn their jobs? Three months after the inauguration, one third of the top nine hundred jobs in the U.S. executive branch were unfilled.

Regardless of what some regard as the political necessity for a change in leadership, it is hard to imagine a more awkward, less managerially effective transition. The White House files were literally empty. Their contents belonged to the defeated. With the departure of the top nine hundred appointed officials went still more files and, perhaps more important, networks of related managers and a whole series of judgments as to competence and bias.

Working with the Politicians

If the tone of the preceding paragraphs sounds incredulous, it is meant to be. Across the United States, managers in companies, states, and cities were waiting to find out what the new team *thought* the game was and how fast they would learn what the game *really* was.

These managers saw one or more of the country's problems as very serious. How the problems are resolved will have major consequences for their prosperity. They have been working with technocratic parts of the government for years. Hence, except where a particular bureaucrat had incensed a group of clients, the moves of the new administration to eliminate the managers held responsible for the problems facing the country constituted nothing more than a delay in a long-term process of negotiation.

The top people in the Reagan administration did not describe agencies and regulations as compromises among competing interest groups but as mistakes to be eliminated. As they learn that they, too, have to compromise and share, their loyal supporters see betrayal. Thus, during the summer of 1982, Reagan was attacked from the right for a tax bill viewed as a compromise. In fact, as with any progress in our system, the bill was a trade among competing imperatives.

As soon as a group has begun to accumulate experience, it learns that our system of politics gives most groups with one or another form of power access to policymaking and resource allocation. What one has to do is to devise a forum in which interested parties can work quietly to see how joint interest can also serve the common good. It is seldom easy. The representatives of technocratic hierarchy tend to perceive the cavalry charge as out of control, unreliable, and unpredictable. The political manager's concern for "irrelevant issues" (read: politically interrelated issues) appears to the technocrat to be dishonest. Often the politician's information appears inaccurate or the interpretation academic. Worst of all, one part of the politically managed system cannot commit another.

In turn, the members of the "cavalry" perceive the technocratic hierarchies as rigid, ponderous, and self-serving. They are particularly incensed with the desire of technocrats to keep data secret. They have little sympathy for the desire to keep private the information that would embarrass colleagues or subordinates. They also have much less sympathy for the value of data to business competitors.

Consequently, politicians typically make public attacks on technocratically managed systems. A most dramatic example of this was when Joan Claybrook did not realize that she had shifted from "Naderite" politician to technocrat head of the National Highway Traffic Safety Administration. On her arrival, she gave a news conference in which she attacked the competence and attitude of the organization whose cooperation she would immediately require. She soon apologized.

This sort of posturing and on-the-job learning at high levels drives technocratic managers to despair. They find it incredible that young and/or inexperienced people are elevated to significant positions by the political process. The rewards to successful campaign staffers seem capricious and disproportionate.

A former dean of a well-known business school served on the Ash Council, which was studying the organization of the executive branch for Richard Nixon. On meeting John Ehrlichman and H. R. Haldeman for the first time, he is alleged to have said, "Those two guys helped run the campaign and now they're going to run the country? God save us."

There is as well a tendency to see the aggressive and visible pursuit of self-interest that characterizes political systems as somehow corrupt. Political managers seem always out for themselves, seeking glamour and celebrity. Skillful use of the media is especially resented, since it seems always to involve distortion of motives and issues. Moreover, big business or big government is always cast in the role of Goliath.

At the same time, political managers often regard the rewards of technocrats as undeserved. Technocratic managers of government departments are viewed as unelected controllers of the policy apparatus; the right to make policy ought fully to belong to the elected. Businesses are seen as venal, rewarded for successful pursuit of private, as opposed to public, purpose.

When we remember how little factual knowledge each has of the other, how seldom one group has worked for any period of time in the other's world, it's not surprising that the results are seldom happy.

The relationship between the Allied Chemical Corporation and the Environmental Protection Agency concerning the Barnwell nuclear reprocessing facility is a sad but instructive example of the problem.[7]

The Barnwell Case

From the beginning of commercial development of nuclear power in the 1950s, both government and business had assumed that spent nuclear fuel would be reprocessed by private companies as soon as it became commercially attractive. The main benefit of reprocessing was that it promised to conserve uranium. By "recycling" the uranium from reactors, the demand for natural uranium could be cut by roughly 20 percent. Plutonium recovered from spent reactor fuel could also charge light-water reactors and this would cut uranium demand by another 15 percent. Finally, recycling plutonium would reduce the need for costly and energy-intensive uranium enrichment facilities by 15 to 20 percent.

Another attraction of reprocessing was that it permitted the introduction of breeder reactors. Reprocessing is linked to breeder reactor development because the plutonium recovered from twenty light-water reactors in one year could charge one breeder reactor. Reprocessing also promised to alleviate the nuclear waste problem.

Allied Chemical became involved in the nuclear power business in the early 1950s when it performed a study of uranium recovery methods for the Atomic Energy Commission (AEC). In 1955, Allied successfully bid on a government request for design, construction, and operation of a conversion facility. The government provided an initial five-year supply of uranium for processing. By 1960, Allied's plant was operating as a commercial and technical success.

In the early 1960s, Allied began serious evaluation of the reprocessing business. After evaluating two new processes, Allied scientists recommended improving the Purex process used in Allied's existing plant.

Reprocessing became an increasingly attractive business proposition for Allied. More and more utilities were buying reactors and these would produce predictable amounts of spent fuel in the 1970s. The government was strongly encouraging nuclear power and commercial reprocessing. The Purex method had been used successfully for years in some thirteen plants, for both defense and commercial purposes. It seemed that the company with the first large-scale reprocessing facility would have the market to itself. One Allied official later commented, "No business area seemed more certain."

In late 1968, Allied applied to the AEC for a construction permit for a 1500-metric-ton-per-year plant to be constructed near Barnwell, South Carolina. Allied proposed to build two basic facilities at Barnwell. One would receive and store spent fuel. It would also separate the spent fuel into plutonium, uranium, and waste. The second was a conversion plant that would convert the reprocessed uranium into uranium fluoride. (Allied was already operating the world's largest privately owned uranium fluoride conversion facility at Metropolis, Illinois.)

In 1969 Gulf Oil expressed an interest in becoming a part owner of Allied's reprocessing project. Negotiations led to a fifty-fifty partnership called Allied-Gulf Nuclear Services (AGNS). The AEC granted the construction permit in 1970. Construction began in 1971 on a site, sold to Allied by the government, adjacent to the government's Savannah River Reservation. There, among other activities, the government operated two reprocessing plants.

Allied estimated that the entire Barnwell facility would cost AGNS more than $100 million and take roughly three years to build. By the end of 1975, when the plant was substantially complete, the actual cost was expected to exceed $225 million.

The overrun was attributed by AGNS to inflation, lower-than-expected construction productivity, and increasingly rigid AEC licensing requirements. In addition, AEC rulings also required the construction of two additional buildings, one to solidify waste and one to solidify plutonium. These two buildings would cost up to $300 million and take roughly three years to complete.

Throughout construction, Allied project management had worked intimately with representatives of the AEC. Both groups had long experience in the nuclear power field.

Two sets of regulatory proceedings would have an effect on Barnwell. First of all, operation of the facility would require the issuance of operating licenses by the U.S. Nuclear Regulatory Commission (NRC). Its Atomic Safety and Licensing Board was already holding hearings covering the environmental impact and the operating license for the separations facility. At the hearings, environmental groups opposed issuance of the license on a number of grounds. Separate licenses and hearings would be required for both the UF_6 facility and the receiving and storage station at Barnwell. Both of these hearings could be contested.

The other set of proceedings, also under the NRC, focused on the environmental impact of wide-scale use of mixed oxide fuel (fuel containing reprocessed uranium and plutonium). These proceedings originated in February 1974, when the AEC announced that an environmental impact statement would be prepared prior to an AEC decision on the use of mixed oxide fuel. (Under the National Environmental Policy Act of 1970, the federal government was required to prepare environmental impact statements for any actions that could have a major impact on the physical or social environment.) In August 1974, the AEC published its draft General Environmental Statement on the Use of Mixed-Oxide Fuels (GESMO). The AEC staff concluded that wide-scale use of mixed oxide fuel should be approved.

In January 1975, the NRC took over the regulatory and licensing functions of the AEC. In the same month, the Council on Environmental Quality, which reviews environmental impact statements, expressed some misgivings about the draft GESMO. The council said the draft was well done but failed to analyze in detail the environmental impact of the potential diversion of plutonium by terrorists or other groups and the possible safeguards to protect the public from such a threat. The NRC agreed to prepare a detailed analysis of the safeguards question. This would require hearings, preparation of a draft statement, a comment period, and preparation of a final safeguards statement. At the same time, the draft GESMO would go through a comment period and a final statement would be prepared. The NRC did not think that a final, comprehensive statement, including a safeguards statement, would be ready until early 1977. The final NRC decision on mixed oxide fuels would be deferred until then.

Allied decided not to invest further. Its 1975 annual report noted:

> In view of the current uncertainties with respect to plutonium and of uncertainties relating to nuclear waste disposal, AGNS has postponed plans to build plutonium oxide conversion and waste solidification facilities at Barnwell but has submitted a proposal to the U.S. Energy Research and Development Administration (ERDA) concerning a program under which ERDA would construct and fund plutonium oxide conversion and waste solidification facilities at Barnwell for demonstration purposes . . . It appears that sustained operation of the Barnwell plant will be dependent upon implementation of such an ERDA program or of some other program not dependent solely on AGNS or the partners of AGNS for financing. Such an ERDA program would require Congressional approval.

These developments occurred in 1976: There was no definitive response by ERDA to the AGNS proposal. The NRC said it would consider interim commercial licensing of facilities such as Barnwell. Environmental groups opposed this decision in court and the U.S. Court of Appeals ruled that the NRC could not issue any license until GESMO was completed. The EPA issued regulations that would probably require the installation of costly equipment at Barnwell for the recovery of krypton. Just before the November election, President Gerald Ford announced that "reprocessing and recycling of plutonium should not proceed unless there is sound reason to conclude that the world community can effectively overcome the associated risks of proliferation."

In April 1977, President Jimmy Carter announced that the United States would "indefinitely defer" the reprocessing of spent fuel and the use of plutonium as a supplementary fuel. The president said the deferment would not cause major economic penalties and would "reduce the risks of nuclear proliferation." Later that year, at the request of the White House, the NRC terminated the GESMO proceedings.

In 1978, the Carter administration announced its opposition to any additional government support for Barnwell. Nonetheless, the Senate voted $18.5 million for research and development activities at Barnwell in fiscal 1979. This money could not be used, however, to "enhance the readiness of the BNFP for reprocessing of irradiated fuel."

By 1978, Allied's equity investment in Barnwell was roughly $105 million. This was 5 percent of Allied's total long-term assets. The $105 million investment was equivalent to an investment of $3.74 per share. In 1977 Allied's after-tax earnings per share were $4.82.

One Allied official, who had been involved with Barnwell from the start, made these comments in late 1978:

> If I had known in 1970 what was going to happen, I would have opposed the Barnwell project. At that time, nothing in the business or chemical world seemed more certain. We had excellent working relations with the AEC staff and strong encouragement from AEC policymakers. When there were uncertainties about future regulatory requirements — as in the cases of waste and plutonium solidification — we made contingency plans as needed. But by 1975, there was just too much uncertainty to go further with the project.
> I think it's tragic that the Barnwell plant has not been put to use. It is an engineering masterpiece, it's environmentally safe, and it could do a great deal to help the U.S. solve its energy problems. Europe, Japan, and Russia are all going ahead with reprocessing, while the U.S. is standing still.

Perhaps the executive is correct. Or perhaps the nuclear reprocessing risks should not be taken. But what an extraordinary way to make a decision. What an extraordinary way to use $100 million of private money.

Certain elements are notable in the Barnwell history. First, it is clear that there were always excellent understandings at working levels between Allied and the AEC. Second, Allied top management seemed to have had a clear understanding of the plans and progress made at the project level — perhaps three or four levels below corporate management in the hierarchy. The linkage between the specialists working the project and the generalists concerned with the portfolio of activities at Allied conformed to the basic norms of a technocratic system.

On the government side, however, the linkage was less effective. At a certain point, technocratic managers had to deal with political superiors. While the policymakers at the AEC supported the project, the AEC had been subjected to reorganization designed to make it more sensitive to "public concerns." Some of its activities were incorporated in ERDA and some in the Nuclear Regulatory Commission. With technocratic power divided, the project was more vulnerable. Working in the context and the electoral politics of the 1976 campaign, antinuclear groups were able to block the project. Finally, it succumbed to President Carter's antiproliferation policy.

Let us leave aside the question of whether there should be nuclear power, or more specifically, whether reprocessing is a good idea. The way in which the decision was managed demonstrated to Allied that it was dealing with a very different sort of organization than it had thought. Substance and commitments were worth nothing if the political climate changed. Logic didn't matter. Nor was Allied's $105 million investment an issue. It was merely unfortunate for Allied.

The president of one of the best-managed U.S. companies put his view of the federal government this way. At a top management meeting he remarked on the failure of a system operated by the federal government that primarily depended for its function on a competitor's product. The competitor's name was in the headlines that week.

That's why I want us to do as little with Washington as is feasible. The ABC Company's system was perfectly reliable. They've just got it wired into an impossibly designed network and the human errors kill you. When things go wrong they turn on the component manufacturer, not the designer or operator. We can do without that kind of publicity. It's a shame because we make the best products.[8]

Call it lack of zest for public life or knee-jerk conservatism, managers of technocratic systems are appalled by the risks of working with political systems. With the possibility of injury to financial position or reputation so high, they withdraw from the field. One banker I interviewed highlighted the problem by contrasting it with the situation in Germany and Japan. "There," he said, "when they go into something, they go in together. Things don't go wrong any less frequently than they do here, but if there are problems, they cooperate to solve them. The government doesn't play politics and turn around to blame its business partner."

We can understand why the U.S. system behaves the way it does if we remember how fragmented it is. While one technocratic system deals in good faith with another, the political ground rules may change and totally unexpected action develop. In this game of musical chairs, it is easy for an organization to find itself odd man out. Given the contract of a technocratic system, the human and administrative costs in dealing with the political system are experienced as intolerable.

Reflect on the fact that a Republican administration seeking to strengthen the economy, employment, and the dollar attacked Export-Import Bank (Eximbank) financing for exports as "welfare for big business" in President Reagan's February 1981 "state of the economy" message. Banking commitments made prior to the speech for the 1981–82 period were endangered, as were the huge export deals they underlay. It is very hard for a technocratic manager to accept that President Reagan's advisers concluded that this "subsidy" was a reasonable item to cut in order to balance other cuts that would hurt poorer consumers.

The Consequences of Fair Division

While a wise old hand may observe incidents such as the Barnwell proceedings or the attack on the Eximbank and chuckle, the aggregate consequences for the country are costly. It would appear that our policies lead us to use public resources in very unhappy ways. The framework that we have developed reveals why in a relatively simple argument. Organizations such as IBM or the Boston Symphony Orchestra have a certain virtue. They pursue a limited objective successfully and with great emphasis on quality. It may happen, however, that for a variety of reasons the world of politics can impinge on the relatively well ordered world of the technocratically managed organization. The consequences are a loss of efficiency as the management of the technocratic organizations shifts attention away from customers to deal with political peers. The self-sustaining characteristics of the organization are lost as each act requires bargaining or negotiation that produces compromise among new demands rather than selectivity. The values of the organization shift as the distraction of the thrust and parry of politics replaces the rewards of long-term objectives pursued with consistency.

The method of the argument is equally simple. We examine some examples of what happens when technocrats begin to play politics in order to survive. Consider again the case of Chrysler.

Chrysler Fairly Divided

To begin, we can note that the political managers picked up the fact that Chrysler was weak only during the summer of 1979. The headlines revealed Congress's concern that some $1 billion might have to be poured into the company. Eventually, after the president of the United Auto Workers, Douglas Fraser, joined the Chrysler Board of Directors and after the union achieved a veto over pension-fund investment policy, a coalition of congressmen and senators was able to drive through a compromise resolution providing some support for the company.

With hindsight it is now easy to see that other beneficiaries of this move were the banks that held large sums of Chrysler debt. With Chrysler stabilized, their chance to be repaid was resuscitated. In fact, by June of 1978, Chrysler had publicly acknowledged in a Securities and Exchange Commission prospectus that it was in dire straits. Its products were obsolete, and it did not have a sure understanding of the market. Its consolidated debts were approximately $10 billion. It required some $7.5 billion to design and produce a new line of cars. Its other assets were marginal. And it was hemorrhaging losses at an appalling rate.

That Chrysler was in trouble in 1978 was not a surprise, for the automobile industry's growth was slowing at the same time that the energy crisis and concern for safety brought new legislation that put new constraints on production. Serious debate turned on whether the free world eventually would see four, five, or six auto companies. In Europe, smaller producers could be seen jockeying for position in coalitions. Peugeot absorbed Citroën and participated in a joint venture to produce an engine with Volvo and Volkswagen. Saab and Volvo discussed a merger, while Fiat struggled with its labor unions and bankers. Meanwhile, France and Italy moved aggressively to keep Japanese automobiles out of their markets.

But no place existed in the United States where interested parties might consider what would be a sensible use of private and public resources.

Should Chrysler be allowed to die?

If so, what kind of aid, if any, should be provided for the workers and suppliers who would be affected?

What might a "rescued" Chrysler look like?

Why was Chrysler in trouble? Was it imports, government regulations, or incompetence that accounted for the problems? Did it matter?

If imports were the problem, should foreign manufacturers be required to build in the United States? How? By whom?

How much money was really involved?

How many jobs could be saved and for how long?

These questions and others are supposed in principle to be answered by the workings of the market. As one task force after another danced around the question, trying to sort out competing interests, a second and larger question was evident. How would the handling of Chrysler relate to the problem of Japanese imports? Would blocking Japanese imports help Chrysler? And if it would, should we upset a major trading relationship on this issue?

To ask these questions is to raise still another, What is in the national interest? To which the literal managerial answer is, Who cares? Short of the presidency, there is no institution with a stake in the national interest viewed comprehensively. And we have seen that the president's ability to adopt a comprehensive program is limited. Questions such as those affecting the contemporary auto industry are not easily answered by some invisible process comparable to Adam Smith's market.

In principle, the presidency should care about the national interest, but its powers are not well suited to the design of technocratic intervention. Issues such as Chrysler pose special problems. The White House staff is organized around three primary categories of policy — domestic, economic, and national security. Chrysler is a "domestic" problem centered in Detroit. Trade is an "economic" problem. And economics are *not* traditionally a matter of national security.

Here we have the prototypical ingredients of the breakdown in government efforts to work with business. The national interest is in the industry, especially the jobs and wealth it creates, but also in its impact on the balance of payments. The institutions with the technocratic capability to plan and allocate resources for the long term have much narrower stakes. The companies compete with each other. Ford may want to solve some of its problems by drawing heavily on its European capability. General Motors is preparing for the future by teaming up with Toyota, Japan's number-one automaker. American Motors is owned by Renault, which is owned by the French government. The UAW is involved in all four companies, but also in healthy industries such as aerospace and construction equipment that are major exporters. The banks hold weak loans. The Environmental Protection Agency, the U.S. International Trade Commission, and the National Highway Traffic Safety Administration all have statutes they are required to enforce. The politicians have regional stakes tied closely to employment and congressional stakes related to jurisdictional power.

The consequences are revealed in the following numbers:

	1960	1970	1980
U.S. Passenger Car Registrations (in millions)	6577	8388	9977
Imports' Share of U.S. Market	7.6%	14.7%	26.7%
Chrysler Sales (in millions of dollars)	3007	6887	9225
Chrysler Profits (in millions of dollars)	32	−8	−1710
Chrysler Employment (average)	102,318	129,127	92,596
Chrysler Return on Assets	2.3%	−0.2%	−25.6%

Source: Mark B. Fuller and Malcolm B. Salter, "Note on the World Auto Industry in Transition" (Cambridge: Harvard Graduate School of Business Administration, 1982).

There is no prospect that Chrysler will soon again be an independent full-line manufacturer of cars. But as it struggled from the brink of bankruptcy the federal government continued to guarantee loans that, though large in absolute terms, are dribbles relative to the problem and largely irrelevant to the fundamental questions of industry prospects and organization.

This would be sad but more tolerable were it not the pattern of U.S. government involvement. In the case of steel, the same pattern can be observed at the industry level.

Carving Up the Steel Industry

In 1977 the U.S. economy consumed an estimated 108 million tons of finished steel. In the same year the United States produced 89 million tons, 71 percent of productive capacity. The 19 million finished tons that were imported came from Japan (40 percent), the European Economic Community (35 percent), and other countries, including Brazil and Canada. With free world capacity utilization below 80 percent and headed down, there were substantial incentives for foreign competition to price near variable cost in order to gain U.S. sales.

While there was some debate as to whether U.S. companies were correct in charging that Japanese manufacturers were dumping, there was no doubt about the Europeans. Their prices in the United States were typically 20 percent below those charged in their home markets. U.S. manufacturers brought suit.

Involved in the problem were the many agencies related to foreign trade, as well as the EPA. Their positions were roughly as indicated in the accompanying chart.

Actors Involved in the Foreign Trade Problem

Department of State	Support free trade and good relations with the steel-producing allies
Department of the Treasury	
Customs Service	Enforce the antidumping laws within the General Agreement on Tariffs and Trade (GATT)
Internal Revenue Service	Raise tax revenues
Policy Staff	Support free trade
Office of the U.S. Trade Representative	Support open trade but manage problems on an equitable basis within GATT
Department of Commerce	
Policy Staff	Support planning; seek a comprehensive approach to strong U.S. industry
Economic Development Administration	Seek subsidies
Department of Labor	
Policy Staff	Provide employment in the United States
Occupational Safety and Health Administration	Enforce safety standards
Department of Justice	
Antitrust Division	Oppose consolidation and discussions that might lead to mergers

Domestic Policy Staff	Support free trade but politics come first
U.S. International Trade Commission	Support free trade
Council of Economic Advisers	Support free trade and reduce inflation
Office of Management and Budget	Balance the budget and reduce expenditures
Environmental Protection Agency	Enforce clean air and water standards

The problem had its modern origins in U.S. steel industry labor practices and in process technology and plant location choices made by U.S. companies between 1945 and 1960. The industry in the United States was dominated by eight large companies that had developed the practice of following U.S. Steel in pricing and in wages. Both had been set industrywide until a series of antitrust cases ended the explicit discussions of prices.

Following the Second World War, U.S. steel companies began to build new capacity, drawing on ore from Minnesota and coal from Pittsburgh and Ohio. Only the Fairless works of U.S. Steel at Philadelphia was built near deep water. Until the 1960s, most of the new capacity was open-hearth technology.

At the same time both Europe and Japan were rapidly rebuilding an industry destroyed by the war. Especially in Japan, the new mills were built near the ocean, where the ore would arrive and product could be shipped. Just as important, the Europeans and Japanese adopted the new basic oxygen technology. By 1965 the pattern indicated in the table on page 141 could be observed. Because the BOF process was less expensive than open-hearth, these numbers reveal a deteriorated competitive position.

The labor history of the industry was especially troublesome, marked as it was by a long series of bitter strikes. Prior to an anticipated strike, customers would inventory steel. When they were

	Open-Hearth	Basic Oxygen Furnace (BOF)
	(Percentage of capacity)	(Percentage of capacity)
United States	72	17
Japan	25	55
West Germany	43	19

unprotected, imports would rise. In 1959, the steelworkers struck for 159 days. During that time, imports surged to exceed exports for the first time, taking 2.8 percent of the market. Following the strike, the companies and unions agreed that the principal benefactors of their poor relationship were the Japanese. Attempts were made to improve the bargaining process, leading in the period 1971 to 1974 to the Voluntary Restraint Agreement. Thereafter, companies and unions bargained in a strike-free atmosphere. And wages rose. In 1976 the wage cost per hour for the average worker in steel facilities was $12.22, almost twice the Japanese level. With maintenance workers out of the average, the gap was wider.

Finally, with the creation of the Environmental Protection Agency during the Nixon administration, and the development of clean air and water standards, the industry was saddled with an enormous bill for equipment that would clean its effluent. It is estimated that of the $18 billion spent by the industry on plant and equipment from 1971 to 1978, 15 percent of that sum was for pollution abatement.

In response to these problems, the industry has liquidated and diversified. Dividends between 1960 and 1978 were 52 percent of profits, and major portions of cash flow have been invested outside the industry.

By 1978 the Japanese industry was in the hands of six giant steel companies assembled through mergers with government blessing. Process equipment was at least as efficient as that anywhere else. Ore and metallurgical coal were purchased and finished product was sold by the world's largest trading companies. The situation in Europe varied from a few comparably strong firms in Germany to very weak and uncompetitive situations in Belgium and the United Kingdom. There was substantial excess capacity posing the threat of high unemployment; governments subsidized their firms at massive rates to keep mills running.

By 1978, then, the U.S. industry was in relatively poor shape, financially and competitively. Some firms — especially Armco, Inland, and National — were relatively healthy, but:

- There had not been a single issue of new equity in the industry since 1960.
- Cash flow did not cover capital requirements.
- The market evaluated shares at very low price-earnings levels.
- The Japanese could land steel on the West Coast of the United States and perhaps elsewhere at or below U.S. mill prices.
- The industry was still estimated as having to invest $6 billion by 1985 to meet EPA requirements.

The response of the industry was a coordinated three-pronged attack on the problem through the steelworkers, their congressional representatives — the so-called Steel Caucuses in the House and Senate — and in the courts where U.S. Steel brought antidumping suits.

The suits posed severe problems for the Carter administration and the network of trade-related agencies. As one trade representative put it, "We knew they were right, but we also knew that loss of access to our market would shut down massive parts of the European industry and that they would then retaliate in agriculture, where we were running a $40 billion surplus."

The bureaucracy staked out positions much along the lines developed above. The answer found, "trigger prices" succeeded in making the industry more viable by raising all prices. They also obviated the threat of the dumping suits. And they made the issue "go away" for a period.

But they did not deal with any of the fundamental issues: the structure of the U.S. industry (the number, size, location, and equipment of the U.S. firms); the excess capacity in the world industry; and the high wage cost in the United States. Again, not one of the technocratic players had the charter and the incentive to deal with the whole problem. And again the politics of their interaction did not make up for the absence of a national viewpoint. Just as within organizations a committee of specialists is not the same thing as a generalist, so a task force of special interests does not add up to the national interest.

The cost is clear. We have an industry that is not as low cost as it might be. Consequently, our auto companies pay higher prices and they are less competitive. Our capacity is below national consumption. That is either sensible given worldwide excess capacity, or dangerous, leaving the United States vulnerable to gouging by exporters during tight periods that might emerge.

There is another cost that also bears analysis. It is evident in the Chrysler and steel cases if we look for it, but is captured best by the past chairman of General Electric, Reginald Jones, who has said that he spent more than half his time in Washington. In order to deal with this network without a head, the top managers of the major technocratic organizations have to join the political world. The greatest cost we pay for our approach to economic affairs may well be the politicizing of the technocracy.

The job of top management shifts from one of direction setting and organization building to one of influencing the public laws and institutions that provide context for the company or bureaucracy. The history of Consolidated Edison of New York further exemplifies the problem of company management in politicized settings. The history of the development of the legislative veto provides a neat example of a pathological stage of the disease in the public sector.

Con Ed Passes Its Dividend[9]

Beginning in 1967, my colleague George Lodge produced a series of studies of the trials and tribulations of Consolidated Edison. For Lodge there is an almost absurd quality to the arrangement of the government organizations, the pressure groups, and the courts through which Con Ed struggled to provide electric power to its market as (1) the customer base changed, (2) laws concerning pollution were passed, (3) inflation raised labor rates and interest costs, and (4) events following the October 1973 Arab-Israeli war altered the availability and price of oil supplies.

Lodge characterizes the situation as follows:

> Like a great dinosaur, Con Ed wallows in its swamp, being bitten to death by smaller animals. There is only one way out — the political order must intervene and plan, in answer to the questions: How much power is needed? At what price? Where should the generating facilities be built? And what technologically is the safest and most efficient source of power?[10]

His conclusion has a ring of inevitability. But we have established that there is no "political order." Unless the Constitution is somehow revised, Con Ed will still face some version of the Federal Power Commission, the Public Service Commission (PSC) of New York State,[11] and various regulatory boards of New York City, Con Ed's biggest customer. In the meantime it is interesting to observe the way in which the company's management reacted to an increasingly difficult political situation.

The beginning was as politically controversial as the situation in the 1970s. The company was first set up by a group of financiers who saw an opportunity for profit in the consolidation of the city's gas and electric companies into a single corporation. This was achieved by 1936, in the midst of a fight with Mayor Fiorello La Guardia over rates that was settled in 1937.

Thereafter, the founders and their children ran the company. Over time, close relations developed between the city and Con Ed. According to *Fortune,* jobs for Con Ed and, more important, the construction contracts it provided for building and the opening and closing of streets were traditionally regarded as part of the patronage system on which the city's politics depended. The extensive construction work also ensured good union relations.

This cozy situation began to break down, however, in the changing economic environment of the 1960s. The performance of Con Ed satisfied everyone but its customers, and they constituted a new political constituency.

Perhaps the earliest and most dramatic step in response to the situation was for the company's Board of Trustees to hire as chief executive Charles F. Luce, a Democrat and former public power executive who was undersecretary of the interior prior to joining Con Ed. (Interestingly, he was not the first public official Con Ed hired in a time of crisis.) At first Luce sought to improve Con Ed's relations with the public through cost cutting, equal employment opportunity, and antipollution programs. He soon discovered, however, that there was much truth to *Fortune*'s 1966 charge that the company he had taken over was "hidebound" with high rates, legions of dissatisfied customers, and close ties to various city and state politicians.

Luce's hope was to respond to his problem by building large-scale, nonpolluting generating capability outside the boundaries of New York City. Nuclear plants were planned for Indian Point and islands in Long Island Sound, and a pumped storage facility was planned for a mountain near Cornwall. The nuclear facilities would permit relatively lower rates and reduce dependence on coal or imported oil, and the pumped storage facility would provide peak load capability that could be brought on line almost instantly.

These basic responses to the company's problems were blocked in the courts and the financial markets. Environmentalists tied up the construction plans while customers, including New York City, slowed rate adjustments that would have protected the company's earnings capability. The oil crisis of 1973 produced a financial crisis at Con Ed.

Approximately 75 percent of Con Ed's electricity was produced by burning oil from foreign sources. As a result of the 1973–74 Arab oil embargo, Con Ed's fuel costs rose sharply: oil priced at $172 million in 1972 cost $293 million in 1973, and on the basis of prices quoted in early 1974, the bill for that year was estimated at $700 million. Unfortunately for Con Ed, under the fuel adjustment clause of PSC regulations, increased fuel costs were not immediately billable to customers. Con Ed's plea to the PSC that the fuel clause be put on a current basis had recently been rejected, and it was thirty-nine days before increased costs of fuel actually consumed would be paid by the customers. As a result, cash inflows lagged outflows by as much as $30 million per month.

Also, as Con Ed encountered mounting difficulties in obtaining scarce fuel for its own generating plants, it had to purchase increasing amounts of power from other utilities, which were not so dependent on Middle Eastern oil. Unlike higher fuel costs, the greater costs per kilowatt-hour of purchased power were *not* recoverable, under a September 1973 PSC ruling, although on January 7, 1974, the PSC largely reversed itself.

As customers' bills began to reflect rapidly rising costs, the company's accounts receivable increased drastically, from $301 million in September 1973 to $367 million in March 1974, reaching the equivalent of fifty-three days' revenue outstanding. Fully one third of all bills were thus in arrears — a record — and the amount of uncollectable bills increased to $10 million for the first quarter of 1974.

Con Ed had, until 1971, followed the industry practice of giving substantial discounts to bulk users of electricity. Yet in the winter of 1973 the company found itself urgently appealing for *reduced* energy consumption. Total electric sendout was reduced in the first quarter of 1974 by 10 percent, this in spite of a "normal" growth of 3.6 percent to 4.1 percent. As fuel was conserved, however, finances deteriorated. Since so many of the utility's costs — taxes, maintenance, labor, interest charges — were high and increasing, and largely unrelated to sendout, it had not been possible to reduce them to match the reduction in revenues.

Higher costs and lower revenues meant drastically lower earnings. Had it not been for an accounting change approved by the PSC in December, which permitted the deferral of fuel costs until the time they were actually billed to the customers — an accounting practice followed by a number of other utilities — Con Ed would have reported a loss in both November and December of 1973.

In December a $314.8 million electric rate increase request was submitted to the PSC. In addition, the company requested a $107.8 million "conservation adjustment" rate increase, arguing that since decreased energy sendout could not be matched by decreased costs, a higher rate per unit of energy sold was necessary to *maintain* the same corporate rate of return. The total rate request represented an increase of 30 percent over a two-year period (1974 through 1975), compared to an average of 10 percent over the previous three years. Approval of the entire increase would have raised the typical customer's monthly bill from $14.97 to $19.20. Although the PSC had granted a temporary increase of $174.7 million in February, this was $100 million less than the company had requested as temporary relief, and under the PSC's procedures, a decision on the permanent increase could not be anticipated until late in the year.

While uncertainty prevailed, Con Ed was forced to delay a planned January offering of $50 million of preferred stock and $50 million of bonds. In March, $150 million of 9⅛ percent bonds were finally issued. Almost immediately they were bid down to a market yield of 10.45 percent, the highest in the utilities industry.

One way out of the rapidly developing "cash crisis" was short-term bank loans. (In 1973, the PSC had forced Con Ed into arrearage financing — over the protests of its Board of Trustees.) Management projected that operating and capital costs would require an additional very large loan by the end of the year. It seemed doubtful that Con Ed's banks would be willing to lend that much. Charles Luce, who had emphasized time and again the company's need for *all* the construction planned for the next five years, reluctantly announced in late March a $46 million reduction in the $629 million planned 1974 construction outlays. Part of that reduction was made possible by the postponement of the completion of an 800-megawatt plant at Astoria, Queens.

In early April, Con Ed offered two of its power plants for sale to the state of New York; a bill providing for the purchase was submitted to the state legislature in May. The outcome of the legislative debate was uncertain. Constituents of many New York City and Westchester County Democrats and Republicans had complained bitterly about Con Ed's higher rates, particularly electric heat rates. These legislators were also concerned, however, that city and county tax revenues would be lost if the tax-exempt New York State Power Authority took over the plants as proposed in the legislation. Furthermore, they were reluctant to believe that Con Ed was really in as bad shape as it claimed. Some demanded a complete audit of the company.

A regular quarterly or semiannual dividend had been paid faithfully by Con Ed and its predecessors since 1885. Although the dividend had not been increased in seven years, Con Ed stock was still acquired for income purposes. To many, especially older women stockholders on Social Security, the average $360 of annual dividends (on two hundred shares) was extremely important. Finally, there was the difficult question of what damage an adverse decision would do to the capital markets.

Nonetheless, on April 23, 1974, the Board of Trustees of Consolidated Edison decided that for the first time in its history Con Ed would omit its common stock dividend. In explaining the unprecedented move, Luce cited the extremely critical cash situation and management's desire to reserve at least some funds for emergencies.

Effects   Prior to the dividend omission, Con Ed's common stock had been selling for $18 a share. The annual dividend provided a 10 percent return, higher than almost any other American utility. Most industry observers felt this had been justified by the riskiness of the company.

On April 23, after opening four hours late on the New York Stock Exchange, Con Ed's stock was offered at $12. By the time it closed at $12.25, it had been the most actively traded stock of the day.

On April 24, Con Ed was dealt another devastating blow. Standard & Poor's reduced the company's bond rating from BBB to BB. Bonds rated in the latter category are usually considered "speculative" and undesirable for institutional investment. The agency said in its announcement, "In omitting the dividend Con Ed had foreclosed itself for an unknown length of time from one of the avenues available to it — namely, the equity market."

Reaction to the Con Ed dividend omission from the management of other major utilities, government officials, and utility analysts was swift and severe. Donald C. Cook, chairman of the American Electric Power Company and long opposed to any kind of governmental interference with investor-owned utilities, stated, "Con Ed is out of the equity market, and New York State is in the power business — forever."

A Salamon Brothers partner, echoing many investment analysts on Wall Street, warned, "Utilities have always been the backbone of the bond market, and Con Ed is causing a harsh reassessment of the utilities." Roger Gilmartin of Morgan Stanley added, "The Con Ed thing has had an immense effect. Until — or if — it is forgotten, it will be very serious."

Analysis   Cutting the dividend of Con Ed was an extraordinary act. Although it was presented as a move taken to conserve funds, its effect was to deprive Con Ed of access to external private capital. For the foreseeable future the company would be totally dependent on government actors for its survival. Luce said through his actions, "If you want to play politics with us by (1) keeping our rates down, (2) driving our costs up, (3) asking us to generate outside the city, but (4) opposing our proposals, we'll play politics with you by (1) selling our plants to you, (2) creating a storm over our financial weakness, and (3) forcing you to let us be profitable or take us over."

It has been an effective move. The state bought the two plants and imported power now meets Con Ed's needs for new generating capability. Con Ed is still alive in 1983. Through conservation efforts, it has been able to stay profitable while participating in the decline of New York City.

On the other hand, by any other standard Con Ed has continued its poor performance. Costs are still dramatically higher than elsewhere; new capacity has not been built; and the Indian Point nuclear facilities are closed while structural flaws are repaired.

Moreover, instead of behaving as a proactive planning entity that seeks to grow while providing energy for the New York City area, Con Ed now is a coping organization. Without "requisite variety," it does less. It reacts to changing circumstances and bargains with strong regulatory and political organizations. Where once Con Ed could count on steady growth by providing service and jobs where they were needed, it is now dependent on strong public bodies responsive to electoral politics. Just as the piecemeal bailout of Chrysler does not buy us an efficient auto industry or put the unemployed back to work, the present arrangement will serve the long-term interests of New York City well only by accident.

Irving Kristol has taken an even more jaundiced view of these events. Writing in the *Wall Street Journal* less than a month after the event, he characterized the politics described above as "the mugging of Con Ed."

Following a sarcastic account of the events, he concluded:

Meanwhile, the 308,000 stockholders of Con Ed have been fleeced. In the state legislature, New York City's representatives are actually insisting that, whatever financial aid Con Ed received, *none* of it should go to the restoration of dividends. This leaves the stockholders forever out in the cold. Almost all of these stockholders are individuals of modest means; 40% are women, elderly widows for the most part. Who is speaking up for them? Not the financial or business community, which seems indifferent to any event that does not immediately affect its pocketbook. Not the media, which has no compassion to waste on stockholders. Not any of those "public interest" law firms, who do not regard stockholders of any kind as part of their constituency. Not even the stockholders themselves, unorganized as they are and utterly unaccustomed to the arts of political warfare.

So no one speaks up for them. More and more, with every passing day, the mugging of Con Ed begins to look like the perfect crime.[12]

Other utilities faced the same problem as Con Ed in varying, usually lesser, degrees of severity. By the spring of 1981 those companies that still had a viable economic base were seeking ways of diversifying in order to protect shareholder wealth. Many companies, however, faced virtual expropriation in the form of rising costs, including taxes, slowed or declining consumption, and ceilings on rates chargeable to consumers. Constrained in performance by politics, the politics of bailout is their only hope for survival.

It is not clear that the way to conserve energy in the United States is to have the healthiest utilities move into new industries and the sick ones transfer to the public sector. But those managements free to allocate their resources recognize their vulnerability to politics, while those without resources can only play politics in order to stay in business.

What has happened is that a series of incremental political decisions, each one defensible in its own terms, has produced an unintended outcome of dubious desirability — low rates, service for the poor when they can't pay, higher taxes, and clean, efficient plants — which, taken together, yield financial losses and eventually a dead utility company. Shifts in the costs of cities, and thus their need for tax revenue; a radical shift in the cost of fuel; an awareness of the medical and aesthetic costs of pollution; a major shift in demographic patterns; and a slowdown in economic growth combine to create a very difficult problem. Because a satisfactory solution means painfully higher costs for someone, no political actor has a stake in finding that solution. Why make a long-term investment in a short-term game? In the meantime, private companies are convenient targets, especially since some are poorly managed.

The process of holding an organization responsible for meeting independently imposed objectives, whether or not they are consistent, changes the task of that organization's management. The demands cannot be ignored even though they are inconsistent. Inability to meet politically imposed objectives ensures failure. Thus the work of the chief executive and his key subordinates is to deal with the day-to-day efforts to eliminate that inconsistency. Where the revenue that might be generated by growth is not available because markets are declining or the ability to provide capacity for that revenue in increasing growth is constrained by politics, then some part of the resources of the organization must be traded for survival. This cannibalization of the organization is the cost of politicization. Tragedies develop when the surplus traded is not slack but critical ability to produce product or service rather than reallocate political control. Whether it be political hacks in key managerial jobs, or "discount prices," or unwise choice of suppliers, the result is often a vicious circle of increasing dependency on political as opposed to market support.

The point is simple to see if hard to deal with. Once a market-based organization becomes dependent on the active intervention of a government agency or bureau for its survival, it must deal with the politics of that agency at least as seriously as it does with its market. Where the politics are negative, as in the case of Con Ed, the organization can be boxed into a Catch-22 of uneconomic circumstances. The steps it takes to survive each year lead it to a political never-never land. Where the politics are positive, as in the case of Chrysler, a fundamentally unsound business proposition can be made a permanent ward of the state. Alfa Romeo in Italy and British Leyland in England are contemporary examples of this phenomenon in the auto industry.

What happens is that managers trade the implicit or explicit promise of economic benefit — usually in modern democracies the benefits are jobs — for immediate economic support. This support takes the form of equity or loans the market won't provide, prices the market won't pay, protection against foreign competition, or even volume that the market would not voluntarily accept at any price. At various times the only reason that French or British agencies bought French or British computer products is that they were ordered to.

The consequence, however, is that the jobs become an entitlement. The workers who fill them recognize that their elected representatives have protected them, not the market. At that point, the withdrawal of protection comes to be regarded as a hostile act, grounds for voting for someone else. Eventually we reach the point that economically obsolete but politically important activity is supported with vigor. The citrus growers of Japan are a glorious example. In a country where miracles of explicit economic redeployment are counted ordinary achievements, the virtually medieval agricultural practices of the nation's citrus growers are regarded as untouchable by the Ministry of International Trade and Industry (MITI) and the Diet. In a country such as the United States, where redeployment can be the political equivalent of bigamy, we have phenomena such as the merchant marine subsidy, which penalizes all of our industry that utilizes coastal shipping, cost us $450 million in 1980, and subsidizes a small merchant fleet deemed irrelevant by the U.S. Navy to our national security.

The Legislative Veto: Politicizing the Government's Technocratic Systems

Ironically, it had often been the case that the technocratic activity of the U.S. government was somewhat immune to short-term targeted pressure from political sources. Executive power clearly reflected swings in political success, but the workings of the bureaucracy were somewhat protected from the more fragmented and instantaneously responsive influence of the legislature. The contemporary use of the legislative veto threatens to change all that.

Beginning in 1932 while Herbert Hoover was president, Congress qualified the power constitutionally granted to the executive for executing the laws by including, on occasion, some provision for legislative review of executive action. Basically the veto involves writing into law a provision permitting some part or the whole of one or both houses of Congress to nullify executive action taken under that law during a specified period, such as sixty days. Between 1932 and 1970 there were 118 instances of a legislative veto provision. There have been more than that since then.

Though the constitutional issue posed by the legislative veto is clear, and though the administrative costs can be quite severe, the motivation for its use is understandable. The Constitution vests all legislative powers in the Congress, specifically the power "to make all laws which shall be necessary and proper for carrying into execution the [other powers granted]." In turn, "the executive power shall be vested in a President."

As the task of governing the nation has grown more complex, Congress has found it increasingly convenient to legislate its intentions and then leave the working out of the detail of its intentions to the executive departments. For example, in response to growing concern over air pollution, Congress in 1970 passed the Clean Air Act amendments. The legislation called for the automobile manufacturers to produce cars that met federally mandated standards by specific dates in 1975. The standards, however, were to be set by the Environmental Protection Agency after an appropriate procedure was established.

Unfortunately for administrative neatness, there existed a great deal of room for debate as to what constitutes a feasible or achievable standard. There was disagreement as well as to how performance should be measured. But suppose that there was substantial agreement. And suppose as well that the EPA in order to meet its mandate set a standard that the manufacturers could not meet without losing their profitability for several years and without loss of jobs in major portions of the industry. Congress might well feel that somehow the standard set by the agency was achieving ends — the weakening of the industry — that Congress had not intended. In those circumstances Congress could rewrite or amend the Clean Air Act. But increasingly some Congress members are seeking the right to review executive acts as they are performed, and where they offend, to strike them down. The legislative veto is their tool. It simply involves attaching a clause to a bill that says, "You go figure out what we meant but if we don't like what you do, we'll strike it down."

The chief spokesman and most effective proponent of the legislative veto is Congressman Elliott Levitas, a Georgia Democrat. Interviewed in July 1978 by the *National Journal,* he said of the veto:

> It is one of the ways, not the only way, but one of the most effective ways to get control over the bureaucracy in general, and specifically that activity in the bureaucracy which issues rules and regulations. That's the whole thing that people in America just don't have any control over. They don't know who's writing the rules. They don't have any accountability because the people [in the bureaucracy] don't stand for election. Yet they are as persuasive and effective as a law passed by Congress. And by giving the elected Congress the right to veto a rule or regulation, we'll have returned to the people the control over these regulations and at the same time sensitize the bureaucracy.[13]

While this remedy is neat, the problem it poses for the president is clear. The legislative veto puts him in a position where he cannot provide unchallenged authority to a subordinate to carry out his responsibility as specified by law. It is not enough for bureaucratic superiors to approve an action, Congress has to approve — or, more correctly, not disapprove. Congress assumes an executive role.

Levitas has made plain his confidence in Congress's administrative ability, but other congressmen have doubts. Richard Bolling, a Democratic House member since 1948 and until 1983 chairman of the Rules Committee, suggested:

> I don't think it's going to work . . . Because I don't think Congress is equipped to be an administrator. Anyway, by taking power back from the agencies, Congress will become confused as to what its role should be. Of course, this doesn't mean that the legislative branch should not be engaged in the oversight of laws it has already written. But oversight is a far cry from actually pulling back power from the agencies and getting involved in administrative decisions.[14]

There is a constitutional issue here that will be settled, in time. For now, the country is left with the power to manage further diffused.

The cost of the legislative veto is clearer if we contrast how standards and regulations are drawn up, and by whom, with the process by which laws are made. A study of the EPA and the toxic substances laws by J. Ronald Fox and Lynne O. Cabot provides useful evidence:

> The Nixon Administration first proposed TSCA [Toxic Substances Control Act] in 1971. Based on conclusions contained in a report of the U.S. Government Council on Environmental Quality (CEQ), it was debated by the 92d (1971–1973), 93d (1973–1975), and 94th (1975–1977) Congresses before it was passed. Disagreement concerning the extent of regulatory powers authorized by TSCA delayed its passage. During this time, the proposed law was the focus of attention and contention among environmentalists, the chemical industry, labor unions, business groups, and public interest lobbies. Even federal agencies joined the debate. Factions in the Commerce Department and the Office of Management and Budget (OMB), for example, were determined to limit TSCA's potential for overregulation of the chemical industry, a prospect that they viewed as weakening an important segment of the economy. However, the Council on Environmental Quality and OSHA were allied with EPA in favor of extending broad new authorities for EPA under TSCA.[15]

The battle between the industry and the environmentalists ebbed and flowed until with the election in 1974 of a new more liberal Congress, the industry concluded that passage of TSCA was inevitable. They initiated a series of discussions with the House subcommittee responsible for developing the bill.

> Participating in the discussions that led to enactment were the Manufacturing Chemists Association (MCA), the National Association of Manufacturers (NAM), the environmentalists, headed by the Sierra Club, and representatives of the AFL-CIO and United Steel Workers. MCA acted as a spokesperson for the larger chemical companies. NAM, a general trade association, and Chemical Specialty Manufacturers Association (CSMA) represented the interests of the smaller, specialized chemical firms. While the House and Senate versions of TSCA differed originally on 52 issues, agreement was reached in conference and the bill

was sent to the White House for President Ford's signature in October 1976.[16]

The bill President Ford signed empowered the EPA to promulgate rules affecting the testing, manufacture, and distribution of all chemicals, substances, and mixtures. Special provisions were made for substances found to be hazardous. The bill did not specify what those chemicals and substances were, how they would be inventoried, who would bear the cost, how proprietary data describing process technology would be protected, or — more difficult — how the law would be implemented so that "the Administrator [would] consider the environmental, economic, and social impact of any action the Administrator takes or proposes to take under this Act." There was not even an indication as to how the four and a half million chemicals listed by the Chemical Abstract Service were to be dealt with, except that the rules for compiling the inventory of existing chemicals were to be completed by November 1977.

The strategy for developing the rules was shaped primarily by Glenn Schweitzer, a former State Department officer with an M.S. in mechanical engineering from the California Institute of Technology. He was named director of the Office of Water and Hazardous Materials of the EPA's Office of Toxic Substances in 1973. He, in turn, delegated the developing of the rule to Cynthia Kelly, a Yale history M.A. who joined the EPA in 1974 after working as legislative assistant to Congressman Donald Riegle of Michigan.

The process of developing the rule involved three day-long open meetings with invited representatives of labor, environmental, and chemical industry groups. These meetings were especially important to the EPA, for they gave agency officials a chance to benefit from the expertise of industry executives while letting them explain the characteristics of an inventory system that would be realistic.

The first draft of the rule was published on March 9, 1977. The chemical industry was satisfied with this version, but environmentalists were not. Representatives of the latter group met with Schweitzer's superior on March 17, and with President Carter's new EPA director, Douglas Costle, on May 12. Comments were also received from EPA regional offices and other government agencies, such as the Occupational Safety and Health Administration (OSHA). The protest evoked extensive discussion and restudy within the EPA. A revised rule was published in the *Federal Register* on August 2, 1977. It represented a considerable change in the earliest published draft, since the scope of the inventory was considerably extended.

Again there were public hearings and scheduled sessions with industry representatives and environmentalists. From September to December there was extensive lobbying. The final rule was promulgated on December 23, 1977.

For present purposes the key contrast is between the breadth of Congress's legislated intent battled out over six years and the concreteness of the task facing the EPA. After Congress finished its work, it left to the EPA the task of interpreting what the law ought to mean. Simply specifying how the list of "existing chemicals" ought to be constructed took more than one year of extensive discussion. When TSCA was passed, the EPA possessed at best limited basic technical capability to analyze the problem delegated to it. This would have to be built up over time. In fact, the entire field of toxicology was in its early developmental stages. Political managers might will that a reasonable and prudent acting administrator would balance the costs and benefits of toxic and hazardous substances, but it would take considerable time and technical work before the administrative apparatus required to carry out that will would be constructed both in the EPA and in the companies.

The question posed by the legislative veto is whether Congress has the skill to enter into this process after it is over — after the various compromises among affected parties have been negotiated — and, as it were, shoot down the contract and reopen the bidding. All that is required is for the parties affected by the rule to persuade the appropriate congressional forum — committee or chamber — that its intent was not followed, and the rule-making process is restarted. The real consequence of such procedures is to extend the political process into the technocratic one. One government official quoted in *Business Week* suggested that:

> All you are going to see are backroom deals to moderate regulations or adverse court decisions. And the action will shift to case-by-case adjudications or large-scale investigations such as the FTC's funeral home or auto studies. None of that is affected by these bills [that extend the legislative veto].[17]

In other words, the technocrats will try to shift their activity to areas free from legislative intrusion. But that intrusion, in turn, reaches further into agency activity. Today the veto is attached to activity as varied as the president's power to reorganize the executive branch; Eximbank loans over $50 million; trade agreements of certain kinds; waivers of the immigration laws; national highway safety rules; natural gas regulation; and all rules of the Federal Trade Commission. Thus, under the guise of increased responsiveness to Congress, the acts of executive agencies are increasingly subject to line-by-line review in the context of year-to-year changes in the political environment.

Were Congress organized to manage itself in a coherent fashion with consistent long-term objectives, this weakening of executive administrative capability might be offset by an equivalent congressional power. But Sam Rayburn is dead and the House is "reformed." Congress would not pass an energy program or even a tax on gasoline, not to mention laws against hand guns. It is this forum of 535 regionally based politicians, 468 of whom are always running for reelection within two years, that seeks to grasp more executive power to make national policy. In this way, politicization threatens the ability of public managers to use limited resources to achieve interdependent national objectives.

But Concern for Fair Division Increases

Why does politicization seem to be an increasing problem? It is all very well to decry the consequence of a shift in resource allocation from technocratically managed systems to political ones, but a useful diagnosis must consider what underlying forces account for the problem. There are two major factors, the slowdown in economic growth and mismanagement. Some would add a third factor, a shift in ideology.

Slower Growth

Lester Thurow has summarized the problem of income distribution in the United States in the title of his book *The Zero-Sum Society.* His basic point is that any of the aggregate problems of the United States can be solved, but only at a cost to an identifiable, politically active segment of society. The sum of the claims of each segment exceeds what is available. In order to stop printing money, somebody has to lose.

Yet for nearly two decades the politics of our country have confused legitimate aspiration with entitlement. Catching the economic surge generated by the 1964 tax cut, Lyndon Johnson rolled out a smorgasbord of programs to create the Great Society. When the cost of the Vietnam War competed with his programs, he delayed until his guns-and-butter policy generated inflation. Supported by grassroots politics that were developed in civil rights, antiwar, and then environmental movements, these aspirations legislated into rights and privileges were extended during the 1970s.

Faced with a growing deficit at home and abroad, Richard Nixon coped with the dilemma of high aspiration and budget cuts through regulation. A host of entitlements was put in place that seemed to have no cost — Congress simply mandated that businesses, universities, and cities would behave in new ways. Were there enough wealth generated by our system to pay for all these good things, our contemporary politics would be different. But there was and is not enough wealth. Our inventiveness in spending has accelerated at the same time as our ability to pay has declined. The slowdown in economic growth that we have experienced, especially after the oil shocks, thereby aggravates the boxed-in sense of zero sum. The willingness of a hard-pressed middle class to fund the aspirations of others disappears. The national consensus based on benefits for everyone that a rising economy can fund disappears, and politics turn divisive.

Just as an inventory permits a manufacturing department to buffer itself from day-to-day demands of sales, the wealth thrown off by a growing economy funds competing, even contradictory, claims. We can subsidize tobacco farmers and fund research on cancer. When funds are short we have to choose (so we cut research).

It is ironic, but just as we have become aware of the real limitations on our resources, we have developed the political sophistication of our special-interest groups to a fine professional edge. "One man–one vote" reforms make these groups potent. All technocratically managed organizations, market or nonmarket, that depend on some form of political charter for protection or subsidy have organized new functional capability to put pressure on a Congress deliberately fragmented so as to be responsive to those pressures. The list of issues addressed is endless, but it includes government employee pensions, veterans' hospitals, maritime subsidies, municipal bond interest tax exemption, airline route structure, natural gas pricing, commercial and military aircraft sales, farm supports, food stamps, medical care, and scientific research. All of these benefits or activities and a thousand more depend upon a government-chartered monopoly or government funds. As growth slows we are increasingly aware how costly are our neighbors' entitlements. Thus doth slow growth make competitors of us all.

As if this were not bad enough, the failure of some of our more important technocratic organizations has added new players to the game.

Mismanagement

A review of the examples of politically managed organizations used thus far is instructive. Chrysler, the steel industry, Allied Chemical, Con Ed, and the agencies that deal with border management do not constitute a very inspiring list.

It is worth asking whether sick organizations are more likely to be politicized than healthy ones. The answer is probably yes, although the evidence is largely the prevalence of supporting examples and the absence of countercases. The question leads us in provocative directions, for sick companies are dependent on outsiders for help even in the absence of government forces (aside from the courts). Despite the mythology of the privately owned company, it is reasonably well documented that the large, professionally managed corporations that account for the major share of our manufacturing, mining, agriculture, construction, and financial services tend to regard owners as a constraint rather than a primary source of motivation. The presence of active shareholders and bankers is almost always a sign of crisis.

Although there have been no systematic studies, the same proposition can almost certainly be made about technocratically managed organizations providing goods and services for nonmarket constituencies. The Department of Agriculture is often criticized but almost never in trouble. Somehow, it is perceived as successfully meeting its constituents' needs without treading on the toes of too many others. It is organizations such as OSHA or programs like Medicaid that seem to be in trouble. Why?

The fate of Robert Moses may be an instructive answer. For many New Yorkers, Moses remains a quasi saint. He opened the suburbs and the beaches to anyone who had a car. The beaches themselves were miracles of beautiful public recreation facilities. The roads and bridges and tunnels were marvels. Yet Robert Caro, in his massive and comprehensive picture of Moses, paints him as fundamentally evil; like Ibsen's master builder, a man trapped in a technocratic vision of middle-class materialistic growth, Moses in Caro's image is a man who evolved from a reformer to a builder.[18] Moses' actual fate would seem to be a shift in the taste or preferences of the voters, *or* the taste and preference of those who interpret events for voters.

Until the civil rights movement and one man–one vote court decisions, those who were hurt by Moses had no voice — nor were they sure they deserved a voice. They experienced a road through their house as material progress, the American way, but bad luck for them. The idea that they were owed real compensation was not widely embraced. And in this judgment, they were correct. Although courts and now amendments to the Civil Rights Acts establish their claim, it is rare for a majority to subsidize a minority for any long period of time. There is generally not that much slack in the system.

What happens to companies or agencies, then, is that either a market's sense of what it wants and who it wants to buy it from shifts, or the community's sense of what it is willing to support with taxes changes. To survive, the organization must shift its product line or develop a new source of support. If management is less than competent, the ability to provide employment may be the only salable service. Here are a few examples. When customers and financiers stopped supporting Chrysler, the United Auto Workers and Congress were natural alternative supporters. The price was a loss of autonomy. When U.S. political leaders in the 1920s lost interest in antitrust activity, the FTC adopted new missions in order to support itself: enforcing textile and garment labeling acts and employing lawyers from Tennessee. When industry shifted south and west, the substitution of telephone communication for mail killed the post, highways and airplanes captured the high value-added traffic, and the eastern railroads had no other customers than the unions and Congress. When local unions and the regular party could not protect Con Ed, it had to turn from the city to the state.

In short, when consumer/voter taste changes, when competition improves or the organization is incompetent, then one of the only routes to survival is to provide something a legislature will buy. The organization is politicized. On the other hand, when a technocratically managed organization can meet the three tests implied above, then it survives with a high degree of autonomy.

An important hypothesis, then, is that politicization of the technocracy is a disease attacking *weak* organizations. This possibility is especially disturbing, for it suggests that there may be a tendency to impose our least efficient form of management on the organizations least able to provide efficient and effective delivery of goods or services.

The crucial feature of a technocratic organization is that it is managed toward a limited set of agreed-upon consequences. It is judged by outcomes. From the perspective of a society seeking productivity and performance from its institutions, the problem with a politicized organization is that process as well as outcomes is judged. For example, energy politics is not simply bargaining over whether the price of energy will be at a given level, it is also the politics of how that energy shall be produced, where it will be produced, and who shall have which jobs. Rather than dividing the surplus of successful operations, political managers divide the opportunities for work and the benefits provided by the operation of the organization itself.

Daniel Bell has spoken to the same point from a broader perspective:

Politics, in the sense that we understand it, is always prior to the rational, and often the upsetting of the rational. The "rational," as we have come to know it, is the routinized, settled, administrative and orderly procedure by rules. Much of life in a complex society necessarily has this character. In going by plane or train to Washington one does not haggle with a taxi driver in the Levant. But politics is haggling, or else it is force. In Washington one haggles over the priorities of the society, the distribution of money, the burden of taxation, and the like . . .

As for politics, what is evident, everywhere, is a societywide uprising against bureaucracy and a desire for participation, a theme summed up in the statement, already a catch-phrase, that "people ought to be able to affect the decisions that control their lives." To a considerable extent, the participation revolution is one of the forms of reaction against the "professionalization" of society and the emergent technocratic decision making of a postindustrial society. What began years ago in the factory through the trade unions has now spread to the neighborhood — because of the politicization of decision making in social affairs — and into the universities; in the next decades it will spread into other complex organizations as well.

Yet "participatory democracy" is not the panacea that its adherents make it out to be, no more so than efforts of fifty years ago at creating plebiscitarian political mechanisms such as the initiative, the referendum, and the recall. With all the furor about "participatory democracy," it is curious that few of its proponents have sought to think through, on the most elementary level, the meaning of the phrases . . . In short, participatory democracy is one more way of posing the classical issues of political philosophy, namely, Who should make, and at what levels of government, what kinds of decisions, for how large a social unit?[19]

From the perspective, then, of economic affairs or policy, politicizing of technocratic organizations infects the mechanisms that we use to produce and deliver goods with debates over who should make decisions and who should benefit.

7 Managers and Wizards

THE FOREGOING CHRONICLE of awkwardness, misalliance, and failure would not be so depressing if it did not seem to be the inevitable consequence of the way we are constitutionally organized to do business. It is extraordinary for the leadership of the most powerful nation in the world to be so confused in its action and contradictory in its statements. Reading newspapers and magazines, one is reminded of Victorian conversations about sex. The participants were either remarkably disingenuous or terribly ignorant.

Careful reading and listening reveal that the problem is not just an impression, it is reality. For example, one voice we often hear is that of the libertarian free enterpriser exemplified by Donald T. Regan, the Reagan administration's secretary of the treasury. What we must do, he says, is unleash individual initiative.

> If we are to beat the inflation problem, only the American people can do it. Only the people themselves can reverse the inflationary mentality, make the necessary saving and investment decisions that will increase productivity, and make the personal initiatives toward more production, getting a better job, upgrading their professions, and generally increasing their living standards.
>
> The President's program provides a dramatic change from existing policies. In fact, it relies on the oldest and most proven economic principles known to this country. It restores our faith in the private enterprise

system, in personal initiative, in individual prerogative and in the traditions of personal saving and investment.[1]

Another voice calls for an active central government. Again making a plea for sensible economic policy, Lane Kirkland, then president of the AFL-CIO, attacked precisely the views expounded by Regan.

A common thread that runs through the economies of countries that have grown faster than our own is their adoption of a coordinated industrial policy that systematically includes the views of labor, industry, and the public. By contrast, we have too long been at the mercy of a series of economic schools, each of which believes that it alone can see the unseen hand. It is time to take our economic life into our own hands, by dealing directly with our many concrete visible problems and sectoral and structural needs. It is time for the United States to formulate a national industrial policy and abandon the irrational attachment to laissez-faire policies that threaten to bring about the wholesale condemnation of entire industries and regions.[2]

Finally, also speaking from the presumed high ground of economic wisdom, George Eads, one of the three members of the Council of Economic Advisers during the Carter administration, attacked the views of both Regan and Kirkland.

[Let us examine] the various failures — both of the market and of our political institutions — that might justify an increased government role in channeling the flow of business investment. In general, market failures are found to be minor or nonexistent; political failures, on the other hand, are found to be pervasive. The call for the establishment of an industrial policy thus ends up being a call for the creation of a new set of political arrangements to deal with problems that the existing political arrangements in large measure have spawned.

The key argument is that an industrial policy would, if anything, be more prone to "political failure" than the admittedly flawed set of institutions it is designed to replace. Therefore, while certain measures might be taken to improve the climate for business investment and improve the ability of labor and capital to adjust to changing market conditions, targeted policies of the sort generally considered as constituting industrial policy should be viewed with great skepticism.[3]

Interestingly, all three statements are drawn from speeches made at a high-level conference held at the University of Pennsylvania's Wharton School of Finance and Commerce in the spring of 1981. Although it is important that the conference and others like it were held, it does not necessarily represent a constructive interchange. With important exceptions such as John Dunlop and a limited number of other actors on the national scene who link the worlds of action, politics, and ideas, most participants in the policy debate talk past each other. Communication? There is dialogue, but no communication.

The reasons are conventional. The participants in the dialogue reflect the very different training, perspective, and values of their technocratic or political experience. They are excited and offended by very different ideas or events; they have different stakes; and consequently they interpret the pattern of history in very different ways. Perhaps most dysfunctional of all, they talk about the problems in a language — economics — that leads them to believe that all agree on what the problem is and only the solution needs to be debated. But the language obscures fundamentally different views about how the world works and what is wrong with it. And the language is grounded in a system of belief that most who use the language probably reject.

When the parties turn for counsel it is often to lawyers. Again with important exceptions, the lawyers exacerbate the problem by shifting its resolution to the adversary process. The same Anglo-Saxon ideological roots on which our Constitution is grounded support a legal process that protects freedom by keeping those in conflict from talking with each other.

As if this were not enough of an obstacle to coherence, the entire process is grist for the electronic and printed news media. Again to protect our freedom, reporters have nearly unlimited access to probe areas of conflict and controversy. What they find becomes raw material for a business that long ago discovered conflict to be the best "peg" for a story. When technocrats and politicians try to sort out a problem so that they can find a basis for consensus, the media chorus can often be heard from the sidelines, questioning motives and giving "equal time" and "balanced treatment" to any voice that provides controversial material. It is a world of the blind in which the one-eyed man is in the zoo.

Before considering how an understanding among responsible managers might be achieved, we must consider more carefully (1) the specific differences of technocrats and politicians in the field of national economic policy, and (2) the special difficulties created by the use of economics as a language for analyzing problems of the economy.

The Technocratic Manager's Voice

Looking ahead, anticipating problems, coordinating policies, operating more efficiently, making decisions on the basis of better information are obviously desirable — desirable for Government, for business, for all of us in this country.

I would give my unqualified endorsement to a proposal showing promise of improving the capability of Government to manage its affairs more effectively. There are a few who would claim that Government could not improve its performance of existing functions. If Government were to manage these presently assigned responsibilities on a steadier course, many of our basic concerns about the economy — and more particularly the concern I feel about preserving personal freedom — would be largely resolved.[4]

As businessmen have increasingly taken part in the public debate, it is possible to discern a pattern in their argument. There is, of course, the constant refrain that the status quo works: "Don't rock the boat"; "Don't bite the hand that feeds you"; or the 1960s southern California version, "Don't knock the war that feeds you." There are, however, two categories of argument that are fundamental to professional business, one having to do with market forces and the other with administration. Both are important, but the second is the basis upon which technocratic managers in business and government can cooperate.

The conventional argument of business — and certainly an important and legitimate one — is the call for better economic conditions, lower costs or higher prices. Business managers are properly concerned with the myriad forces at work that can raise the cost of their raw materials, labor, and capital relative to the prices at which they can sell their goods.

The economic argument can take many forms. It can bear on relations with foreign nations from which raw materials derive; or it can simply be a protest against a utility that seeks to pass on costs that it has incurred because of higher energy prices. It may bear on the tax structure of one state compared with others that makes it harder to recruit engineers and in effect necessitates higher salaries. It often deals with the cost of capital to consumers — high interest rates depress both auto and home sales. Very frequently it deals with the terms of competition: "predators" such as large, technologically advanced competitors or efficient off-shore manufacturers are to be prevented from using new products or price as a weapon for attracting customers.

It is a vast and sometimes cacophonous argument, and it serves to keep our politics informed about the specific impact of economic conditions on the many actors in our economy. There is a tendency in some quarters to see conspiracy everywhere in this argument. The last ten years should have laid that notion to rest. Big business on the whole spoke poorly for itself and has performed accordingly. Real return on investment has been dismal for a decade. But much more interesting, studies such as Bauer, Pool, and Dexter's reveal that big business — even within an individual company — is a house divided.[5] Divisions of multibusiness companies have opposing views on public questions. More visible and dramatic, companies seeking to cooperate in vehicles such as the Business Roundtable find that they have opposing interests.[6] We may not have the Athenian Senate, but C. Wright Mills's ghost and even John Kenneth Galbraith can be assured that countervailing economic forces are at work, even within the "planning system."

A second interesting argument made by business — passionately held and voiced, but poorly phrased — is the case frequently made for a public policy that permits effective administration.[7] There are two dimensions to the argument, one having to do with internal conditions of the organization, the other with external conditions.

The internal argument is very simple — management has to have the ability to alter the configuration of activities so that economic efficiency can be pursued and resources reallocated in response to changing markets and technology. An early version of this argument was made in the context of "managerial rights." During the 1920s and 1930s it was often raised by those opposing legislation that would facilitate the organization of unions.

George Lodge has analyzed that particular version of the argument and concluded that it derived from a "Lockean" interpretation of the rights flowing from property. In the United States the ideological grounding of our individual freedoms in property gave custodians of property the right to do with it what they pleased. Organizations of workers that interfered with that pleasure threatened the basis of individual freedom. As Lodge has pointed out, the economic basis for that argument eroded as ownership separated from management; and the ideological basis weakened as Congress and the courts recognized that some rights were based in organization membership. Nonetheless, in many forms and many places the idea still lives that a manager can do what he wants simply because he owns something.

More important, there is a much more neutral argument for management rights that has nothing to do with property. It is a position that derives from a view of executive responsibility: if the chief executive is responsible for the effective use of the resources entrusted to his leadership, then he must have a certain degree of cooperation. Recognizing that his authority over others rests on their consent, he cannot manage effectively unless there is a willingness on the part of subordinates to accept direction. In a crude form this is what people commonly think of as the power to define jobs and organize the work flow. In effect, the right to manage in this sense is implicit in the technocratic contract. In return for a manager's commitment to provide compensation and satisfactory working conditions, an employee cooperates. These would seem to be very basic ideas, but with the evolution of the social agenda in the United States and elsewhere, both mores and laws have changed so as to severely constrain this administrative ethic.

Large organizations require a very high degree of specialization. In turn, in order to function, there must be an equally high degree of cooperation among specialists. That sort of cooperative effort is not easily commanded or measured. The subordinates who contribute their cooperation loyally have in turn come to expect rather extensive due process in their dealings with superiors. To a remarkable extent this due process has slowed down the working of conventional hierarchical management.

We now even read about managerial burnout — the situation when competent bosses collapse from the strain of dealing with complex, conflicting human forces over long periods of time. They know what needs to be done, but they can't work the system to get people to do it.

The struggle of a manager to analyze and influence behavior within subtle constraints of emergent norms of due process may be an anachronism. Increasingly, the right of subordinates to due process is grounded in legislation. Beginning with a variety of labor laws, but continuing with civil rights, equal opportunity, and safety legislation, the rights of specific groups of employees have been codified. It is common to hear a manager say, rightly or wrongly, "I'd like to fire X but I'd be sued." Legislation also constrains investment decisions by affecting plant location, product and process specification, and marketing practices. In Europe it is not uncommon for unions to have the right to advise and pass on even such decisions as the hiring of a management consulting firm.

There are those, mostly academics and politicians, who would argue that these changes are for the good, that this is the wave of the future. But in order to understand the public statements of those responsible for technocratically managed systems, it is not necessary to take a position on the correctness of the argument. Most managers are obsessed with how difficult managing is getting to be. Given that there is extensive competition worldwide, that there are as well excess capacity, high energy costs, high interest rates, and inflation, then when managers are asked to implement a wide range of separately legislated social objectives (each of which requires time, attention, and money), they come to regard such legislation as directed against the purposes of their organization. Because it takes time and uses money when neither is available, many businessmen have come to regard such legislation as antibusiness.

As they fight to defend the administrative integrity of their technocratically managed operations, they come to be regarded as "anti–social progress" by those supporting one or another of the "liberal" agenda items. In the same way, however, government managers of the operating agencies also feel pressured. The food stamp program manager mentioned in chapter 2 made the following remarks. Speaking of the new regulations supporting verification that were signed into law in May 1980 and implemented by the Department of Agriculture beginning in January 1981, Blanche Bernstein noted:

> One may ask why did it take Congress and USDA so long to do what obviously needed to be done? . . . It is again an illustration of the triumph of a combination of special interest groups and their supporters in Congress, as well as in state and local legislative bodies, over the majority concerned to serve the needy but to do so with reasonable *effectiveness and efficiency* as well as compassion. [*Emphasis added*][8]

"Effectiveness and efficiency," Chester Barnard's metrics of organizational performance, are always at the core of the internal administrator's argument. But they drive the logic that supports administrative arguments concerning the environment of the organization as well. For technocratic managers to function, they require enough stability in their surroundings to establish the routine climate within which subunits of the organization can interact in a predictable manner. The more predictable a system, the more it can be planned and scheduled so as to be efficient.

Instability in major environmental conditions is not merely disconcerting, it can paralyze a large organization. If an auto manufacturer was very unsure whether the U.S. government would end its policy of encouraging cheap gasoline, it would also be unsure whether it should spend the large sums required to tool up for a very efficient small engine. Faced with consumers seeking large engines and substantial evidence that Congress would not back President Carter's conservation policies even at the modest cost of a ten-cent-per-gallon tax, two of the Big Three auto manufacturers waited for clearer information while investing in conventional concepts. They were then poorly equipped to respond when Ayatollah Khomeini's actions led to a doubling of prices.

The key problem posed by uncertainty about major issues such as tax rates, interest costs, and energy prices is that they pose high levels of risk. Big risks are especially difficult for the managers of large organizations to deal with. The variance in possible outcome dwarfs the authority delegated to subunit managers. Moreover, since a successful commitment is likely to be regarded as impetuous but lucky, and an unsuccessful move regarded as clear evidence of poor judgment, the lower-level manager responsible for activity affected by uncertainty is likely to avoid taking any action. Rare is the organization with systems and top management like those at Texas Instruments, which are designed to seek out big opportunities for discussion and absorb major risks at the top.

More typical is the career executive at the Rural Electrification Administration interviewed by students of mine in 1967. Asked why after many years he had chosen to avoid promotion to the leadership of the agency, he said: "Washington is like the ocean. Below the surface there are stable patterns — currents that run deep. Up on the surface, it may look calm, but there are big waves and storms. A person can get hurt."⁹

In a world where unsuccessful investments are regarded as punishable failure, managers are only sensible if they take risks acceptable to them personally. A turbulent environment poses precisely the dangerous, unacceptable sort of risks.

For managers of technocratic organizations, the late 1960s and the early 1970s in the United States were often paralyzing. As lawyers competed to legislate or litigate a perfect society, new standards cropped up overnight. With a sudden rush, managers were held accountable and sometimes criminally liable for a substantial range of activities previously outside the purview of legislation. At the same time, the precise standard by which they had been measured changed, sometimes increasing in severity so that early attempts to comply with the law were made obsolete, sometimes decreasing so that foot-dragging or stonewalling competitors were left with an advantage over the "progressive" cooperator. Barnwell is one example of a politically obsolete investment, but imagine also those who thought of tooling up to provide generating equipment for Con Ed, or air bags for the auto industry. The psychologist B. F. Skinner has shown in his laboratories what great uncertainty can do to the behavior of pigeons. When managers feel like frustrated pigeons, they speak out.

The Political Voice

If the manager of a technocratic system is measured by his customers or his clients, a manager of a political system is measured by his constituents. In the contemporary United States, voters expect their representatives to be visible. Modern technology in the form of television and jet planes makes this possible. On a daily basis it is feasible for a legislator to step in front of a camera, take a position on an issue, and be seen by viewers in his or her district that evening. If the politician is an important personage, the political motivation of his acts or statements will be interpreted by commentators that evening or the next weekend.

The modern politician has to have a position on most issues facing the country. It is hard to be neutral. A reply to the effect that "since air bags seem expensive and their benefits unclear, we ought to study them carefully," is likely to be headlined SENATOR HITS AIRBAGS.

To deal with this problem of exposure, the legislator's staff — or the president's, the governor's, or the mayor's — works hard to anticipate and deflect problems. Since appearances count immediately and substance works out over the years, dealing with a problem means having an answer that can be delivered convincingly in thirty to sixty seconds. Our politics also tolerate groups like the National Conservative Political Action Committee (NCPAC), so that it may also be necessary to defend in thirty to sixty seconds a twenty-year voting record against irresponsible but persuasively packaged charges of gross malfeasance.

The legislator must also represent. Members of Congress have come to play the role of ombudsmen helping their constituents to deal with the Army, the Post Office, the Passport Office, the Small Business Administration, the Eximbank, or some other element of the "bureaucracy" that is unresponsive to a local problem. This is a time-consuming role, demanding attention from at least two or three full-time staff. But it is the bread and butter of a politician seeking a reliable loyal base of voters.

Equally important to a politician seeking success are a limited number of specific issues. These are the questions that are especially important to the district or state. They are often economic, involving jobs at a company or a military base. Employment in the auto industry, for example, has always been of great significance to representatives and senators from Michigan. Perhaps more dramatic, source selection for the TFX airplane turned into a battle between the states of Washington (Boeing) and Texas (General Dynamics). Also important, however, are the ideological questions such as gun control or abortion that may be highly salient in particular localities. These local manifestations of national policy are crucial to the survival of a politician.[10]

Back in Washington, the legislator seeking to acquire influence over such issues needs allies to support him on votes. In the marketplace of Congress, having influence means having something to trade. Trading requires control over line items in budgets or procedural bottlenecks in the legislative process. Typical important posts are House Appropriations Committee subcommittee chairmanships, or membership in the House Rules Committee, but Congressman Wayne Hays of Ohio built up significant influence through control over the physical facilities and support staff of the House. Regardless of the specific method, achieving useful power requires specialization on issues or in procedure.

Managing the relation between substantive issue and political process requires a delicate touch. In a world where appearances count, some reality does as well. As a consequence, the position of a politician is calculated to appeal at home but also to build credits among political colleagues. It is a world of theater in which you play to the audience as well as to the other actors. And the critics review you daily.

One congressman has suggested that under present circumstances one could not build the Tennessee Valley Authority. The vast majority of legislators could not justify to their districts the use of locally raised taxes to help out farmers in Tennessee. Indeed, it takes the seniority and power of men such as Senator Jesse Helms of North Carolina to protect the tobacco subsidies. One would have thought that two decades after the surgeon general's report on the hazards of smoking it would have been easy to attack tobacco during a budget-cutting exercise such as the one in the summer of 1981. But where a congressman has the power to block action others want, it can be used in trade even to support a product widely understood to be hazardous to health and even where the blocking action can hurt the national interest. In the spring of 1981 Helms demonstrated his power to the new administration, holding up appointments to the State Department from his senior position on the Foreign Relations Committee.

For the individual politician the major economic issues such as trade, inflation, productivity, and innovation are very difficult to deal with at the level of reality. On such broad national economic issues progress requires investment. Investment requires saving, either directly by individuals who consume less, or indirectly by the government printing money and reducing the consumption of those with fixed incomes through inflation. It is hard to have broadly appealing theater in Lester Thurow's zero-sum society. This, of course, accounts for the form of President Reagan's New Economic Program. Under the guise of a program with evenly shared but marginal and presumably temporary costs, an attempt is being made to increase investment with funds made available from reduced consumption. To achieve this shift in spending patterns a great purgative is being administered — called tax and spending cuts — that will substantially depress lives, especially of the working poor and the lower middle class. And our international competitive position will be affected. In this theater, politicians seldom address themselves directly to the needs of professional managers. The world of political issues tends to cut across organizational needs until they get local or adversarial: jobs in Massachusetts versus jobs in Arizona; jobs in Detroit versus jobs in Nagoya, Japan; railroads versus trucks; big banks versus little banks; regulated versus unregulated — all these are translated into a theater of good versus evil. The complexities of modern economic life must be translated into a morality play with one-liners and sixty-second summaries before there can be political action.

Speaking of the same phenomenon in the context of Senate hearings, one observer noted that:

> Within each day, drama and conflict between witnesses were needed primarily for the sake of the press. Press coverage was an important goal if the hearings were to attract the public attention needed to secure

political support for regulatory reform. To sustain the interest of the press, one must produce a news story, a newsworthy event, each day. It would have to be clear, focused, and comprehensible.[11]

Stephen Breyer, then on Senator Edward Kennedy's staff, remarked:

> The more you can have, the more important thing you can have, the better. And what counts as important would be a revelation, somebody doing something. You have to have action rather than words. "Ford announces new CAB policy," that's a story. "Forty-two college professors criticize CAB" is not a story. "Forty-eight consumer groups say the CAB is ridiculous" or "CAB can't answer Kennedy's questions," that's no story.
> It is a matter of revelation and event.[12]

In the morality play, it is usual for big business and big government to be cast in the role of Goliath to some political David. Precisely the needs for stability discussed earlier make technocratic organizations vulnerable to charges of unresponsiveness. Human weakness being what it is, the drive for efficiency is often enough associated with stupidity or venality so that there are examples of malpractice to use as evidence when throwing bricks at big bureaucratic organizations.

If a politician has any reservations about exploiting the occasional rotten apple, the practices of investigative journalists make it irresistible. What else is news except big organizations leaning on small people, corruption or sin in high places, self-serving bureaucrats ignoring the weak? And what better way to get media coverage than to lead the chorus against Goliath?

The Economists: Wizards Who Oversimplify

In 1962 Robert Peterson published a parable in the *Quarterly Journal of Economics* titled "The Wizard Who Oversimplified." The story concerned a king who sought training for royal children who would have to play chess as adults. The wizard constructed a course based on checkers. Eventually, after examining the relationship of the training to the problems he had in mind, the king disposed of the wizard.

The task of developing a reasonable debate around the conditions appropriate for economic efficiency and development is made more difficult because the "science" relevant to the debate is based upon the idea that economic activity is carried out by small fragmented units. Obviously, many important producers and customers are not small, but the theory of how the economy works exploits a powerful simplifying assumption. Basically, if units are so small that they can only respond to but do not influence their environment, then in simple environments their behavior will be highly predictable. That predictability permits the construction of a model of the whole economic system that describes the quantity and mix of goods produced, and the prices of inputs and outputs.

If the assumptions on which the model is built hold, a remarkable range of predictions can be made. Not only that, the outcome of performance in the economists' "atomistically competitive free market" is an extraordinary state of affairs called Pareto optimality. When the market has finished its invisible working, that bundle of goods and services has been produced at lowest total cost that maximizes consumer utility. In fact, no individual's position can be improved without cost to another.

This would seem on the face of it to be an extremely just state of affairs — unless, of course, the income one obtained from participation in the market was inadequate to live on. Or, if there existed other economic systems side by side with the modeled one that achieved higher standards of living. Or, if consumers' concept of utility changed periodically, so that the experienced value of what was achieved was different from what was anticipated. Or, if there were unanticipated joint consequences, such as pollution, from individual action.

But before considering the lack of "competitiveness" in the economy or the accuracy of the economists' predictions, there is a more fundamental issue to be dealt with. The problem is that the assumptions underlying the economic model are not only very simple, they are also very strong and wildly unrealistic. As a consequence, the economy does not always work as described — even if outcomes sometimes appear to be as they were predicted. The cost is that economic policy premised on the simple assumption often leads to unintended — and dysfunctional — consequences.

A few experiences of this sort would, presumably, lead to a disenchantment with the model. But the general equilibrium promise is so attractive in the abstract — free market, minimum cost, maximum utility, Pareto optimality — that there is an implicit tendency to regard the assumptions as prescriptions and departures from the assumptions as problems to be remedied. Because atomistic competition is theorized to lead to good things, business that violates the atomistic condition is bad per se. You don't have to look at the consequences of their behavior, just prosecute big companies.

In the fifteenth century Galileo was prosecuted for his understanding of modern astronomy. Today we go the church one better and prosecute the sun for being in the center of the system and thereby violating our deeply held beliefs about God's work.

This might seem too harsh an indictment of a field that is generally regarded as the strongest of the social sciences. After all, Nobel Prizes are given in economics. That would seem to be a rather strong endorsement of the empirical grounding of the field.

In fact, economics has contributed much to our understanding of how the economy works. But the major advances have tended to be at the level of the macroeconomy, involving overall patterns of activity. There has been very little work focused on the behavior of individual industries and, within economics, next to no study of individual firms or consumers. That empirical work has been left to business schools, social psychologists, and management consultants.

The theory of the firm, so called, is in fact elegantly developed surmise. The literature of the field has something of the character of a chain letter. The journal articles relate well enough to each other; it is only the reality that is difficult.[13]

The particular areas that pose the most problems in the sense that conventional economic treatments depart from reality are:

1. The structural conditions that yield lowest delivered cost to the consumer.
2. The bundle of attributes that the consumer actually purchases.
3. The relationships among producers, consumers, and government most conducive to efficient performance.
4. The consequences for domestic economic affairs of the steady development of world trade.

These four areas are not subtle; they are central to the function of the economy. Nor are they independent. A web of interdependence connects them. Yet in economics they are usually discussed as separate topics.

Cost to the Consumer

Given the populist aura surrounding the development of antitrust law as well as much industry regulation, one would think that an early question to be explored by economists concerned with industrial organization would be a determination of the conditions that yield lowest delivered cost to the consumer. In fact, there has been very little study of this question. Instead, public policy has developed and been elaborated on the basis of political ideas about what industrial structure was most congruent with constitutional democracy in the United States.

The economic historians Alfred Chandler and Thomas McCraw have shown how, in response to new technology and widening markets, the structure of core industries in the United States, Europe, and

Japan experienced concentration more or less independent of the local legal system or culture. In the United States this trend has been resisted, almost without concern for the economic consequences of resistance. Protection of competitors rather than consumers is the consequence of much regulation.

In fact, the Boston Consulting Group has claimed that its industry studies reveal concentration to be a normal and healthy part of serving the consumer. These studies show total unit costs falling as cumulative volume climbs. In one industry after another it has been the giants that delivered to the consumer the benefits of scale, new technology, and the administrative economies of vertical integration. This line of thought might lead one to conclude that declining real price to the consumer should be taken as a crude measure of positive performance — even if associated with increasing concentration. On that basis we would have rewarded IBM and Xerox for their innovation rather than attacked their success.

An inquiry to the Federal Trade Commission in 1980 revealed that — at least to the knowledge of the policy planning staff — there had never been a study that arrayed industry according to the trend of real price. When a crude first approximation was carried out, the results were suggestive. In only some industries did concentration have apparently negative consequences for consumers.

Michael Hunt has suggested that the answer is to be found in the strategies of the individual firms.[14] Where there is a me-too, follow-the-leader pattern of behavior, size and concentration may yield unattractive results. But where firms follow asymmetric strategies, the results of direct rivalry among giants may be very positive. A later study by Michael Porter[15] showed that the organization of the industry distributing the products of a supplying industry could have a very powerful effect on behavior in the producing industry. The 1982 Nobel Prize winner George Stigler is reputed to have put the same point more crudely. "Price competition," he said, "is 90 percent Sears, Roebuck and 10 percent the number of competitors."

All of the foregoing accepts much of conventional economics, and merely suggests that technology favors scale more than economists have allowed. Price is still an adequate measure of performance.

But another problem with the traditional economic view is that it badly oversimplifies the concept of product, especially in empirical analysis. There are two major dimensions to the problem — private and public.

What the Consumer Buys Defines the Product

In 1948 Timex introduced a high-quality pin-lever watch to the market dominated by the Swiss jeweled watches. By Swiss standards of the day, a Timex wasn't a watch. Swiss firms were selling "jeweled precision timekeeping instruments." Later, after Timex took half the market, the Swiss discovered that most customers were buying "adequate reliable timekeeping" while a few were buying jewelry.

In the same spirit as the Swiss, economists insist on leaving Sears, Roebuck and Company out of the major home appliances industry. The fact is that the appliance customer buys features, reliability, and service at a price. In the range of functions from design to manufacturing to distribution to selling to service, Sears performs all but the manufacturing function. In contrast, General Electric performs all but the retail selling function (they do sell to home builders). A small company such as Tappan neither retails nor services. As Michael Hunt has shown, the strategies of GE and Sears shape the industry. Sears has perhaps the greatest impact of all. It is in the industry, if that industry is properly defined.

Another example of the same phenomenon is the so-called ego-intensive good, such as cosmetics and fashion garments. Here, the retailer is a key factor in what the consumer buys. Seeking to enhance his or her own self-image, the customer needs to be reassured that the product is "right." The increase in price of a T-shirt when "Bloomingdale's" is added to its front is a simple example of the point.

Still another example is the clear preference of airline customers for the airline with the most flights scheduled on a particular route. Market share increases disproportionately with capacity share. In industrial goods, excess capacity can have a similar impact. Customers will buy speed of response as well as product.

Perhaps the most dramatic example occurred in computers. There, in the early years of the industry, a number of firms made awkward attempts to sell machines to customers. What was true then, and seems just as true today, is that most customers want to buy reliable electronic data processing — they don't want machines. The customer's concept of his need defines the market, not the producer.

The problem for traditional economics is that the definition of the word *producer* gets complicated. What are we to make of manufacturers without factories? How do we measure concentration? What does it mean that the vertically integrated manufacturer with assured source of supply is selling something different from the single-stage producer?

The Product the Consumer Buys Often Includes Public Goods

Still more difficult for traditional economics is the contemporary approach of Congress and state legislatures to the purchase of public goods. Whenever there is a choice between persuading the public to pay for a program directly through taxes and imposing the costs of the program indirectly through regulation of industry, our legislators choose the hidden approach.

Examples of this phenomenon are so extensive as to defy a complete listing, but a few illustrations are useful: (1) We are buying clear air and water with pollution laws. (2) We are buying racial integration of the society through equal-opportunity laws. (3) We are buying political fragmentation through the antitrust laws. (4) We are buying redistribution of income through the exemption of unions from the antitrust laws. (5) We are buying better health through auto safety specifications.

Perhaps the most easy to understand and diagnose is the last example. Studies have shown that the leading source of auto accidents is the driver. He drives too fast, he is often poorly trained, and he drinks. The next source is roads: poorly designed, poorly lit, and poorly signed, they cause problems. The next is the car itself. However, our auto safety laws attack car manufacturers, not the states or the drivers. While they have helped reduce death and serious accidents, their effects were dwarfed by the reduction in the speed limit to fifty-five miles per hour.

The point here is not that Congress may buy public goods in a way that is deceptive or not cost effective. The point is that we are now asking companies to produce a wide range of goods, including — perhaps most important of all — stimulating, fulfilling, steady, high-paying, healthy jobs located within the fifty states.

International Markets

One of the dramatic vignettes in the recent world economic scene was the spectacle of Zenith suing the U.S. government to enforce dumping laws on television sets, and the Consumers Union fighting to protect imports. What was happening?

In color television, the Japanese used their position in their large home market to drive down the cost curve. Net wages were nearly the same as for the U.S. industry. Yet, by applying superb process engineering, they had achieved both lower unit costs and higher reliability than their U.S. competitors. Sony, Matsushita, Hitachi, and Toshiba enjoyed roughly a 75 percent world market share. When their higher yields permitted introduction of a one-year warranty, costs for one prominent U.S. firm allegedly rose from 2 to 9 percent of sales.

In order to penetrate the U.S. market, the Japanese — except for Sony — had engaged in illegal practices, dumping product (selling below cost) and paying kickbacks. Over a period of years, the economic staff in the Treasury Department proved reluctant to prosecute the importers, seeing it as an interference with "free trade" and with the probable consequence of higher prices to consumers. Zenith sued to force the government to enforce the international trade laws. Somehow the fact that the low-priced Japanese sets could hurt the U.S. economy was not factored into the Treasury Department's equation. Theory promises a benevolent result from unfettered markets. Eventually, after the Japanese companies were convicted, the question of fines was settled. Zenith sued unsuccessfully to force the Treasury to publish why they were settling a $400 million finding of damage for $77 million. The specifics of the Japanese behavior remain hidden.

Motorcycles provide an even more dramatic example, perhaps because we have more data. A 1975 study produced for the British House of Commons by the Boston Consulting Group revealed the impact of Japanese economics on a traditionally strong British industry — motorcycles. In 1960 the Japanese produced large numbers of small cycles but exported only 4 percent of their production. They used this base, however, to invade the low end of the British market. Less sophisticated in both manufacturing and marketing, the British withdrew from the low-price segment. The Japanese developed volume and experience in progressively larger models, displacing the British, who sought short-term profit by withdrawing from these price-competitive markets. Followed throughout the world, the consequences of this strategy were market shares of 87, 88, 74, and 70 percent in the United States, Canada, the United Kingdom, France, and Germany.

The volume base this gives Japanese production is such that the British study estimated all but the smallest of Honda's products in the United States to be selling at a premium of 24 to 43 percent over prices in Japanese markets. The return on investment for the Japanese producers is high.

The same Japanese strategy has succeeded in jeweled watches, cameras, automobiles, and steel. It has not succeeded in pin-lever watches, in chemicals, in drugs, or in major home appliances, to take a wide range of examples. Why? Has fragmented competition in the United States produced efficiency? No. In pin-lever watches, Timex simplified the design, then mass-produced and marketed a good product. They crippled a Swiss industry responsible for 8 percent of Swiss employment. In chemicals, the major U.S. manufacturers have practiced experience-curve strategies for years. With the Germans they are the leading producers in the world. In drugs, Japanese industrial engineering — key to low cost in assembly-based manufacturing — has left their drug companies totally dependent on U.S. and European patents.

In major home appliances, GE, Whirlpool, and Design and Manufacturing have made the investments in efficient manufacturing process and scale to block any Japanese advantage. In fact, television and major appliances are a dramatic and instructive contrast. In one industry imports have captured virtually the entire U.S. market. In another — similar with respect to manufacturing and distribution — the U.S. manufacturers are pre-eminent. The consequences of superior strategy for U.S. balance of payments and employment are obvious.

The point, however, should be clear. Conventional economic analysis does not seek out the distinction made above. In fact, no market ought to be considered in solely domestic terms until study justifies that conclusion. The gale of competition blows from all points on the compass but particularly from Europe and East Asia. In Japan, it is primarily aggressive, modern, volume- and experience-conscious companies exploiting all the world's markets that account for that country's success — not just Japan, Inc.

At exactly this time our ideology leads us in two irrelevant directions. Each represents an attempt to re-create the Acadian glories of some primordial "free market." The libertarian approach, represented by the Reagan administration, is to call for a reduction in government intervention — let the market work its way. How this helps a steel industry that faces government owned or subsidized industry in Europe is unclear. Nor is it apparent whether the military aid or farm programs that support our two principal export industries are included in the libertarian prescription. The fact is that government is, and has been, everywhere in U.S. business life, subsidizing the building of canals, railroads, airlines, and private homes; providing through patents incentives to innovation; protecting trademarks; and providing standards for weights, measures, and performance.

At a minimum there is a contradiction to be faced between nonintervention and free trade. As has been most evident in the case of autos, free trade as a unilateral policy can threaten the survival of U.S. industry where our competition overseas is playing by different rules. Are we willing to see in the United States the sort of deindustrialization now sweeping the United Kingdom at least in part in response to Margaret Thatcher's orthodox libertarian economic policies? The 1981 and 1982 agreements to restrict imports of Japanese cars and European steel suggests that Ronald Reagan and company are made of more pragmatic stuff. While seeking adjustment they will protect important parts of the industrial base.

The basic problem is that a market is a mechanism, not an end in itself. A free market is a remarkable invention for allocating goods and services — but allocation is the end, not having a market. Where the consequences of the market's performance can be anticipated to be politically unhappy, there is likely to be intervention. There must always be political support for the consequences of allocation. Support in turn depends on the existence of some consensus as to how the benefits and costs of the system should be shared. For that consensus to exist, there must be awareness of the needs of other parties to the consensus. If these conditions are not met, there is likely to be political movement to reorganize the market.

There is a paradox here. The implication of the foregoing discussion is that for the efficiency of an impersonal free market to be enjoyed, the personality of the participants in the market must be recognized in some important ways. A good example of this principle at work can be found in the 1787 Federal Constitutional Convention in Philadelphia. There, one goal was a system of government remarkably like a market. All freeholders would vote. But on important issues, how they would vote could be anticipated. Before they would bind themselves to a set of rules for governing, both the small and large states, those with slavery and those without, had to assure themselves that the mechanism they were devising would not produce unintended consequences that were unhappy for their constituents. When there was an effective consensus, and only then, the Constitution was ratified unanimously.

A frequent fault in the libertarian argument is to forget the necessity for a consensus underlying the market. That consensus is going to be hard to find if there are states, parties, interest groups, or individuals who can predict what seem like broadly inequitable results from the workings of the market.

Oddly enough, the economists who enter debate on the liberal side pose a different version of the same problem. When the consequences of market performance are not as they or their political constituents desire, their instinct is to intervene in the market in order to produce the consequences that they associate with a proper working of the system. Does deflation produce unemployment? Inflate. Are wages too low? Legislate a minimum wage. Are small firms hurt by big ones? Break up big firms.

The remarkable legislative record of the Great Society program is grounded in efforts of economic analysts to see how markets could be modified to produce different — more desired — results. The fact that the efforts were piecemeal and uncoordinated is often noted. But that criticism presumes there is some reason to notice interdependence. In the simple, static world of economics, most of those interdependencies simply do not exist. Nor do the exigencies of technocratic or political management systems. Long lags and imperfect execution are treated as reflecting incompetence or "bureaucracy" or "politics" rather than the time and friction that are inevitably required if large groups are going to do anything.

Again the fault is in not looking at the reality of the economy underneath the model to consider the consequences of intervention. The problem for both libertarian and liberal economists is that the political economy is a vastly more complex place than they choose to research. At the most simple there is a political economic system with second- and third-order relationships that are hard to predict. (One could, as well, recognize the social phenomena that complicate analysis and action.) The language of economics tends to hide the political economy below, and that makes it easy to ignore the political context of prescription. "Higher saving and investment" must mean that someone's current standard of living will decline in the short term, but the words are neutral. The liquidation of the kulaks by Stalin involved "saving" in the technical use of the term.

More generally, economic analysis does not deal directly with the political content of its normative conclusions. As a result of any intervention in the economy, some groups will be better off and others worse off, because of the action of government. Even if the position of all groups improves some, relative positions will shift. Since it is human to compare (not to mention covet), these shifts all have political implications. For the concerned policymaker, aspects of a situation that ought theoretically to be irrelevant may be more important than the direct economic consequences involved. Individual citizens and interests thus tend to find economists using "scientific" theory and language to justify political acts.

More important in the present context, the economists' advice is likely to be based on an analysis that does not take into account the actual behavior or the stakes of technocratic and political managers. For example, it is conventional in economics to regard the rate of business investment as a function of the cost of capital, and for the cost of capital to be reflected in interest rates. Accordingly, if money is cheap, business will invest; if money is dear, investment will slow.

Actually, investment does not behave that way very regularly. In the two decades between 1960 and 1980 business investment corrected for inflation grew 70 percent of the time, although the cost of money corrected for inflation increased almost as often as it declined (eleven years down versus nine years up). In other words, 35 percent of the time, business increased investments even though the cost of capital increased.

Economists know that in practice the relationship is weak, but they have usually avoided facing up to the underlying reason. The head of one of the world's leading investment banks put the point clearly. Discussing the role of theory in corporate investment practice, he noted, "I have never seen an investment that was regarded as strategically sound and important not made because of the cost of capital. For that matter, I've never heard the 'cost of capital' discussed during consideration of a major investment."[16] In contemporary settings, very few major capital investments would ever be made if they were evaluated by "proper" economic analysis. At interest rates of 20 to 25 percent, the present value of investments that do not begin to return earnings for five or more years is likely to be negative.

In my own studies of investment behavior in large firms in the United States and abroad, interest rates were rarely if ever mentioned. The problem for subunit managers was to generate opportunities for investment that met the criteria of profitability and risk by which they would be measured. The problem for senior managers was to find and support investments that fit the strategic thrust of the company.

Forces affecting the perceived profitability and strategic importance of an investment have more to do with phenomena such as:

Competitive behavior. Is market share threatened or can it be expanded?

The perception of risk. How stable is the environment in which the business will operate? Will government action change these conditions, for example, through new environmental and safety regulations?

The availability (as opposed to the cost) of capital. The portfolio of investments must be measured against funds flow.

Management control. An executive group will rarely make moves or use capital in ways that threaten its control over the organization.

If business managers are persuaded that the potential returns on investment are poor, they will invest elsewhere or not at all, regardless of capital's cost. The changes in taxes and financial markets that economists propose will seldom have direct short-term impact on these four factors except to increase perceived risk.

Political managers also take into account a wide range of noneconomic factors. Quite understandably, they focus on the present and anticipated consequences of action as perceived by the constituencies to which they are beholden.

Who bears the cost of this action?
Who enjoys the benefit?
How does this distribution of cost and benefit bear on my chances for reelection or reappointment?
How does this distribution bear on my party?

Two examples of the consequences of this process at work are President Carter's energy program and President Reagan's nonprogram for Social Security. Economists who have studied the energy problem in the United States have been in relative agreement on one thing: the price to consumers must be allowed to rise so that the market (1) will allocate it to its most important users, (2) will induce conservation, and (3) will call forth new sources. Yet, ten years after the 1973 embargo, gasoline in the United States remains relatively untaxed. Congress has demonstrated a total unwillingness to penalize driving in the same manner that the rest of the industrialized countries have done.

There is also agreement among economists that the economy cannot afford the cost of a Social Security system or veterans' pensions tied to the Consumer Price Index. But there is a nearly universal political unwillingness to address these sacrosanct uncontrollables, although their growth in the last five years has been almost 100 percent and their role in fueling inflation is undisputed. The point is not that economists are wrong in urging higher gasoline prices or the de-indexing of Social Security, but that their analysis is only a piece of the problem that must be diagnosed before effective action can be prescribed.

For the policy debate to be useful to technocratic and political managers it must be formed with a managerial perspective. Suppose the conventional theoretical foundation is abandoned as a justification for using the economists' model. Suppose instead that the "free market" is recognized to be a plausible argument for modeling the U.S. economy because it is reasonably descriptive of our decentralized political arrangements. Then we might consider what difference it made that the atomistic operating units so useful for conceptualization were not adequately descriptive of the behavior of large producing units. It might be appropriate to drop phrases such as "imperfect" or "monopolistic" competition to describe interaction among large producers, sellers, and buyers, because it is obviously not wise to use pejorative language to describe arrangements that may be preferable to the available alternatives.

If it were possible to develop a framework for analyzing an economy made up of large institutions interacting with each other and the myriad smaller ones that also were functioning, then it might well be discovered that the center of the system had one or more important roles. The visible guidance of these large entities might seem important.

Beyond such basic functions as maintaining public safety and a stable currency (although success here hasn't been too great), government might turn out to have a role facilitating (1) efficient production, (2) effective innovation, and (3) mobility of materials, capital, and labor. Were parts of our government to carry out such roles, both the technocratic and political leaders would require as a basis for action a reasonably good understanding of our system. It would be necessary, for example, to understand the importance of learning and continuity in production; of the dynamic quality of competition, the extent to which arrangements that seem locked in at one moment change with technology, taste, or simply the strategic creativity of an aggressive manager; and of the unpredictable, destructive, and cleansing force of innovation on all economic arrangements.

Comparison of Growth per Annum in the United States and Japan

	United States	Japan
Industrial Production		
1950–60	3.5%	18.2%
1960–73	4.5	12.6
1973–79	2.7	2.3
Balance of Trade		
1969–72	−$1.6 billion	$4.2 billion
1973	0.9	3.7
1974	−5.3	1.4
1975–80	−120.3	61.7
Wage Index/Consumer Price Index		
(1967=1.0/1.0)		
1970	1.05	1.39
1975	1.12	2.42
1979	1.04	3.31
Unemployment		
1970	4.9%	1.2%
1975	8.5	1.9
1980	5.8	2.2

Sources: *OECD Main Economic Indicators* and IMF, *International Financial Statistics.*

It could well be that in the absence of any very clear or precise understanding a government would seek to lower the profile of its responsibilities. One extraordinary manager of an extremely large and successful business, a man who knows and uses power, typically responds to calls for central, coherent, long-term planning by pleading, "I'm not that smart." If we are "not that smart," perhaps we should promise ourselves a different sort of government — one more restrained in the tasks it undertakes.

More likely, however, is the prospect that the Japanese model will be found enticing. The pattern of business and government in apparent blissful cooperation under the benevolent tutelage of the Ministry of International Trade and Industry, the Ministry of Finance, and the Bank of Japan may have an irresistible seductive power. After all, the comparative performance of our two systems, shown in the table on page 195, gives us few grounds for satisfaction. In the next chapter, then, we pause to consider the usefulness of the Japanese model for the United States.

8 The United States Isn't a Company, It's Not Even Japan

FROM TEN THOUSAND MILES AWAY Japan has great appeal to Americans. To begin with, the Japanese produce good cars and television sets. The family is important; crime is low, as are inflation and unemployment. It seems to be such an orderly society. Observing the U.S. scene, technocratic managers are driven to take apparently radical positions.

James Balog, chairman of William D. Witter, Inc., has been quoted as saying:

> We wouldn't run our families the way we run the economy. We try to have a boom during an election year at the price of recessions in between. Corporations plan and the government should, too. Planning could help us to look beyond the next election.[1]

When he was president of Atlantic Richfield, Thornton Bradshaw voiced the opinion that

> we should not strive to bring about more government intervention in economic matters, but we surely need to make the intervention more rational. Since so many government regulations are nothing more than stopgap efforts to compensate for failure to plan, it follows that government economic planning of a high order — including, especially, the setting of specific goals and plans for achieving them — would reduce the amount of government regulation with which we have to contend.

I advocate such national planning as a means of saving the very market system so often considered to be inconsonant with it.[2]

The plea for order is not unique. Most observers who have given serious attention to our economic affairs see a need for more coherence in government behavior and less factious, adversarial behavior between business and government. When one considers some of the contradictions evident in even the most central arenas of economic policy, it's not hard to see the merit in the argument. The material quality of life that is sought as a base for civic development requires a healthy economy to generate the wealth to pay for it. But it is important to remember what is implicit in each one of these manifestos. Efficiency and effectiveness over any period of time call for continuity in administrative arrangements, selectivity in resource allocation, and stable hierarchy in power over the management process. These are attributes we achieve with technocratic organizations. To paraphrase Lerner and Loewe's Professor Henry Higgins, what commentators such as those quoted are asking is: "Why can't a country be more like a company?" If women are getting to be more like men, why can't the United States be more like IBM? And if we can't be IBM, can we be like Japan?

It should be simple to agree that the terms one accepts when employed by a technocratic organization are different from those associated with citizenship in the Republic. For all the very real consideration for the rights of members that governs the workings of modern corporations, they remain, in Roland Christensen's words, "undemocratic hierarchies run for the pleasure of their leaders."

Presumably such corporate models of society would be easy to ignore. The problem is that we continually forget why we adopted the particular form of government that is the U.S. Constitution, and instead concern ourselves with government efficiency. We then seek to make the government more "businesslike." In no small measure this is because we have chosen to use the federal government to accomplish a very wide range of activity — from defending the country to delivering the mail; from the management of our major parks and forests to the protection of recreational boaters; from the conduct of basic research in a wide range of fields to the delivery of housing and health care to certain groups such as veterans. The purchases of the federal government are now 7 percent of the GNP, and state and local purchases are 13 percent; together, federal, state, and local government as an employer ranks ahead of the manufacturers of durable goods, mining, construction, or transportation and public utilities.

Under such circumstances, waste is noticeable as well as annoying. It also provides politicians out of power with targets for criticism — government bureaucracy. In this spirit, the story is told of a management consultant hired to study productivity in a government agency. At ten one morning he visited an office where the executive, feet on the desk, was reading a newspaper. After checking that there was no work-related reason for the reading, he proceeded to the next office, where he again found someone reading the paper. "I think," he said to his client, "I've discovered your problem here. It's duplication."

To deal with such problems in government it is ritual for business managers to be brought in to study, reorganize, and help manage. Two examples are the President's Advisory Council on Executive Organization, chaired by Roy Ash, which brought forth the Domestic Council and the Office of Management and Budget for Richard Nixon, and the extension of Robert McNamara's Program Planning and Budget across the whole of Lyndon Johnson's administration. Both Ash and McNamara addressed themselves to the government as if its primary activities were to be managed with technocratic systems.

In introducing the recommendations of the Council on Executive Organization, Richard Nixon articulated clearly the technocratic pipedream of many new presidents: "A president whose programs are carefully coordinated, whose information system keeps him adequately informed and whose organizational assignments are plainly set out, can delegate authority with security and confidence."[3]

Ash clearly shared Nixon's hope, revealing that one of his inventions would replace the political ebb and flow of staff with technocratic continuity: "I expect the Domestic Council staff to provide continuity in planning, with as many as 75 percent of its members staying on through a change in administration."[4]

As he began to staff his new organization, Nixon continued with the same theme. Announcing the appointment of George P. Shultz as chairman of the Office of Management and Budget, he voiced "the hope that Mr. Shultz would reorganize and 'streamline' the government, 'bringing real business management into government at the very highest level.'"[5]

In seeking businesslike government, Nixon was not pursuing a partisan Republican ideal. In fact, Robert McNamara had made reliance on modern management an article of faith in the preceding eight years of Democratic administrations.

Business Week quoted Lyndon Johnson and his director of the Bureau of the Budget, Charles L. Schultze, about "spreading the McNamara doctrine." Said Johnson, "This system of cost effectiveness will improve our ability to control our programs and our budgets rather than having them control us." Continued Schultze, "Our major need is a much wider application of improved methods, techniques, and systems analysis to the definition of program objectives, the measurement of performance, and the weighing of alternatives as the basis for decisions."[6]

McNamara, the fountainhead of this spirit, expressed himself clearly:

> Some critics today worry that our democratic free societies are becoming overmanaged. I would argue that the opposite is true. As paradoxical as it may sound, the real threat to democracy comes, not from overmanagement, but from undermanagement. To undermanage reality is not to keep free. It is to let some force other than reason shape reality. That force may be unbridled emotion; it may be greed; it may be hatred; it may be inertia; it may be anything other than reason. But whatever it is, if it is not reason that rules men, then man falls short of his potential.

. . . Rational decisionmaking depends on having a full range of rational options from which to choose, and successful management organizes the enterprise so that process can best take place. It is a mechanism whereby free men can most efficiently exercise their reason, initiative, creativity and personal responsibility. The adventurous and immensely satisfying task of an efficient organization is to formulate and analyze these options.[7]

Alexander Hamilton in the first *Federalist* speaks in this same mode:

. . . the vigor of government is essential to the security of liberty; . . . in the contemplation of a sound and well-informed judgement, this interest can never be separated; and that a dangerous ambition more often lurks behind the specious mask of zeal for the rights of people than under the forbidding appearance of zeal for the firmness and efficiency of government.[8]

But in discussions of the value of a democratic republic and of the sharing of power provided for in the Constitution, he and James Madison, his partner in the *Federalist* undertaking, make clear that the architecture of our system was designed to preserve liberty against all forms of tyranny, including a clear-minded majority seeking efficiency.

The two great points of difference between a democracy and a republic are: first, the delegation of the government, in the latter, to a small number of citizens elected by the rest; secondly, the greater number of citizens, and the greater sphere of country, over which the latter may be extended.[9]

Focusing on the electors, Madison notes:

By enlarging too much the number of electors, you render the representative too little acquainted with all their local circumstances and lesser interests; as by reducing it too much, you render him unduly attached to these and too little fit to comprehend and pursue great and national objects. The federal constitution forms a happy combination.[10]

Turning to the resistance of a republic to factions, he argues,

The smaller the society, the fewer probably will be distinct parties and interests composing it; the fewer the distinct parties and interests, the more frequently will a majority be found of the same party; and the smaller the number of individuals composing a majority, and the smaller compass within which they are placed, the more easily will they concert and execute their plans of oppression. Extend the sphere and you take in a greater variety of parties and interests; *you make it less probable that a majority of the whole will have a common motive to invade the rights of other citizens.* [*Emphasis added*][11]

And considering the same issue in the context of the apparatus of government, he suggests that:

In order to lay a due foundation for that separate and distinct exercise of the different powers of government, which to a certain extent is admitted on all hands to be essential to the preservation of liberty, it is evident that each department should have a will of its own . . .

But the great security against a graded concentration of the several powers in the same department consists in giving to those who administer each department the necessary constitutional means and personal motives to resist encroachments of the others . . .

This policy of supplying, by opposite and rival interests, the defect of better motives might be traced through the whole system of human affairs . . .

Whilst all authority in it will be derived from and dependent on the society, the society itself will be broken into so many parts, interests, and classes of citizens that the rights of individuals, or the minority, will be in little danger from interested combinations of the majority . . . Justice is the end of government. It is the end of civil society.[12]

This is the crux of the matter. The administrative weakness of our political management system was built in from the beginning by some of the best minds our civilization has known. Their concern was justice, not efficiency; the preservation of liberty, not the best use of economic resources; accountability and legitimacy, not efficiency and effectiveness.

The division and sharing of power was artfully designed to divide the interests of those who govern, to open the workings of a system so that a determined minority could subvert the will of a coherent majority if one could be found. It was designed so that the weakest individual has a chance to defend his property from the strongest, with the hope that often he will succeed. The notion that the whole would be better served by withdrawing resources from one part or group without their concurrence, but in order to serve others — the idea of hierarchically imposed selective resource allocation — is anathema to U.S. constitutional government.

And yet from the earliest times economic issues — especially the contradictions inherent in the aggressive promotion of our agricultural exports and protection of our manufacturers — have plagued the federal government, weakening the executive and crowding the legislative agenda. Slavery and the Civil War were only one aspect of the fight.

Today, as we debate the proper way to respond to our economic problems, it is worth keeping in mind both the age and the importance of the issues. The criteria used by Hamilton and Madison to argue for the Constitution make useful yardsticks with which to measure the political danger inherent in one or another proposal. The calls for consensus and cooperation, for a reduction of due process, are in fact calls for a rewriting or reinterpretation of the Constitution in the interest of more effective management of the society.

Though obviously we are not about to yield up to some national general manager the kind of powers wielded by Thomas Watson, Jr., at IBM, we are being asked to consider lesser changes. Because the Japanese economic challenge is so effective and because the contrast between Japan's system and ours is instructive along precisely the lines of the previous discussion, it makes sense to consider it here.

The United States Is Not Japan

For the United States, a nation that likes winners and forgets easily, the Japanese were first of all the camera makers who made Nikon, Canon, Pentax, and Minolta the superiors of Leica, and the watchmakers who pushed the Swiss Omega and Tissot, as well as the American Longine, from their pinnacles. Later, somewhat less amusingly, they would take the U.S. black-and-white television market, the color television market, the motorcycle market, and most irritating of all, more than a quarter of the automobile market. Unknown to the general public, they took the West Coast steel market, and the tanker market, and a share of ball bearings and zippers, and they are now moving on semiconductors.

For a generation brought up with the idea that Japanese products were shoddy, the sheer quality of the products is amazing. For businessmen used to the idea that Japanese labor is cheap, the discovery that Japanese productivity is higher in some industries, that design is better and automation further advanced, is a surprise worth learning about.

For government administrators and political scientists brought up on a diet of sometimes inspired but often catastrophic incrementalism, the idea that this economic surge has been planned boggles the mind. It is one thing to lose a jungle war to "zealots in black pajamas"; after all, we understand that our civilian-led and staffed military was not designed for so subtle a conflict as Vietnam. But an economic war is another matter; surely the American economy ought to be pre-eminent.

The "numbers" refute us. As noted in chapter 7, the Japanese have managed to achieve a performance superior to the United States' in many dimensions that we care about: high growth, low inflation, low unemployment, and positive balance of payments. They have done it by following a systematic economic strategy at the country and industry level. While there has been luck, there has also been a good deal of management.

The popular explanation is Japan, Inc., the idea that if the United States has a problem behaving like a company, Japan does not. Japan in this caricature is like a group of tourists from Tokyo following their flag-carrying leader in orderly fashion. It's not quite clear who carries the flag for the nation, but MITI (Japan's Ministry of International Trade and Industry) is now notorious as the gang that plans the group's itinerary.

As in any good cartoon, there is an element of truth in this presentation. But more than a thousand years of history, as well as a remarkable effort of governance by public and private institutions in the second half of this century, also play a part in the story.[13] At the beginning there was an island society divided into hundreds of warring clans unchecked by a sacred but powerless emperor. The threat of China was a unifying force, but except to drive out the foreigner, Japanese feudal society could not cohere until the noble house of Tokugawa seized power. At this point coherence — in the form of Tokugawa control — was achieved with a vengeance. Roads and bridges were kept too narrow for armies to move, and nobles or their hostage families were a continuous physical presence at the court in Edo.

Two hundred fifty years passed before the rigid hierarchical society created by the Tokugawa shoguns was effectively destabilized by the arrival of Commander Matthew Perry in Tokyo Bay in 1854. Having observed what "trade" with the Western industrial powers had done to China, Japan wanted none of it. Yet Perry's gunboats left little alternative. Indeed, between 1856 and 1865, despite distracting wars in China as well as the U.S. Civil War, the shogun had signed a series of humiliating "unequal" trade treaties that unilaterally reduced Japan's right to levy import duties that might protect its infant economy.

The next sixty years saw a remarkable and successful effort of Japan's leadership to catch up with the West and achieve something near to equality. In 1868 a group of young nobles overthrew the shogun under the guise of restoring the emperor. They proceeded to transform the government and the political institutions on which it was grounded, destroying in the process the hierarchy that had served to hold back progress. They reformed the social order so as to dismantle feudalism. They modernized the army; introduced Western technology, compulsory primary education, and a modern infrastructure of telegraph and railroad lines; supported the development of a powerful merchant marine; encouraged manufacturing and mining; and built a banking system and reformed the currency.

Their basic strategy was "rich country, strong army." Through industrialization came the strength necessary to protect Japan from foreign tutelage. Measures of her success were her victories over China and imperial Russia in the Sino-Japanese (1881) and Russo-Japanese (1904) wars. But what Japan won in war she usually lost in peace. And the series of peace and disarmament conferences following World War I confirmed that Japan was still regarded as an inferior by the great powers of the West.

The 1920s saw an increase in protectionist tariffs in the United States at a time when Japan was running record balance-of-payments deficits, and industrial exports seemed the only way to solve the problem of paying the bill for food for Japan's growing population. Austerity and a strong yen helped until the Great Depression further eroded export markets. The answer was a series of Keynesian "demand-side" measures that righted the Japanese economy and permitted it to resume its growth.

The irony for Japan was that her very accomplishments made her more dependent on the West both for markets for her new manufacturers and for access on favorable terms to the raw materials of the developing world. It was precisely this trading advantage the West would not concede; nor would it permit Japan a navy of a size that would enable Japan to supply her needs by force. But as the depression aggravated the economic conflict, and as Japan's drive for raw materials took her further into Manchuria and China, war emerged as a nearly inevitable consequence.

Nineteen forty-six found Japan bombed flat, with a GNP 50 percent below that of 1933. But — and this is the central point of this entire recitation — she retained the experience, and hence the learning and institutional memory, from one of the most extraordinary surges of economic, political, and social development in world history. When in the early 1950s she regained full control over her destiny, she could recall the basic conclusions of her analysis from the late 1920s. Without food, natural resources, or power, Japan could not live as a rich country unless she imported. To pay for the imports required exports. To truly prosper, one's exports had to command high prices based on value added. Such goods could only be found in advanced manufacture and, in turn, be sold to advanced markets. With this understanding the rest was just execution — good government, good education, good business management, and good luck.

Because the remainder of this chapter focuses on government, education, and business, it is worth pausing to note the elements of good fortune that helped Japan. Most involved the preoccupation of the United States with other matters.

To begin, Japan was fortunate in being defeated by a great general and statesman who had studied and come to respect the Far East. Douglas MacArthur was the perfect transition leader between army/emperor and a strong civil service. He was also able to foil the efforts of former New Dealers to give Japan strong industrial trade unions and strong antitrust laws.

Even MacArthur might have not prevented the occupation from destroying Japan's sense of how to manage itself had the Korean War not intervened, making Japan's economic strength more important to the United States than her economic democracy and providing a great market for her infant manufacturing industries. The cold war that continued after Korea kept the best scientific and engineering talent in the United States focused on weapons and space. When we thought about it at all, Japan's economic success seemed heaven sent — one nation in the alliance the United States didn't have to worry about. On the other hand, we seldom recognized international economic matters as having a bearing on the domestic scene. Those policymakers who did favored free trade.

Earlier chapters have made clear that the postwar United States had no coherent economic policy. But even had we been aware during the 1960s that Japan was successfully consolidating its beachhead in our markets, the "greening" of America made sure that the politics of love and civil rights would dominate any concern for economic productivity. Teen-agers listened to rock music on Sonys and Panasonics. Environmentalism and consumerism would set the agenda for political debate. If the 1980s are zero sum, the 1960s were affluent. The questions debated were about how to use our wealth well. Big business, when it was discussed, was a target for contempt and attack, not concern.

Finally, Vietnam provided the ultimate distraction for the U.S. economy and politics. And the unwillingness of Lyndon Johnson to raise taxes to pay for that war put us on the inflationary course from which we only now may be extracting ourselves.

As we consider Japan's successes, it is well to remember that although in the early 1980s we might feel ambivalent about the cost to U.S. industry of her export drive, throughout the preceding three decades the United States did not work very consistently to do anything about it. Orderly market agreements in cheap shoes or textiles just redirected the attack toward a stronger sector of our market, or led the Japanese to manufacture in a third country. Only Richard Nixon's floating of the dollar and OPEC's high oil prices have caused the Japanese momentarily to break stride.

Most of the success, however, is not luck. In the context of Japanese history and culture, they have built and managed systems for government, business, and education that are remarkably effective. Critical to an understanding of their workings is an appreciation of the interrelatedness of family, school, business, and state in Japanese life.

A Japanese student of mine, Masatake Ushiro, has provided some useful ways of expressing some essentially different aspects of Japanese life in a "note" written for students at the Harvard Business School.[14] He points first to the relationship between the individual and society. In the United States, we value individualism, equality, and contractual relationships.

"Before a Japanese recognizes himself as an individual he tends to recognize his position in a group," Ushiro wrote.

> I am the second son of my family. I am a member of Mitsubishi Trading Company. Whereas Americans express freedom as a lack of constraint, and act it out as a lack of obligation to others, the Japanese recognize interdependence in human relations as "a consciousness of the order of things emanating from a certain view of life and the world."
>
> It is also given that people are unequal in capability. Much more important is the fact that persons belong to the same group or share the same feelings. "One of the same is more important than equal."[15]

Ushiro points next to property, viewed in the United States as the fundamental guarantor of individual rights. After feudalism broke down in Japan, property came to be held by the village or the family. Property rights were held by the father, who always passed his position and his rights to his first son. If he had no son, he adopted one — often a son-in-law — who would take the father's name. Thus at Matsushita, the company that makes Panasonic electronics, Mr. Matsushita was succeeded as president by his son-in-law, who took the name Matsushita.

A family chief in Japan was not morally allowed to sell his property, since he was not so much its owner as he was a holder of property passed on to him for caretaking by his ancestors. In contrast to the American view that property is something you can do with as you please, the Japanese father was obligated to keep it, protect it, and pass it along to his descendants. Property exists in time, and was thus owned by a family over time. Should a man exploit his legal right to sell, he would be regarded as a common criminal.

As the Matsushita example suggests, this ancient idea relates to the conception of Japanese companies today. The firm in a real sense is felt to be the property of all its members. Property is held by a "family."

The employee of a Japanese firm refers to "my company." He says, "I am a member of the Mitsui Bussan Kaisha." He belongs to the Mitsui family, even though he may have no right to represent Mitsui officially. And he is proud of his membership.

Today, the great growth of Japanese industry has shifted ownership of most companies from families to banks and insurance companies. As in the United States, corporate leadership is chosen by representatives of stockholders. Once he has been chosen, the president plays the role of eldest son who succeeded the family chief. He often will choose his successor, and generally plays many roles of a father caring for a family.

Japanese managers believe that it is their responsibility to look after all aspects of their subordinates' lives. In the evenings, the Tokyo restaurants are filled with bosses talking with employees — about their work, certainly, but also about their home lives.

In fact, senior executives are likely to play a major role in finding suitable wives for their junior executives. Thereafter they may play a role as godparent as well as mentor.

Another aspect of the family life of companies is sometimes visible at train stations in the morning. A large semicircle of white-shirted men will stand around a man and his wife. The man in the center will walk around the ring, bowing, and close friends from the group will come out to him and bow deeply. He is an executive being transferred from one office to another, and his "family" has come out to say good-bye.

Not surprisingly, in a society that reveres the concept of membership, competition plays a different role than in the United States. We see competition as defining what is good. The best is the fittest that survives. In Japan, there is also competition, but it can be discarded when the shared goals of the members are not served.

There is a great deal of competitiveness in Japan. The country's history is full of bloody conflicts between feudal lords. Today there is still strife between leadership groups using the usual weapons of economic and political power. But the chief ammunition has come to be the talent of young men emerging from the highly competitive Japanese educational system.

Ezra Vogel states in his excellent and extensive study of the question posed in this chapter that "if any single factor explains Japanese success it is the group-directed quest for knowledge. In virtually every important organization and community . . . devoted leaders worry about the future of their organizations, and to those leaders, nothing is more important than the information and knowledge that the organizations might one day need."[16]

The foundation for this data gathering and use is a superb system of basic education. Japan is almost completely literate (compared to perhaps 20 percent illiteracy in the United States). Such comparative evidence as exists reveals high levels of performance in mathematics and physical science, as well as history and geography, across major parts of the society. There are national standards for the curriculum, textbook publishers must be certified, and the government subsidizes the poorer prefectures.

Since education is a person's route to success in a world where the best jobs are in the biggest firms, where lifetime employment begins right after graduation, every youth is motivated to get the best education he can. What he does in a few days of competitive exams decides his future.

Almost all the leaders in every field are graduates of a handful of famous universities. This procedure means that a poor boy can rise to great heights in Japan. It also means there is intense competitiveness.

This competition reflects the rivalry in all aspects of Japanese life, including business. Firms are always struggling for a larger share of the market. On the other hand, there is also a strong sense of cooperation among business groups and harmony within businesses. Japanese companies are organized into thousands of associations — for example, one for each major petrochemical. These industry groupings, in turn, are organized in aggregate associations, the largest and most important of which speak for Japanese industry. At each level, these groups consult and receive guidance from the relevant desk, or bureau, or minister at the Ministry of International Trade and Industry.

The habit of cooperation is ingrained. Ushiro offers a particularly apt explanation in the legend of Mori Motonari.

"Motonari was a famous feudal lord who lived 400 years ago. In his old age, he was worried about the safety of his territory. Fighting and disorder ranged throughout the countryside. One day he called his three sons to his bedside and he gave each of them an arrow and said 'Break it.' Each of them did so easily. Then he gave each of them three arrows and said, 'Break them.' They could not. Then he said: 'If you are alone, you won't be able to survive. If you cooperate, you will prosper and protect your family.' "[17]

Japan's history has been filled with threats from outside. And they have always been able to put internal fighting aside in order to drive off invaders. Competitiveness, therefore, is subordinated to the common interest in protecting the Japanese family and seeing it prosper. It is not Japan, Inc. It is the Japanese family.

Remembering the story of Motonari, Ushiro says that it is easy to understand the role of government in Japan. "Government plays the role of the father. He does not impose plans. He says, 'If you wish to survive, cooperate instead of fighting among brothers. If you want to fight, go ahead.' "[18]

The Ministry of International Trade and Industry has laws that permit firms in industries where there is overcapacity to cooperate in antirecession cartels. But if firms will not cooperate voluntarily, they are not forced to.

The government, of course, plays a very important role. It is the reconciler and coordinator. As with the Japanese manager, its role is to build a consensus among competing proponents from politics and industry. Here it is important to remember that the common educational background of business and government leaders creates a shared understanding.

It is also important to recognize the quality of the study and analysis provided by government ministries. MITI and its related agencies gather and study a staggering range of data and have done this over a period of years with great success. They carry out this study with the goal of helping private industry; and they perform the work using the best minds in the country. For it is the best of the university graduates who go to MITI. If companies tend to cooperate with MITI, perhaps it is because the executives of those companies have been following the lead of the men at MITI since school days. In a society that values information, MITI, the Ministry of Finance, and the Bank of Japan have the best. It is natural to follow such guidance.

Ambassador Edwin O. Reischauer has noted that it is this cooperation that gives the government more delicate control over Japan's economy. Governments can cause business to move out of a slowdown or dampen an inflationary situation more quickly. He notes that the spirit of cooperation shows up in labor relations as well, where loyalty to the company-family is much stronger, and more highly rewarded, than loyalty to the union.

Since Japanese companies hire for life, they train workers to be productive for life. They don't pass their market problems on to their workers.

Loyalty, cooperation, and lifetime employment have also made the Japanese less resistant to technological change. They are aggressive innovators because no member of the family, executive or worker, will lose his privilege of belonging. Someone else may be promoted who is better equipped to handle the technology, but the whole family will prosper.

In short, continuity and stability are hallmarks of the tightly interwoven worlds of family, business, and government that make up Japanese society. Yet this system is also able to be selective. It is able to move beyond mere cooperation, because government is provided other sources of influence that are legitimate and yet not at all directly accountable in conventional Western ways. By U.S. standards, Japan lives closer to the edge. Industry relies heavily on debt, as do the banks. And the government provides far less security in the form of pensions and welfare for the individual. As a consequence industry pays a great deal of attention to its bankers, and the bankers in turn are very sensitive to the behavior of the central bank. The Bank of Japan in turn has tremendous independence in the use of its power. For example, in late 1973 after the embargo following the Yom Kippur War, the Bank of Japan together with the Ministry of Finance initiated an eighteen-month period of austerity in which they shut down consumption in the Japanese economy, slowed oil imports, stimulated exports with an undervalued yen, and then, when the economy righted itself, strengthened the yen against the dollar to help pay for the growing oil requirement. This austerity period, which involved thousands of business bankruptcies and brought to a halt growth in real per capita consumption that had averaged 8 to 9 percent per year during the previous ten years, was managed despite a government that held a bare majority in the Diet.

Just as the central bank has power, so does MITI. Licenses for imports and joint ventures, permits for expansion, access to incentives, and advice to the banks as to which companies deserve support during periods of tight money all flow from MITI, based on the judgment of its officials. Selectivity is rampant, based on an ideology of obligation that legitimizes dependence.

The situation of individuals is not different from companies. They too are dependent, but — interestingly — not on the government. Individuals must rely heavily on their companies and their own savings for old-age pensions. With social security that is low by U.S. and European standards and no tax deduction for interest on borrowings, it is not surprising that the Japanese save roughly three times more of their personal income than do Americans. It is especially understandable when we remember that income is geared to seniority and retirement age for all but the most successful executives was fifty-five up until 1980, when it was changed to sixty. There is a long period after leaving work that must be paid for.

Within families there is similar dependence of wives on husbands and children on parents. Divorce is legally easy but socially difficult. Women are accepted in the workplace until the time when they ought to be married. Thereafter, liberation is a Western concept.

More generally, while it is remarkably easy to move forward after a group has decided which plan to adopt, it is very difficult, if not impossible, for an individual to move ahead on his own. In his otherwise adulatory book, Ezra Vogel lists the "costs and dangers" of the Japanese system:[19]

"Smothering individual rights, individuality, and creativity." This includes "respecting bureaucrats and looking down on the citizens," and isolation or ridicule of deviant individuals or groups.

"Ignoring the variant, the opposition, and the little man." There is discrimination against racial minorities, opposition groups are given little standing or recognition, and the central governing groups are drawn from cadres formed five and six decades before they reach real power.

"Condemning the misfit." Those not happy with the track into which they have been slotted when young have virtually nowhere to go. Suicide rates for the young are comparatively high.

"Stimulating excessive nationalism." The Japanese have raised the nontariff barrier to an art form. In this sense the combination of Japanese culture and competitiveness with close business-government relations makes the lot of the foreigner who would do significant business in Japan very difficult. Generally, the more time one has spent outside Japan the less chance one has of rising to the top of a Japanese organization. Foreign born are excluded from a wide variety of positions.

"Becoming immobilized." When one significant member of a group refuses to go along, it can immobilize the group, since it is "not considered proper to force a decision on an unwilling party."

In other words, there is a less attractive side to the technocratically managed family. In *Time* magazine's 1981 report "How Japan Does It," an American working at Sony's very successful plant in San Diego remarked that the Japanese plant management "do not realize that some of us live for the weekend, while lots of them live for the week."[20] He captures in that simple phrase the essence of the American system. We separate family from office, weekend from workplace, politics from business. Our entire history reflects an effort to eliminate potentially arbitrary restrictions on the individual flowing from a monarch, family ownership, or professional management. We go to great institutional lengths and pay a high price to avoid being a national family, to protect the deviant, and to reward individuality in all its manifestations.

What, then, should we do? Vogel argues that we should learn from Japan and develop an industrial and trade policy, a small core of permanent high-level bureaucrats, a communitarian vision, and aggregations of interest groups.

The problem is that it is by no means obvious how we can invent effective mechanisms for developing a coherent industrial and trade policy that is legitimately and accountably representative of our very incoherent national economic interests. To whom would the small group of permanent bureaucrats be accountable? If to a wide group, then how can they reconcile the demands of efficient farmers for access to foreign markets with the demands of inefficient manufacturers for protection; how can they balance Boeing's need for export-import financing with claims that foreign competition in steel is unfairly subsidized? Our inability to shape policy is not so much the lack of initiative as it is the lack of mechanism to trade off wide-ranging conflicting interests. Our Federalist vision is of a heterogeneous community.

If on the other hand a small group is accountable only narrowly, then what is the source of its legitimacy? In so imperfectly understood a world as ours, expertise won't do. There must be a political base.

John T. Dunlop has addressed himself to this problem in his essays in *Business and Public Policy.* [21] In the same vein as Vogel but in a somewhat different spirit, Dunlop has called for high-level tripartite negotiations of government, business, and labor to replace the chaos of policymaking described in earlier chapters.

The view developed in the next two chapters is close to Dunlop's. But many approaches to tripartite groups in government pose two important problems that need to be noted. The first, oddly enough, is a lack of effectiveness. Tripartite groups have proved to be excellent mechanisms for reconciling divergent economic interests as long as cooperation helped all parties to the agreement. But the experience of the British under the National Economic Development Office with their tripartite industrial groups is that they were incapable of making progress once significant parties to the discussion had a great deal to lose — for example, if it made sense to shut one or more entire companies down while leaving others open. Yet where there was overcapacity in an uncompetitive industry, that was often the most sensible solution.

Where a group has the power to impose economic harm, then it tends to fall apart or raise a second problem, legitimacy. What right does a cooperative group have to impose harm on a member?

Where are the solutions that meet both the technocratic tests of efficiency and effectiveness and the political tests of legitimacy and accountability? We seem boxed in by administrative infeasibility and ideological dogma.

The way out of the box we have created for ourselves is not obvious. There may well be no clear-cut solution. But there may be some clearly acceptable partial and incremental steps that can be taken that will put the country in a better position to manage its destiny.

9   Small May Be Beautiful, but Local Works

OUR BASIC PROBLEM in achieving technocratic coherence is a political barrier erected by the Constitution. Suppose we return to the argument of Madison and Hamilton to look for some suggestion of a solution. Or, more candidly, suppose we apply what we know about the problems of large organizations to the paradox we have defined and see if the conclusions are not consistent with the Federalist argument.

It is worth reviewing the political objectives first, lest they be forgotten. The architects of the Constitution sought a form of organization for government that would be highly sensitive to the needs of the many constituencies present in the thirteen colonies. The operations of the government were placed in agencies directed by and accountable to a legislature that had line-item control of the budget as well as the power of oversight. The legislature was organized in two parts. One house, the Senate, was considerably more able to achieve continuity, selectivity, and a stable hierarchy than the other. The House of Representatives could be expected to be more responsive to shifting local interests. In short, technocratic agencies were accountable to politicians, and politicians to the voters. Coherence in the system over time could be achieved only (1) if there was a considerable degree of consensus among the governed — at a minimum after the fact — and (2) if the leadership could define or express that consensus in a way that seemed to fit the needs and opportunities of the period. The legitimacy of the government was guaranteed by the fact that "the society itself will be broken into so many parts, interests, and classes of citizens that the rights of individuals, or the minority, will be in little danger."[1]

The threat perceived by Madison was that if the number of electors was too great, the individual would be "unduly attached" to local circumstances and "too little fit to comprehend and pursue great and national objects." In this context, the question posed in chapter 1 and at the end of chapter 8 can be put more sharply: Doesn't the performance of our system of political management over the past decade suggest that the fragmentation in which its legitimacy is grounded renders it "too little fit to comprehend and pursue great and national objects"? But in the absence of a national consensus or an ideology that places positive value on consensus, how can our heterogeneous society achieve a more comprehensive outlook?

The direction of an answer would seem to be provided by the Federalist analysis. Somehow the number of things that the government has to deal with needs to be reduced. The remarkably responsive tool that is our federal system must not be used to resolve myriad local political conflicts. Either the major forums for analysis and choice are drowned in trivia, or the political work of local government is delegated to a federal technocratic system that is not especially capable of trading off local interests.

The congressional staff has grown large and the executive agencies powerful because local conflicts are elevated from one level to another in search of a federal solution. But at the federal level, the limited time of political leaders means that detail must be delegated. When rival modes of transportation or retailing, or rival cities, take their differences to Washington, the answer must be delegated to some organization competent to deal with the substance of the matter. Imagine that the two mothers disputing rightful possession of the baby brought their conflict to Congress instead of Solomon. It would take a staggering investigation to establish legitimacy in this instance. We know enough now about the human heart, for example, to recognize that the mother most concerned with the child's welfare might not be the natural one. Somehow the interest of society in natural motherhood would have to be balanced against the interest in quality care. Absent a Solomonlike leader to find justice, a good deal of imperfect bureaucracy is required to provide society with good sense and due process in its decision making. Most of the time the bureaucracy resolves the problem by cutting the baby in two.

One way to avoid this dilemma is to take less to Congress, to elevate fewer issues to the federal level. Otherwise, the very nature of the large organization we call government means that elevating a conflict does not elicit study and choice at a high level. Rather, it means that the issue is reassigned for study and choice at a low level in a different part of the government organization.

Forums Have a Logic

In other words, if cities A and B or companies A and B take their dispute to the federal government, of necessity it will be delegated back to a bureau or staff with a narrow enough scope to deal with the issue. There is operating here what might be called the Laws of Forums.

- Forums are places where basic organizations such as companies or agencies reach agreements with each other. We will call these basic forums.
- Sometimes, because the benefits of cooperation are obvious, basic units come together to enjoy the positive benefits of interaction. Many trade associations have this characteristic. Organized markets are also positive, or "benign," forums — a stock exchange, for example.
- Some forums are places where members conspire to exploit others. In business these take the form of cartels. The benefits of association

are not generated by the interaction of the members, but rather through the exploitation of nonmembers. These could be called "malign" forums. A price-fixing conspiracy is a malign forum.

- Sometimes, when the usual consequences of unorganized interaction are negative, a forum must be imposed from above. Externally imposed mediation of a labor dispute is an example.
- Quite frequently high-level forums are assembled from many basic forums. State governments have this relationship with cities; and the federal government has it with the states.
- An informed forum is a "local" one composed of basic technocratic units. There is no such thing as a high-level informed forum, only a different local one.
- The negotiation required for substantive resolution of problems requires a local forum.
- Since the rules for resolving disputes in a forum may favor one party or another, much political maneuvering around an issue consists of attempts to shift disputes to more favorable forums.
- Referring a dispute to a higher-level forum results either in having the dispute shifted to a different basic forum or in politicizing the issue.

The working of these laws is such that the politicization of the technocracy and the technocratization of politics often take place when technocratically managed institutions in conflict try to escape from the particular outcome they face by elevating their dispute. What then happens is that discussions move from local offices to the White House or Capitol Hill. What happens there depends upon who does the staff work on the issue and how it fits on the agenda. Someone's local problem becomes woven into the political fabric of the day and rather dramatic results can follow. Thus, the border management solution was killed because it moved too early, pushed by the wrong offices. By analogy, the IBM 360 series lived because its political opponents were disenfranchised. Progress was made in New York's state prisons because Benjamin Ward moved to meet many of the correction officers' perceived needs. The issue of reform was negotiated, not elevated.

Elevating an issue may have other surprising consequences. It permits skillful politicians to totally alter the face of the issue so that all substantive questions evaporate. In 1981, U.S. air-traffic controllers may have believed in the legitimacy of their grievance over working conditions, but their rejection of a negotiated solution gave President Reagan the opportunity to stake out a dramatic political position on illegal strikes, which destroyed their union.

It must be so. The president or any senior official cannot give adequate time to every issue deemed important, and certainly cannot get immersed in the technocratic substance. The clearest example of the problems that can arise is provided by the Carter administration. The Camp David agreement between Israel and Egypt would seem to have been a model of how Carter would have liked to proceed on all issues he saw as significant — a week devoted to intense substantive study and negotiation. He would have liked to have handled energy and welfare reform in the same way and at the same time. He did not seem to understand that Camp David was a low-level forum for Israel and Egypt, but that Washington is usually *many* levels removed from the basic units in conflict over alternative sources and development programs for energy, or alternative approaches to income redistribution. Consequently, he had his cabinet officers develop detailed programs remarkably soon after taking office. One insider commented on the result.

[Energy Secretary James] Schlesinger went off, assembled a small academic corps around him, and came up with an absolutely ingenious plan that the president bought. He said, "Here's the answer."

Carter made twelve speeches on energy over a period of three and a half years and that's one of the factors that contributed to his low ranking in the polls. He was selling something that is the most distasteful change sociologically that this country has ever faced. "We must shift from cheap energy to expensive energy." Can you imagine a worse program to run on?[2]

In his memoirs of his years as secretary of health, education and welfare, Joe Califano describes the transition from candidate Carter's 1976 campaign promise at the Clinton, Massachusetts, town meeting (that on May 1, 1977, Califano would propose to the Congress a "comprehensive revision of the entire welfare system") to President Carter's abandonment of the battle after he had sent a 136-page bill of compromises forced by limited resources, interest groups, and politics to the six committees of Congress that claimed jurisdiction over the matter.[3]

In the presentation of the Reagan economic program in 1981 we saw the reverse — the president as politician, purely political. The visible work of the White House was all process, completely focused on the economic program. Symbolic of the utter lack of precision in the president's effort was the graph he used to support his televised speech of March 1981 presenting the program to the nation. The graph had no labels or numbers on it. Reagan uses his highest-level forum only to communicate, to persuade, to reshape voters' perceptions of their own interest.

A clear example of Reagan's approach is provided by the speech he made to the NAACP's 1981 annual meeting. At a time when black unemployment approached 15 percent, and that of black teen-agers 40 percent, the president defended cuts in government social programs on the grounds that black people would remain dependent on welfare support forever unless his economic program of tax cuts brought growth to the economy — and with growth, jobs. Whether or not he persuaded his audience, he very clearly sought to provide a new way of interpreting their circumstances and interests.

If the procedural aspects of the Reagan presidency can be taken as an example of how politicians can avoid technocratization, then the budget battles also exemplify the need for a forum where substantive problems can be worked out. This need is inevitable if fewer issues are to be taken to the federal government for substantive resolution. This need can be met in at least two ways. (1) Negotiate conflicts directly, using existing local forums. (2) Recognize the need for new intermediate-level forums for managing — above the local level — and create them.

Negotiation Avoids Escalation

The first approach is deceptively obvious. Negotiation, like motherhood, is clearly a "good thing." But it is very hard to negotiate if one does not recognize the existence of a legitimate opposing interest, and it is common to find opponents denying each other's existence or legitimacy. Workers, or small companies, or environmentalists are sometimes characterized as "a small minority of disgruntled nuts," rather than articulate leaders of potentially important groups with conflicting stakes. The instinct to discount the existence or the variety of stakes of others is particularly unfortunate because it delays the kind of problem solving that reveals a solution, in which there can be a joint interest.[4] This has come to be recognized as a truism in collective bargaining, but has much more general validity.

Warren Christopher has addressed the subject with eloquence.

> . . . I propose to invite your attention to a practice — a simple practice, but one of such importance that I raise it to the stature of principle.
> The practice is talking. It is communication.
> . . . Talking . . . includes listening — and hearing. Authentic diplomacy is a two-way endeavor . . .
> More and more problems that touch us cannot be solved unless there are agreed, collective solutions — solutions that can only be attained through diplomatic means. Cross-boundary pollution, energy shortages, the declining resource base, surging populations, terrorism — these are just a few of the most urgent matters on the global agenda. No country can either blast or buy these problems out of existence. Broadly based, negotiated solutions have to be found. For that, talking is indispensable.[5]

The urge to talk, to negotiate, is seldom acquired at birth. In the United States we value competition but denigrate competitors. Our history, ideology, geography, and education system make it easy to regard "others" as nonpersons, obstacles to opportunity that it is our manifest destiny to exploit. Cities, companies, regions, or groups that block progress are perceived and handled as if they were the American Indian. They are the enemy to be exterminated, not potential members of a common forum with a different point of view.

Much of the time parties to a dispute do not know each other, live near each other, go to school together, or have any understanding of what makes life difficult from day to day. Projecting from our own background, we make the wrong forecasts. Confronted with what seems to be aberrant behavior, we make the wrong evaluation. Dialogue breaks down. The gap widens.

Readily available to exacerbate this national tendency is a legal system that justifies conflict as the route to truth and relies on a cadre of mercenary fighters who sometimes see their livelihood as dependent on the existence of conflict.[6] Given their disposition, it is not surprising that when they serve as legislators they write law that relies upon the adversary process of the judicial system to handle disputes over low-level detail. Consequently, when parties to a political dispute elevate an issue to Congress, it is likely to be settled in principle only. The detail of the solution will be delegated to the courts, where truth can be sought in battle.

Negotiation, in other words, is not a natural way of doing important business in the United States. The increased prevalence of litigation has led many observers of society to see litigiousness as another evidence of a fragmented society. Fred Friendly has characterized the general pattern of behavior discussed here as a lack of comity, or social harmony, and in the context of some remarks pointed toward another problem.

Modern Americans have a kind of adversarial disease which, when controlled, works. When out of control, which I suggest it may be, we have battles between the First Amendment and the Sixth Amendment, battles between those who want to do something for poor people and those who want to do something about inflation. We've reached the point where there is such a lack of comity that the very thing we prize the most, the democratic system, may not be working.

And what's that got to do with journalism? Everything.

Every time I read a news story that doesn't work, or listen to the radio and it doesn't tell me what I thought I was going to understand, if I analyze it — and too often I don't — it's because I'm aware that the reporter doesn't know what he or she is talking about. We live in a world that's litigious, cantankerous, adversarial, full of journalists who love to use the word "controversy." It's almost a byword — if you have a weak story, you put the word controversy into it, and that hypes it. If you want to hype it more you say "very controversial." But most of all you have journalists like me, like you, explaining things they don't understand, whether its El Salvador, productivity, what's going on in Poland or at Three Mile Island, or in South Africa. This is not because they are venal or sloppy people. It's because they are not given enough time. We live in a world in which the gatekeepers, whether they be television producers or newspaper editors, don't really have time to let people understand what they're reporting. You have people writing about productivity who have no sense of understanding the problem of productivity in this country. They don't know whether it is a problem of labor strife, of depression, of reform, of health benefits, or of management out of control.[7]

Our sources of information, in other words, have trivialized the news in part by encapsulating it in short bursts comparable to spot advertising, but also — and more damaging — by converting news into entertainment (the model for which is Howard Cosell's Monday night football: apparently knowledgeable analyses of violence). Whether or not an event is adversarial, it is a "better story" if it is about controversy. And the easiest way to find controversy is to treat participants in an event as adversaries. Reporters behave this way because they do not have the time or the background to behave otherwise. It is no accident that Roone Arledge, the inventor of Monday night football, now heads ABC News.

Sadly, our schools and colleges operate in much the same mode. Political economy and physical science, the two fields that might help individuals to understand their changing world, are seldom available in the general curriculum. Instead, students are presented with what George Cabot Lodge has called "disciplinary tunnels," such as economics, psychology, or physics. "If a student seeking a holistic view advances toward the light at the end of the tunnel, he finds an old professor with a candle, digging deeper."[8] Within a given school the disciplines in their departmental organizations compete for resources and status. There is little within the formal reward system for faculty that would lead them to cooperate across disciplines. Within a given discipline individuals compete for advancement with research evaluated by other members of that discipline.

As a consequence, it is hard for someone who wants to understand how business works to find a place to learn. Most teachers don't know. They have seen business only as a customer. It is equally hard to learn about government, even local government. And it is very hard to learn about the rest of the industrial world that competes with us. As a consequence we get most of our information from journalists.

But on the day that Friendly's paragraph was first drafted the *New York Times* carried no story about England, France, Italy, Spain, Japan, Singapore, or Brazil.[9] A one-inch squib indicated that there was opposition to the neutron bomb in West Germany, and the business section carried a story indicating that the West Germans coveted U.S. gene-splicing technology. Conflict in Poland and the Middle East dominated the international news, and the air-traffic controllers' strike the domestic news. The allocation of attention was typical.

The consequence is that technocrats and politicians perceiving themselves at odds are very unlikely to be exposed to information or people who will have a more comprehensive or informed view. They may meet people from "the other side," but they too are likely to think of any issue as a zero-sum game. John Dunlop evokes this same picture.

> Increasingly, at local and national levels, the community is calling upon the skills and qualities of business executives. Both groups [business and

government] are thrown into much contact with each other, typically in a sharp adversary position, usually with legal staffs. They have different backgrounds, approach issues with different time horizons; see the press and media in quite different roles and have quite different institutional objectives; and frequently have quite different personal values. They see the role of the law in society in substantially different ways, one to change and the other largely to preserve. The business perspective often tends to be international, while the government administrator is much more narrowly national. They are also often separated by a gap in age and experience. It is little wonder that beyond difficult substantive issues and values they do not find it easy to communicate with each other.[10]

There would seem to be a small movement away from confrontation, especially in such areas as labor relations, antitrust and regulatory enforcement, and community development. The trend is important, for each conflict worked out locally frees up the federal mechanism for consideration of the "great and national issues." At the same time, those seeking a new national consensus, such as George Lodge, Ezra Vogel, and Robert Reich, might want to consider the implications of what they have in mind. They might conclude that a far less ambitious objective would be appropriate.

The Route to Consensus Is Local

Quite often, when parties seeking a technocratic solution examine an issue, it develops that there is a fundamental need for a forum that is "higher" than the parties in the sense that it can adopt a more comprehensive point of view for study and then organize action or redistribute costs and benefits over long periods of time. There are instances in which physical factors such as a river, or economic forces such as a foreign competitor, make the benefits of cooperation among rivals dramatically apparent. But the lines of state or local organization and the distribution of costs and benefits are such that direct negotiation will not help. The basic forums are inadequate. In such instances it makes sense to invent a new forum that permits technocratic management at a higher level of aggregation than the single unit. Usually, old organizations do not disappear or even "report to" the new one. The creation is an overlay.

This second approach has many precedents. Despite our natural focus on cities, states, and companies, all sorts of organizations have been devised to deal with issues that cross these conventional boundaries. In fact, as long as the parties to a problem can recognize their long-term interests in a joint solution it has often been possible to devise a higher-level organization intermediate between the parties and the federal government to deal with the problem. Sometimes the federal government must act as an enabler or a facilitator, but that is a very different role than problem solver.

The economic historian Ellis Hawley and his colleagues at the University of Iowa have called attention to Herbert Hoover's extensive efforts to have the federal government play this role during his years as secretary of commerce and later as president. Hawley reports, "Essentially, [Hoover] believed, he had created the type of governmental tool that he had envisioned in 1921, one that functioned as an economic 'general staff,' business 'correspondence school,' and national coordinator, all rolled into one, yet preserved the essentials of American individualism by avoiding bureaucratic dictation and legal coercion, implementing its plans through nearly 400 cooperating committees and scores of private associations and relying upon appeals to science, community and morality to bridge the gap between the public interest and private ones." Hawley evaluates this approach as flawed in substance rather than form, and doomed by macroeconomic collapse; he seems committed to the potential correctness of Hoover's philosophy and design.[11] In a similar vein, Thomas McCraw's positive assessment of the work of James Landis and William O. Douglas at the Securities and Exchange Commission is based on their very careful use of a talented, small staff that could structure and manage incentives so that industry associations of accountants, investment bankers, and security dealers would cooperate in the self-policing of their industry.[12]

There is an interesting analogy here to group-level organization and the recently designed "strategic business units" in large companies, or the sort of administrative system used at Texas Instruments. Companies have accepted a kind of multidimensional organization that might help us to manage in government. A review of its history is therefore useful.

Around 1920, in order to manage the growth of increasingly diverse companies, managements invented the "product division" form of organization. Previous to this development, companies were organized by function — sales, manufacturing, engineering, and so forth. In order to achieve coordination across functions it was necessary to take issues to the top. This became an increasing problem as diverse products required different packages of functional policies. Consumer goods, for example, had to be marketed differently from industrial ones. As well, the relationship of marketing to production and engineering also needed to be coordinated.

The answer, organizing separate sub-businesses or divisions around each product cluster, worked until great growth presented top managements with too many divisions to manage.[13] It was then natural to cluster divisions into an intermediate-level group. General Electric, for example, assembled its refrigerator, washing machine, dishwasher, dryer, and stove divisions — each a business with annual sales over $100 million — into a gigantic home-appliance group.

Groups worked fine, and then supragroup "sectors" were invented for some very large, diverse companies. Oddly enough, some of the same problems facing the country cropped up in the large companies. Real substantive understanding was located in the divisions, and despite the existence of groups or sectors, resources were being allocated in a highly fragmented way by groups Hamilton would have described as "too little fit to comprehend great and [corporate] objects."

To address this newly comprehended need, business corporations began in the 1960s and 1970s to invent SBUs — strategic business units — clusters (forums) of already organized operations that ought to be able to plan and coordinate their long-term commitments across conventional and otherwise useful organizational lines. Exemplifying this point are the comments of General Electric's chief executive explaining his decision to his immediate executive core:

First, talking about Operations — we are going to retain the basic organizational structural pattern that has served us so well in the last twenty years. We are going to keep Groups, and we are going to continue to reaffirm that the Department will be the basic building block of our organizational structure. We are going to *superimpose* on the organizational structure the Strategic Business Unit *concept.* [*Emphasis added*][14]

In an analogous way, various mixtures of existing conventional public and private organizations have joined to work around strategic problems they cannot otherwise address. Examples of this sort of overlay activity are numerous.

In order to manage a wide range of joint interests in Minneapolis, St. Paul, and surrounding suburbs, the Twin Cities Metropolitan Council was created.

In order to deal with the joint problems of New York harbor, the states of New Jersey and New York joined to create the Port Authority of New York and New Jersey.

The New England River Basins Commission has studied numerous problems that affect interests of the several states.

The Chemical Industry Institute of Toxicology was created by the major companies in the industry in order to provide a legitimate body of high expertise to which much detailed development of knowledge related to the implementation of the Toxic Substances Control Act could be delegated.

The National Coal Policy Project brought electricity producers and users together with environmentalists to identify those areas under dispute that could be resolved outside political or judicial forums.

The examples listed above and discussed below are chosen for their diversity and because they have been studied. There are others. The importance of this approach is that:

1. It permits one to embrace a whole problem.
2. It provides the possibility of defining larger communities of interest.

3. It provides an intermediate forum for negotiating outside the boundaries of the adversarial system.
4. It provides technocrats a depoliticized forum for work.

Examples of Intermediate Forums

The Port Authority of New York and New Jersey provides a clear example of a prominent form of intermediate-level organization.

> [The Port Authority] was created to settle a century-old dispute between New York and New Jersey over control of transportation on the Hudson River and in the harbor. Railroad development on both sides of the Hudson was rapid and haphazard, with each line using separate terminals. The states battled over rail transportation, vying for competing terminals and bickering over regulation of railroad rates. New Jersey argued that rates to the New York side of the harbor should be higher because the rail cars had to be ferried across the bridgeless Hudson. In 1916, New Jersey interests brought formal complaints before the Interstate Commerce Commission to force the railroads to lower their rates to the New Jersey side of the river, arguing that equal rates throughout the port district unfairly imposed on New Jersey part of the costs of the ferry services and of terminals in New York and Brooklyn. The resulting railroad rate case dragged on until 1918, when an interstate commission was established to study the problem. (Ferry service was threatened by ice on the Hudson in the severe winter of 1918.) Two years later, the commission proposed the Port Authority compact. The stated purposes of the new authority were to resolve the counterproductive competition among the railroads by creating a comprehensive transportation plan and to promote the economic well-being of the port cities. The authority was designed to coordinate regional terminals, transportation, and other commercial facilities and to stimulate development of the port district.[15]

While the great work of the authority always had little to do with railroads, the essential ingredient can be seen at work. A broader view is necessary to rationalize the unreconcilable stakes of the individual states, cities, and railroads.

Another example is the New England River Basins Commission, which, before its elimination by the Reagan administration in 1981, was a federal-state planning partnership composed of representatives of the six New England states and New York, ten federal agencies, and six interstate agencies. The NERBC was created in 1968 at the request of the governors of the member states. Its primary responsibilities were:

- to be the principal agency for coordinating water and related land resource plans throughout New England.
- to prepare and update, in cooperation with its state, interstate, and federal members, a comprehensive, coordinated joint plan for managing the region's water and related land resources.
- to recommend long-range priorities for meeting the region's most important natural resource information planning and management needs.
- to undertake studies needed to carry out these missions adequately.

Although the commission's tangible accomplishments were not nearly as grandiose as those of the Port Authority, it did provide an expert and neutral definition of the New England water situation. The effects of individual actions on the system were examined; and that determination was used to match up costs and benefits of action. Private beneficiaries were asked to absorb and meliorate social costs. Collective and/or coordinated action was made feasible. And consequently the number or organizations that must negotiate — as opposed to transact — business with government units was reduced. For example, the commission dealt successfully to resolve a conflict on the Connecticut River in the early 1970s between hydropower generation and water quality, recreational boating, and salmon restoration interests. At that time, the five mainstream power dams on the Connecticut had been operating as peaking plants; they ran on weekdays, but closed down at night and on weekends to build head, thus blocking flows along the main stem.

That practice resulted in flows, particularly during late summer, that were inadequate for assimilation of sewage effluents, were insufficient for salmon and other anadromous fish runs, and that created an unpleasant setting for recreational boating. Federal and state interests were involved. The Fish and Wildlife Service wanted a minimum flow release that was greater than the power companies wanted in order to minimize lost power-generating potential. A compromise on the required rate of release was eventually worked out and confirmed by the commission.

A more permanent example of a postwar regional commission is the Twin Cities Metropolitan Council. There, a group of public figures combined with business leaders to persuade the Minnesota state legislature to create an intermediate-level group that could act for the contiguous networked government made up of two cities, Minneapolis and St. Paul, and their suburbs. People joke that this experiment in regional government succeeds because Scandinavians are used to cooperation, but the council now provides a forum where zoning, water resources, sewage, roads, and other issues where interests are interdependent can be resolved with all elements of the region considered.[16]

The General Principle

Seen in the light of the preceding discussions, many intermediate-level activities apparently ought to be recognized as having extreme potential importance. We are, in effect, reinterpreting institutions that others saw to be necessary in order to go beyond the confines of conventional public and private organizations. Although each institution was the child of necessity, the pattern of such institutions suggests a way of freeing up the higher levels of government.

The essential ingredient in each case is the value of a broader view. The benefit of overlay organizations is to provide an embracing perspective from which parties can "talk" more effectively. Another benefit is the possibility of discovering or defining larger communities of interest. Individual parties that regarded themselves as adversaries can see from the more elevated group-level perspective that if they can cooperate they may be able to move their rivalry to an altogether more hospitable arena. They can move from a zero-sum to a positive-sum game.

The reason is straightforward. Market transactions or conventional legal contests are, as promised, invisible but powerful processes for moving incrementally from one position to a slightly better one. But the focusing of energetic self-interest on the contest of competition or trial is a poor way of discovering that there is a quantum improvement possible outside the arena of battle.

A favorite alternative in some parts of the world obviously is central planning. As noted in the discussion of the Japanese, centralized government guidance provided a route past all sorts of excessive conflict. The French rely on similar central leadership. The Germans use their three largest banks in an analogous way.

But our search here is for a more decentralized approach, one appropriate to the United States. Our focus is on voluntary confederation of otherwise autonomous private groups. Examples of this form of cooperation are numerous but far too infrequent. Usually they are defensive reactions to failures or attacks from outside the traditional arena in which organizations operate that are too severe to ignore. The U.S. steel industry provides an excellent example. There a violent history of labor-management battles was slowly replaced by collusion that eventually — with trigger prices and relaxation of antipollution laws — came to include the government. An effort to achieve similar arrangements could be observed in the auto industry beginning in the spring of 1981 and in the revolutionary Ford and General Motors labor contracts of March 1982.

There is some hope that the automobile companies can negotiate their way out of their suicidal labor contracts. The precedent has provoked much discussion. But the defensive alignments of business, labor, and government, called "tripartite" above, often have a fatal defect. Unless they lead to a permanent change in the conditions that left the industry vulnerable, they merely constitute a political coalition capable of shifting income from one part of the economy to another. They do not solve a problem. They move it. For example, unless the U.S. steel industry is able to achieve costs competitive with the Japanese and the Germans, trigger prices will represent a continuing subsidy from steel consumers to the industry. It will not be easy to catch up. Wages are very high in the U.S. industry, and the front end of the business — ore and coke — is relatively old and costly.

More interesting than the defensive groupings are the cooperative ventures that create new capabilities. The Chemical Industry Institute of Toxicology (CIIT) has this characteristic, but so do the National Coal Policy Project and the Twin Cities Metropolitan Council. Each of these organizations has been able to diagnose problems ahead of crisis, thereby obviating the need for adversary action and to a considerable degree avoiding politicization.

The Chemical Industry Institute of Toxicology

In 1974 corporate executives in the chemical industry began to recognize the size and complexity of moral, political, and economic problems posed by the toxicity of their products. The discovery by producers that exposure to vinyl chloride monomer (VCM) was causally related to certain forms of cancer, and the bitter controversy over how VCM would be controlled, provided gory evidence of what might lie ahead as other commodity chemicals were studied. Quite clearly the products could be dangerous. But the scale of the problem was so great, the technical knowledge so limited, the cost of testing so high, and the cost of protecting against hazard so astronomical that time and resources would be required to deal with it. On the other hand, the political inflammability of the issue was enormous. There was virtually no chance that the EPA or OSHA would be allowed to move slowly.

The chemical companies — Love Canal and kepone notwithstanding — had a remarkable record of concern for the hazards of their products and processes. Leading companies had laboratories focusing on safety and pollution before the Second World War. There was, therefore, basic sympathy with the goal of protecting the public's interest. But the VCM experience, as well as some of the claims of "public interest" groups, indicated that if things went wrong whole portions of the industry could be shut down quite unjustifiably. The industry did not think it in the public interest to cease manufacturing products whose hazards were manageable. The problems were that (1) the industry was suspect, (2) the costs of testing the thousands of existing products was very high, and (3) the people trained to test the products for industry or government were very scarce. CIIT was an ingenious response to all three problems.

In 1982 CIIT provided a solution to fundamental problems — the absence of needed toxicological knowledge and of less costly screening processes, and the dearth of trained toxicologists. Given what was perceived as the inevitable and in some instances appropriate intervention of the federal government, the challenge was to keep the process of developing standards for the thousands of chemicals produced as sensible and economic as possible. The industry's ingenuity was reflected in its ability to create an institution with (1) the technical strength that technocratic managers in government and business would respect and (2) the obvious autonomy that provided a clear basis for a claim to political legitimacy.

The latter accomplishment represents a major victory, for one of the greatest problems with any collaboration of public and private technocrats is that the venture will appear "captured" by narrow or even venal interests. The point is perfectly expressed by one author who made a comparative survey of the British, French, and Italian experience with their versions of central planning. Having noted that one leading authority, Andrew Shonfield, thought very highly of long-term cooperation among French technocrats, he commented, "Referring to the pioneering effort of French planning in this field in the fifties, Shonfield summed it up as a 'voluntary collusion between senior civil servants and senior managers,' producing, as he saw it, a 'conspiracy in the public interest' although whether and why it is in the public interest he seems to take for granted.''[17]

Virtually any proposal for voluntary cooperation across traditional institutional lines poses this problem. *Whether* activity is in the public interest and *why* is at the heart of constitutional analysis. Shonfield ends in neglecting the threat posed by the French technocratic alliance. The central questions of government must never be taken for granted.

The National Coal Policy Project

The problems that this leads to are exemplified by the National Coal Policy Project (NCPP). The report of the project provides a useful summary of all but the passions involved.

> The National Coal Policy Project brought together leading individuals from industry and environmental groups to seek consensus and provide guidance on the important national policy issues related to the use of coal in an environmentally and economically acceptable manner. The participants in the Project demonstrated that a process, other than an adversarial one, can be used for resolving industry and environmental differences.
>
> While the participants are members of industry and environmental groups, they took part in the Project as individuals. Therefore, the recommendations contained in *Where We Agree,* the report of the National Coal Policy Project, are those which the individuals believe are workable, compatible with their personal beliefs, and in the national interest . . .
>
> Unlike many other coal studies, the Project did not attempt to forecast the expected or the desired future levels of coal production or use.
>
> . . . the two sides agreed that while such a forecast might be interesting in an academic sense, it was more important that the ground rules or criteria for using coal be determined . . .
>
> The National Coal Policy Project is also different from the many studies which have set out to develop a complete set of national policies.

Instead, the Project concentrated on those areas in which the production, transportation, and use of coal have resulted in conflict between industry and environmental groups.[18]

Some sense of the intensity of the process for those involved is provided by *Fortune*'s account. The instigator of the project, and the leader of the industry representation, was Gerry Decker of Dow Chemical. He described the first meeting, in January 1976, with some twenty representatives of ten major environmental groups as "the roughest meeting I had ever sat through." "When Decker explained his idea for adopting the 'rule of reason' to working out differences over coal, the environmentalists responded with skepticism and scorn befitting able practitioners in a litigious and Machiavellian age."[19]

But perseverance and skill prevailed. Sponsored by the Center for Strategic and International Studies at Georgetown University, the project moved forward and eventually published its extensive recommendations in two volumes entitled *Where We Agree*. Action, however, was a different matter. The political management system follows no "rules of reason." In 1981, the project's recommendations were the basis for two pending bills, one concerning the siting of power plants and the second regarding the technology of pollution abatement. By 1982 the bills were dead. More tangible accomplishments were the impact of NCPP proposals on the rules and practice of the Office of Strip Mining of the Department of the Interior, and the rules for cogenerated power of the Federal Energy Regulatory Commission.

Forums Are Not Always Benign

Before proceeding further along this path, it is important to recognize the many pitfalls. To begin, the tobacco industry's response to the health threat posed by cigarette smoking is at least as typical of an industry-level response to a problem as is CIIT or NCPP. If one takes the view that cigarettes are incontrovertibly a significant contributor to disease, then the work of the industry's research center has to be regarded as a form of vigorous and successful obstructionism, rather than a lower than federal response to a public problem.

Robert Miles's study of the industry provides a clear picture of this sort of response:

> The Surgeon General's Report marks what many industry observers would characterize as a primary unequivocal and direct threat to the legitimacy of the Big Six [cigarette companies] . . . The response of the Big Six was stepped-up sponsorship of the Tobacco Research Council and its research studies of major gatekeepers and institutions in the medical and scientific communities . . .
>
> Financial support of the Tobacco Research Council the year after the Surgeon General's Report almost doubled the total cumulative support that joint venture had received during the previous ten years of its existence; by 1975, its cumulative funding had reached a level that was almost seven times the level it had achieved on the eve of the publicized announcement in 1962 of the formation of the Surgeon General's advisory committee. But the Big Six did not rely totally on the research grants awarded by this formal joint venture.
>
> In addition, they pooled other resources to make special grants to particular institutions. For instance, in 1963 during the time the Federal Trade Commission (FTC) was formulating its proposal to require health warning labels on all cigarette packages and advertisements, the Big Six awarded an unrestricted research grant of $10 million (more than its total previous funding to the Tobacco Research Council) to the American Medical Association (AMA) . . . [Other grants followed to the AMA and distinguished medical schools. In 1973,] the Big Six announced that they not only had ". . . funded more scientific research on smoking and health problems than any other source, government or private," but that ". . . the tobacco industry is now providing more financial support for smoking and health research than all of the private health agencies combined . . ."[20]

Miles concludes that "both the pervasiveness and the timing of the research grants awarded to major medical centers and research organizations leaves little doubt that resource dependencies were being established that might in many subtle ways tend to co-opt the interests of important gatekeepers in the medical and scientific communities."[21]

This approach to a problem is not unique to any particular industry. But the attitude of companies toward public problems is critical as proposals for business cooperation with government are developed. What sort of behavior can we expect, problem solving like the CIIT or stonewalling like the Tobacco Research Council? Richard Vietor, a historian who has reviewed the widely used "industry advisory council" format, is not sanguine.

When President Richard M. Nixon established the National Industrial Pollution Control Council just two weeks before Earth Day, 1970, his stated purpose was to "encourage the business and industrial community to improve the quality of the environment." Operating at the height of environmentalism, the NIPCC had a tremendous potential for serving the public interest by applying business management skills and expertise to a serious national problem.

However, it did not achieve the goal, joining instead many other advisory councils. For half a century advisory councils have been criticized repeatedly by the Justice Department, Congress, the White House, and a host of reform-minded citizens. Criticisms include lack of accountability, monopolistic behavior, and undue influence over public policy.[22]

The problem highlighted by Vietor is that the group became deeply involved in the politics "of the 1972 campaign to the extent that of NIPCC's 224 individual members at least 102 are known to have contributed substantial amounts to Nixon's re-election campaign." Of thirteen illegal corporate contributions revealed by Senate investigation, five were by NIPCC members.[23]

Vietor concludes that NIPCC is atypical only in its considerable influence and lack of circumspection. The problem is endemic in committees set up by the president to temper criticism of unpopular programs. Although the overt charge to the committee may be to provide study and advice on an important economic problem, the inherent political function "transforms advisory groups into agents of self-interest."[24]

Setting Vietor's point in the framework for analysis developed above, we can conclude that the National Industrial Pollution Control

Council may well be a prototypical example of the politicized overlay group. Rather than operating as an intermediate-level forum for technocratically managed institutions, the NIPCC was chartered by the president to operate on a salient political problem using chief executives of *Fortune* 500 companies. If ever there was an example of elevating a problem to a political forum, the NIPCC would seem to be it.

There seems, in other words, to be evidence that the rather appealing overlay format is substantially dependent for its success on the specific origins of the institution in question, its structure and procedures, as well as the motives of its membership. Once created, the institute or commission or authority takes on a life of its own. It is legitimate because of the auspices of its creation, but it is not always accountable.

The nature of the problem varies. The National Coal Policy Project, the least permanent of the overlay groups discussed here, was attacked by environmentalists left out of the project. For example, the Environmental Policy Center, a lobbying group, in de facto alliance with the bureaucracy responsible for implementing the laws that had been reviewed by the project, criticized the project as illegitimate because it was "unrepresentative." One critic specifically attacked the use of arenas other than the Congress, the executive branch, and the courts to resolve public policy disputes. Since implementation of the project's recommendations was, in fact, subject to constitutional due process wherever it applied, it is hard to see why the procedure has been attacked except that the recommendations may not have been satisfactory to the groups not involved. Moreover, evidence suggests that precisely such due process could and did block implementation of many of the recommendations of the project. The project may have been more independent than some would have wanted, but conventional governmental process was able to control the result. My reading of the project's final report is that progress was possible only where technocratic organizations perceived the project's recommendations as sensible and adopted them directly. Otherwise it lacked the power to implement its recommendations into reality.

An opposite version of this problem is posed by the overlay organization that finds a way to become self-financing. Recognizing precisely the limitations that due process imposed, Robert Moses and his imitators adopted a form of organization that earned revenue. The revenues from early projects were then used to fund new projects well beyond any narrow interpretation of their legislated charter. As well, they complemented their financial strength by writing extensive administrative authority into bond indentures, which were then defended in courts by these executives and their financial sources as constitutionally protected contracts. With administrative control and funds assured, these executives pursued their objectives in a virtually unaccountable fashion until one or another political leader fought tenaciously enough over a period of years to reassert public control. Robert Moses summarized his view of the problems posed by unaccountable power quite directly and clearly: "If the end doesn't justify the means, what does?" and "Once you sink that first stake they'll never make you pull it up."[25]

As one who as a child enjoyed the beaches Moses built but grew up to regret the impact of his roads, I find that Moses' self-defense neatly reduces the scope of the problem we face: effectiveness and lack of immediate accountability are directly related. Create an organization that has the breadth of perspective and the resources to work on a problem, and you create an organization that will offend or abuse a minority. That it proceeds legitimately may not be sufficient restraint if its powers permit it for long periods of time to override the constitutional protection provided fragmented minorities. Or, phrased as another law of forums, "Create an effective forum, and to some degree you have an unaccountable one."

Interestingly, the problem has a private counterpart. It is now well understood that major corporations are owned by shareholders but controlled by professional managers. As share ownership has diffused, these managers have also become unaccountable in all but the most extreme circumstances of economic failure. Decades can pass and an entrenched core group can continue to control substantial assets, despite a dismal economic record. The recent wave of hostile take-overs is the first reassertion of the market's power to hold a management accountable for the use of assets under its control. Generally, it is hard to dislodge the management of a self-financed organization, be it a backward copper company or a turnpike authority.

The problem, then, is the misuse of power that is intentionally freed from close political restraint. One answer that has the potential for serving a modern need is "sunshine," or the relatively complete disclosure of an organization's actions.

Disclosure as a Control

The basic idea of sunshine is to rely on the norms of society for protection against abuses by an institution's technocratic managers. Sunshine — the opening of decision-making processes and records to public scrutiny — provides latent politicization. If the press, or opponents of some move, are dissatisfied with the behavior of an organization, sunshine provides access to the data required to mount a grounded critique.

The approach has a considerable history in the United States, going back at least as far as Charles Francis Adams's use of disclosure to regulate pricing by the railroads of Massachusetts. More recently, Alfred Kahn, Jr., became an enthusiastic proponent of sunshine while chairman of the Civil Aeronautics Board. In his view, the process improved not only the legitimacy and accountability of the regulatory process but also its efficiency and effectiveness. The performance against technocratic criteria was enhanced by the deadlines inherent in publicized meetings and the incentive for thorough preparation that public exposure to review provided.

It is, of course, one thing to support sunshine when the chairman of a commission has an agenda that includes the wish to limit the impact of his considerable statutory authority on an industry he believes would benefit from deregulation. As well, the commission's proceedings are still a decision-making process, not a negotiation. It would be another thing to use sunshine to hold less structured forums accountable.

John T. Dunlop has pointed out that "each group that is party to negotiation and to an agreement has diverse internal interests, and an internal consensus or formal approval by each party is required to permit the consummation of a negotiated agreement. A great deal of the negotiations process is devoted subtly to communications about internal priorities and reactions to various proposals and counter-proposals."[26]

He goes on to point out that since parties to a negotiation often begin the process with large or extreme initial positions that give nothing away or involve no compromise or trading of internal positions, reaching an agreement then involves a change in position such that some initial goals are abandoned. Because it is necessary to explain the concessions made in terms that make sense to constituencies represented, and because that process at a minimum must go on in the language of those represented rather than of those with whom the deal has been struck, Dunlop notes that "negotiations are not fruitfully conducted in public, in the press or media."

On the other hand, it is quite possible for a neutral party of high public credibility to be present at the negotiation. This can be a government official or a private individual of appropriate stature and reputation. A surrogate for sunshine, this kind of presence can lend an aura of legitimacy to a process otherwise devoid of even apparent authority. But it does not solve the fundamental problem of control.

Accountable or Effective?

We can consider the problem before us in terms of the accompanying table. There are a number of institutions or types of organization available for the resolution of conflicts in the development and execution of policy. These are listed on the left in rough order of decreasing accountability to the political process and responsiveness to political forces. But these institutions can also be evaluated in terms of their contribution to effectiveness and efficiency in the resolution of substantive problems. It would seem that as one descends the table, effectiveness increases.

Institutions Arranged by Accountability and Effectiveness

Example	Accountability to Those Who Are Not Members	Ability to Produce Goods & Services Efficiently
Congress	High	Low
The courts	High	Low
A new executive agency	Relatively high (New underfunded agencies are often politically responsive and inefficient.)	Relatively low
An independent agency (e.g., the Civil Aeronautics Board)	Relatively high (but less responsive than nonindependent)	High, within narrow limits of character and alternatives provided by constituency
An advisory commission authorized by Congress (e.g., the New England River Basins Commission)	Medium	High for analysis and negotiation within limits of budget and scope
An independent institute funded by foundations (e.g., the National Coal Policy Project)	Medium	Good for negotiation and study. Limited for action.
An independent institute funded by companies (e.g., the Chemical Industry Institute of Toxicology)	Limited	Good for action within narrow limits of charter

An old executive agency (e.g., the Forest Service)	May be very effective serving a narrow constituency	
A public authority (e.g., the Port Authority of New York and New Jersey)	Low	Good for study and action limited by revenue base of authority and charter
A private company	Low	Good for study and action limited by revenue base

The dilemma is clear. The contradictions implicit in the administrative requirements of efficiency on the one hand and accountability on the other are fundamental. We are stymied. As a matter of logic or architecture there is no way of designing structure or procedure that can be relied on to satisfy the dual economic and political test.

Nonetheless, the same diagnosis provides a powerful argument for timely voluntarism. What cannot be guaranteed by law or logic can often be achieved by informed, temperate, and persistent efforts to invent solutions of policy and structure that meet the needs of a region or an industry. Almost inevitably, to be successful such an effort must begin before a problem has been politicized and, even more important, before it has been elevated to the national political arena.

Early efforts to manage an issue voluntarily help to reduce the range of issues with which the one in question is interwoven. Border management does link immigration, drug control, and southwestern and northeastern politics, but it need not involve civil service reform and the Panama Canal. Certainly one wants to keep issues to be managed out of the entangling web of presidential politics.

But the fundamental virtue of early discussion is that it provides immediate acknowledgment of the existence of a potential community of interest. Those with stakes can be "included in." When labor and management form a joint committee, or a group of towns forms a district commission, or environmentalists and energy users organize a project, a great barrier is surmounted. The legitimacy of opposing viewpoints is acknowledged along with the potential value of study, negotiation, and cooperative action.

Once community of interest is accepted, it is possible to exploit some of the attributes of the Japanese system. Local consensus can replace contract, and the costly adversary process can be relegated to the smaller number of instances where comity has broken down.

The word *local* should be emphasized. The United States is and will long remain a highly heterogeneous society. It makes no sense to seek a national consensus on most substantive issues as long as there are so many fundamental bases for disagreement. We are not Sweden — a population of eight million with common geography, culture, and history. Nor are we Japan, with family as a basis for political organization.

But in smaller — overlay — groupings we can find areas of interest that reward efforts to negotiate. To begin, those who are "included in" have some reason to make the agreement work. As at Texas Instruments, the organization will be unclear and each member will have overlapping responsibilities. But a recognition of somewhat larger interests that balance competitive stakes may be facilitated. The potential benefits of negotiation should be apparent despite more confused structure. Especially important, the costs of continued fragmentation to individual units should be clearer. The 1980 election can be interpreted to mean that many groups in the United States have recognized that piecemeal attempts to solve problems in the federal arena have in fact reduced our ability to invent coherent local solutions.

Another less obvious value of overlay groupings is that they may permit business executives to contribute as managers and problem solvers rather than amateur politicians. Irving S. Shapiro, the former chairman of E. I. du Pont de Nemours & Co., has noted that "Businessmen have a unique ability to develop facts and analyze alternatives. They have an obligation to bring these talents to bear in solving the nation's problems."[27] It is easy to discount Shapiro's point, but probably wrong. Over time the managerial community's habits of problem solving and orderly action can be an important resource.

The Search for Global Answers

There are many who would see well-intentioned formation of overlapping voluntary coalitions to be a fragile foundation for the improvement of a society. Both Lodge in his exposition of a new American ideology and Vogel in his celebration of the Japanese see the need for something far more embracing. For historical and demographic reasons, however, the chances of a national consensus are slight. At least in the short run, action is necessary and possible in more obviously tractable areas. The western slope of the Rockies does not seem to have the water required for all desired uses, and the existing treaty is not satisfactory to the states where the water rises. The old industrial areas of western Pennsylvania and the northern tier of Ohio, as well as Michigan, Indiana, and Illinois, need resuscitation. Fishing, recreation, mining, and defense interests must be reconciled in ocean treaty negotiations. Cable television, word processing, and fiber optics promise a revolution in communication that threatens AT&T's $80 billion fixed investment and the mountainous debt that financed it. The eastern railroads need reorganization.

The list is long and important. It will not go away. Nor is it adequate to abandon these problems to the states and business under the ideological banner of free markets and Federalism. The problems were elevated to Washington precisely because they involved conflicts that could not be treated easily in local forums. To the extent that the elevation took place in the 1960s it was likely to have been entwined in the Great Society — "aimed at cradle-to-grave security, income transfer, elimination of poverty, pervasive regulation"[28] — which we learned later did not work and could not be afforded. That set of programs needs dismantling. But we must move forward, not back to a past that never was.

Great Society programs failed for a wide variety of reasons. Some were poorly drafted. Some imposed symmetry on local activity where there was none. Some appear to have undermined the motivation of individuals. Others interfered with the ability of the society to create the wealth needed to pay for the quality of life the programs were to deliver. And others did not fail — except to achieve aspirations that had been raised to unrealistic heights.

But the programs shared, more or less, a profound and common flaw. They presumed that there existed a process for handling conflict among local interests that could be designed at the center. Even where the goal was "local participation" the design of the form was "top down." The White House and its executives' arms were engaged in an effort to manage what Madison and Hamilton had designed to be unmanageable.

Rather than take the time to encourage the invention of intermediate overlays that met the needs of local situations, our political leadership strayed where even the most successful corporate executives feared to tread. They reached down to intervene in the detailed functioning of technocratic organizations. In doing so, they ran into the law of forums — they had to either create new local forums to do the substantive work or politicize existing forums.

Under political time constraints they sought rapid change in the most complex situations, whereas corporate executives allow a decade in vastly more simple settings. A young lawyer by the name of Liebman returned to Harvard Law School's faculty from two years of battles in the Lindsay administration and pronounced Liebman's Law — "All reorganizations don't work."

But the metropolitan experiment in Minnesota has worked. The post–World War II joint venture to clean up Pittsburgh also worked, and the evidence of that effort and others cited above points to a fascinating conclusion. Many problems have rough substantive boundaries. Metropolitan areas, rivers, coal mining basins, and industries define natural groupings of activity that benefit from cooperative study and analysis in the sense that community of interest can be established and analyzed around tangible issues with practical consequences. In such settings the politics of action are somewhat simpler, since choices are more specific. The Minnesota legislature did not approve an academic's vision. They dealt — in increments — with a steadily more capable reality supported by a coalition of wide-ranging interest groups.

The evidence is that there is enormous room in American life for overlay organizations generated from the bottom up and then made legitimate and more effective by higher-level government. Even so vast an issue as trade policy can be dealt with, if the interests of those with stakes are recognized and adequate overlays are created so that both technocratic and political needs are met. In order to develop a sensible set of industry positions, as well as congressional support for the eventual outcome of the Tokyo round negotiations of changes in the General Agreement on Tariffs and Trade, special trade representative Robert Strauss and his deputies Alonzo McDonald and Alan Wolfe built a network of industry committees and close congressional liaison. Partially freed from the press and the separation of powers by the Trade Act of 1979,[29] Strauss's staff was able to manage a complex series of discussions with industries affected by the trade negotiations and our trading partners in a manner that satisfied Congress as to the process if not all the outcomes. It is an elegant example of what can be done.

But we have to want it. The key multinational trade negotiations personnel were moved elsewhere and the structure allowed to atrophy soon after the Tokyo round was completed. Indeed, it is discouraging that both the administration that saved the Tokyo round and made it a potential success and the U.S. business community concerned with the invasion of imports and our ability to export made no special effort to preserve the structure and procedure put in place. The fact is, most people concerned with the consequences probably do not know that anything has happened.

This unhappy surmise has a crucial place when we turn from

diagnosis and broad prescription to action. We cannot hope to have sensible negotiation or invent and preserve overlay organizations if our technocratic managers and politicians are ignorant. We need business and other local units of our society to generate and take part in overlay organizations and upper-level government to encourage and make legitimate this activity, but neither can happen until the participants and those who report on them in the media develop both an understanding of why it is necessary and a willingness to contribute.

The Way to Intermediate Solutions

Education

Not surprisingly, the first recommendation of an academic author is a call for education. Those in business, in government, in the academic disciplines that advise them, and in the media that report on them all require a crash course in how things work. A wide variety of approaches is consistent with the present argument and makes sense. Summer seminars for judges have been developed; why not for reporters, editors, and public- and private-sector managers? But the scope of the effort must be wide. There must be commitment to the idea that local-level managers shape national policy. Plant managers, district directors, and police chiefs must have a working sense of how the United States and its principal economic competitors are organized to manage themselves and compete, how companies compete, and how cities work.

On-line education is also valuable. The Business Roundtable is thought of as a lobby. But for the men who built it, the learning accomplished by involving one hundred fifty chief executives in national political life was a primary objective. The participation of government executives in comparable cross-government exercises should be encouraged as well. Some of the thinking behind the Senior Executive Service is congruent with this notion.[30] On the other hand, some designers of learning for these managers still seem to think of even high-level civil servants as functionaries. The key to our analysis is that top-level managements deal with abstractions except in the choice of personnel. It is the operating managers who make the outcomes we call policy.

Overlay Forums

At the same time that education proceeds, we must learn to value and encourage the creation of overlay forums. This can happen in a number of ways. To begin, the successes are worth hearing about, although there is a terrible risk that our uninformed media will treat something like CIIT or the Multinational Trade Mechanism as "news," to be first hyped, then debunked, then embroiled in "controversy," and then forgotten.

Whether or not the media get it right, we ought to have a series of comparable published studies of the many sorts of commissions, institutes, committees, and projects. This would be a sensible task for schools of administration to carry out and for foundations to fund.

Next, there ought to be a bias on the part of the federal government to deal with such larger groups. On a trade issue, for example, the special trade representative should make a practice of encouraging the development of industry positions. These will be of varying quality and varying fairness to industry participants. But, and this is the point, no satisfactory position is likely to be developed and implemented without such an industry effort. In Germany and Japan, our two principal industrial competitors, such institutions are a critical part of the economic policy process.

In the same way, cross-agency efforts at cooperation should be supported. It is probably too much to expect Congress to rationalize its committee structure to fit some modestly coherent framework, but it helps Congress coordinate its activity if the executive branch can indicate where coordinated planning and budgeting would be useful.

A more ambitious proposal would expand the scope of the Trade Mechanism, empowering it to study and make proposals concerning domestic industrial issues as well as international trade. With skillful leadership, the mechanism might again be considered a natural forum for cooperation among working levels (basic forums) in the White House.

Free the Managers

If our companies are going to take part in significant efforts to manage through overlaying organizations, then two significant adjustments in the law may be necessary.

First, we probably have to give up the myth that ownership of shares of common stock of a widely held company is the same thing as ownership of a company, in the sense that ownership conveys a right to manage. A company using its resources to support activities such as CIIT should not have to concern itself with what Wall Street will think. If we wish corporate management to take a more long-term comprehensive view, then we should not leave them vulnerable to whims of brokers seeking transaction fees who pretend that fictions such as quarterly earnings per share have any fundamental meaning. Some have taken this further, noting that such a shift will also necessitate a more powerful, managerial board of directors.

Second, we need to adjust the antitrust laws so that cooperative efforts that meet whatever new tests we create for disclosure and accountability are not subject to prosecution. What one part of the federal system encourages must not be blocked by nineteenth-century politics.

Learning to Manage the New Roles

Finally, business needs to think through the implication of a pattern of behavior in which the corporation is engaged in several potentially overlapping regional and industry activities. After all, their principal raison d'être will remain the creation of wealth through production of goods and services. Cooperation may generate public wealth or provide conditions conducive to successful enterprise, but technocratic managers still have demanding work to accomplish in their base organizations.

Very few companies have worked out to their satisfaction a way of organizing participation in nonbusiness activities. Certainly when chief executive officers such as Reginald Jones of General Electric indicate that they spend more than half their time in Washington, it means that they have not figured out how to organize the work involved so that it can be delegated. At the very least it raises questions of the "who's minding the store?" variety. But more perplexing is the problem of what chief executive officers of multinationals should do when each of a dozen countries wants half their time. What research has been done suggests that this is a central question to be faced in the organization of the corporate office.

In addition to encouraging overlays, the federal government has to develop its ability to hold them accountable. For while it makes sense to devolve responsibility for technocratic management to local units more able to do the work, such delegation becomes abdication without both the information that will permit control and organizations with the capability to act on negative signals.

In this respect sunshine can be put to good use. There is much that the office of the president can do to organize and disseminate information. If it is understood that the federal executive is not trying to manage the outcome but rather is seeking to monitor the process by which outcomes are developed, then there is a good chance that we can make considerable progress on a number of local fronts. This turn of events would be doubly happy. Not only would we enjoy the benefits of local solutions but also our federal government would be that much freer to deal with those conflicts and challenges that are the "great and national objects" of our society.

10 Who Leads?

THE DESIGNER of a new house was meeting with the planning council of an English village, seeking the required permits for construction. "You can't have the pipes in the walls like that," said one council member. "If you do, you can't get at them when they freeze."

There is much in the discussion of organizations in America that follows this logic. The premises are from an era that preceded central heating. But just as they may influence construction in Great Britain, they influence policy and behavior in the United States.

In 1958 Edward S. Mason wrote an important critique of the philosophical base of the enterprise system in the United States under the title "The Apologetics of Managerialism."[1] Reflecting the theoretical and ideological premises of economists, he noted that because large firms were not perfectly competitive, it followed that their powers were at least partially unconstrained by the market. The discretion that this gave management was irresponsible power in the important sense that the managers were not clearly accountable in the use of their capabilities.

Much of the discussion of corporate activity continues in this vein. There is an almost desperate desire on the part of the intellectual community to confine firms to a world of Newtonian mechanics where natural laws would permit close predictions of their behavior. When these laws are found absent, then a search develops for voluntary codes or government reviews that will somehow keep big companies "responsible." But the way in which "responsibility" is imposed often politicizes the corporation.

The argument of this book points in a different direction. Large, technocratically managed organizations need no apologetic. They are, like the sun rising in the east, inevitable in a world seeking a high material standard of living. The legitimacy of such organizations must be grounded in their *performance*. They have no inherent political status. They are tools used by all modern industrial societies.

If a large, technocratically managed unit appears to perform poorly, inquiry into the causes should be made by the board of directors responsible for the unit. Perhaps it is the wrong organization for the job. Perhaps top management should be changed. Perhaps the task is impossible. But partially unaccountable performance is a fact of life in large organizations. No matter how "tightly" managed a company, there is always activity about which top management knows nothing. Attempts in response to performance problems to impose comprehensive accountability can only politicize a technocratic unit.

The clearest example of this phenomenon, because it is so extreme, was Mao's Great Leap Forward. Writing in 1970 of administrative arrangements in China, Ezra Vogel described them as "politicized bureaucracy."

> A very high level of political commitment is expected of everyone in the bureaucracy . . .
> The demands which can be placed on cadres go far beyond performance of special tasks . . . They are expected to perform almost any work that might be assigned them.
> The burst of political activities and the pressures generated within the bureaucracy are disruptive of ordinary routine procedures . . .
> Since for political reasons the concern for competence has been diluted, competence cannot be evaluated on strictly universalistic criteria.[2]

That the attempt to impose embracing political tests on all activity has slowed China's economic development is now acknowledged by the Chinese. A petrochemical plant has its own logic that is dictated by neither Karl Marx nor Adam Smith. It cannot be politicized, only designed, sited, and managed more or less well. Whether China can overcome its heritage of a feudal past, Russian engineering education, and Maoist thought as fast as its internal politics requires is another question.

But if large technocratic organizations are not efficient or effective when politicized, it remains true that a very large political audience is interested in corporate performance across a long list of dimensions. A study sponsored by the closest thing we have in the United States to a forum of big businesses, the Business Roundtable, lists twelve:

(1) Marketplace Performance, (2) Profit, (3) Financial Reporting, (4) Public Disclosure, (5) Legal and Ethical Behavior, (6) Quality of Working Life, (7) Employee Citizenship Rights, (8) Health, Safety, and the Environment, (9) Technological Innovation, (10) Political Participation, (11) Social Performance, and (12) Executive Compensation and Perquisites.[3]

How should we reconcile the very real need to examine corporate performance with the equally real costs associated with political interference in technocratic management? It is fair to say that I have no comprehensive answer and that I am extremely suspicious of arguments that pretend to.

We are not smart enough to make big central solutions work. Fortunately, we do not have the education and experience appropriate. And our Constitution poses a fundamental obstacle. Earlier, the political/technocratic framework was used to make this argument in detail. Summarized in the analysis of forums, we have seen that in the United States virtually anything that is centralized is politicized.

The principal consequence of politicization in economic affairs is protectionism. Political coalition building requires a kind of equity that defeats the selectivity in resource allocation, organization, and reward required for good technocratic performance. Consistent with this analysis, it was argued that lower-level, intermediate forums of industry or region have demonstrated the most potential.

This line of argument points toward a need for educated understanding on the part of those who evaluate and interpret business and government performance. As we seek to invent new mechanisms for the cooperative balancing of competitive interests, perhaps the most important proposition to remember is that political and technocratic systems are both different and valuable.

The Wisdom of Difference

In an era when *equality* has achieved a meaning almost synonymous with *equity,* when even androgyny is celebrated by some as a wave of the future, it is probably dangerous to suggest that it is good that political management systems and technocratic management systems are so very different. But in a way that is the most important conclusion of this book.

The genius of the constitutional fathers is that they anticipated and valued the diversity of U.S. society at the same time that they distrusted the ability of any central technocratic structures to manage the affairs of the society. Hence they sought to provide the potential for strong political leadership of the country side by side with unfettered management of technocratic institutions.

Global economic interdependence has shattered many of the premises on which the argument for unfettered technocracy rested, but a central state technocracy is avoidable if we can recognize that altered circumstances have changed the desirable, or tolerable, balance between competition and cooperation. There must be emphasis on the duties of free citizens and institutions toward each other as well as on their individual rights. A great deal of progress can be made if political and technocratic managers, along with the rest of us, come to understand and appreciate the characteristics and the value to society of the two systems.

The Virtues of Technocracy and the Vicious Circle of False Expectations

Technocratic managerial institutions are good for achieving efficient and effective performance. They can also be remarkably rewarding places to work.

Trouble develops either when the institution performs poorly against its own goals, as when a company loses a share of the market to competitors and experiences losses, or when society's expectations for performance shift and the goals of the organization do not, as in the instances when the Corps of Engineers ignored environmental concerns during the early 1970s.

There are two kinds of reaction to such situations, one helpful and the other harmful. It is useful to consider first the analogy with humans. When a person has a fever or behaves strangely he or she will often seek a doctor voluntarily. Usually health is restored. The cycle experienced is benevolent. But sometimes the sequence is less positive. A person is depressed because of some family problem. Performance at work suffers. At work the problem is poorly diagnosed. Behavior is misinterpreted and the reaction of superiors and peers is to criticize and exert pressure. Depression increases, followed by drinking. Performance further deteriorates. Alcoholism may follow, along with severe antisocial behavior. Social pressure can then become enormous and the individual may simply break down. Or, following a violent act, the person may be imprisoned. The cycle is one of vicious deterioration. The only way out is to introduce the seriously sick person to a hospital environment, where various kinds of support and treatment can be provided. Often health can be restored.

The exact same cycles can help or hurt technocratic institutions. When a business's profits decline, bells ring all over the system. If it is part of a larger corporation, superiors immediately inquire. Corporate specialists and outside consultants may be assigned to help out. Eventually new managers may be brought in. The same sequence would occur in an independent company, except that if new management were required it might take longer.

But sometimes a business performs in ways the society finds unacceptable. For example, in the late-nineteenth-century United States, small merchants and farmers believed themselves exploited by the pricing practices of the railroads. Eventually the Interstate Commerce Commission was established to set prices and conditions of business. These prices provided inadequate funds to cover depreciation. Many roadbeds deteriorated.

After bitter strikes, railroad unions were recognized and wages and working conditions were regulated by contract. New forms of transportation emerged: cars, trucks, modern barges, and even airplanes. The mail and an increasing proportion of passengers and freight shifted to seek lower prices or better services.

With prices fixed, capital condition deteriorated, and labor cost fixed, the railroads found themselves unable to respond. Railroads that sought to drop unprofitable services were denied the ability. Those that sought to raise prices where competition permitted were frustrated. Those that sought to cut cost or price were often blocked. Yet competitive pressure steadily increased. Between 1950 and 1970 the railroads in the northeastern quarter of the United States more or less collapsed.

The cycle can be observed in many of our sick industries:

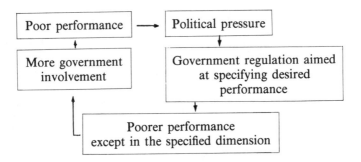

The same cycle afflicts government institutions such as cities and the U.S. Postal Service.

New York City achieved great wealth as a liberal center of trade located where there was a superb harbor at the mouth of a key river/canal route into the interior. Later its importance continued as a rail terminal, a corporate management center, and the world capital of finance and communication. It developed schools, services, and cultural institutions worthy of its wealth. But the decline of New England commerce left the city less central geographically and the growth of the West left New York on the periphery. Technology permitted the decentralization of finance and corporate management. Law firms and advertising companies moved to join their clients. At the same time, the interstate highway program opened the suburbs; the developing states of the Southeast drove the poor off the farms; and the resultant tremendous demographic shift in New York City raised costs and lowered the tax base.

At no time was the reaction of the city government to deal with the causes of the problem — the decline in competitive performance of the city and hence its wealth. Instead, the symptoms were attacked through rent control, high levels of welfare payments, and high wage costs extracted by strong public unions. These, in turn, hastened the economic decline of the city.

Today the problems of our sick cities are as difficult as the rehabilitation of alcoholic criminals. There are no broad remedies. They need to be fixed neighborhood by neighborhood. The economic base that permits Boston to retrieve itself is different from the one available in Cleveland. Federal funds or other facilitating activity may be required, but money chasing ideas has seldom solved a substantive problem. It takes effectiveness and efficiency in the local circumstance — in short, good technocratic managerial systems.

Local coalitions such as the one in postwar Pittsburgh between Democratic mayor David Lawrence and Republican financier Richard King Mellon will be required to organize and manage the many individual efforts required. But creating such coalitions requires political management so that technocratic management can function.

The Virtues of Political Systems and the
Vicious Circle of False Expectations

The problem of rehabilitation in the nation's cities is as good a setting in which to exemplify the virtue of political management as one can find. For surely, no one believes that there is any simple centrally prescribable remedy. Mayor David Lawrence's work in post–World War II Pittsburgh is a good example of the tasks that must be performed. In 1945 one couldn't see the daytime sky in Pittsburgh through the smoke, and streetlights were often required late in the morning. The downtown area was a commercial wasteland of dumps and empty warehouses. Slums linked the downtown to the more prosperous midtown.

What needed to be done involved planning: new office buildings, housing, and civic buildings had to be constructed, slums cleared, highways built, and parking provided. Most important, an ordinance affecting the entire region had to be passed that would provide for the control of smoke. In an America that is now more concerned with the excesses of the Environmental Protection Agency than its achievements, it is hard to imagine what smoke control meant in "Steel City" in 1945.

David Lawrence and Richard King Mellon did what great politicians do. They communicated to others their understanding that life in the city could be markedly better. They led the creation of an intermediate-level forum — the Allegheny Conference — to study the many interrelated substantive problems at the appropriate level. And then they used their political skill to phrase the problems facing the city so that their respective constituencies would see the solutions being proposed as responsive to their needs.

Lawrence had to explain to the poor and the union workers why "clean coal" was worth the price, and why tax abatements for a parking garage were not a rip-off. While issues were still in doubt, he had to use his political machine to win elections. Mellon had to bring along suspicious conservative business leaders, and when the Pennsylvania Railroad lobbied the legislature to block the regional smoke-control ordinance, he had to remind them that the Mellon interests and their friends could use other railroads. But in the context of Lawrence's and Mellon's political leadership, technocratic institutions loaned money, built buildings, and planned highways, making a reality of the opportunity politics had created. Performance by the technocratically managed institutions was key.

For political systems, the vicious circle begins when expectations are excessive so that performance falls short. The gap between expectation and result leads to two negative consequences. (1) The next campaign is likely to be fought on the grounds that performance was poor rather than that expectations were unrealistic. (2) At the same time, disenchantment with the poor performance of the "government" may express itself in low pay and low status for government workers, which can lead to precisely the poor performance imagined. These specific failures are likely to lower expectations somewhat, unless a political battle raises them again to unrealistic levels. This vicious circle is illustrated below.

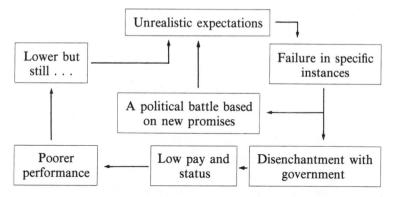

Perhaps the clearest and most unfortunate example of this vicious circle is provided by the battle of the Reagan budget. In 1982, the U.S. economy could be diagnosed as:[4]

1. Consuming too much energy, which requires expensive imported oil.

2. Uncompetitive with other nations in certain important industries.
3. Burdened by regulations, social expenditure (for example, indexed Social Security), and a defense budget that it cannot afford.

Unrealistic expectations are fostered by the positions on either side. President Reagan has argued that tax cuts that favor consumers will restore the competitiveness of industry so that we can afford higher defense budgets and existing — indexed — Social Security. The liberal Democrats have argued that we can afford what we consume if we just tax business a bit more and spend less on defense. Poor performance is inevitable as long as the three fundamental problems are not addressed.

Both parties have further contributed to the problem by campaigning *against the government* that they sought to lead *and* continuing salary ceilings that make it impossible to distinguish among levels of rank or performance and generally ensure that government service is an economic sacrifice to those with marketable skills.

The weakness of politics is that it takes strength — either a good organization or high credibility — to argue for delayed gratification. In the contemporary politics of sixty-second television blurbs, there is no such thing as investment. Present costs are too tangible, and future benefits too ephermeral, when compared with painless remedies. We tell the alcoholic that he can keep on drinking as long as he votes right.

We cannot revitalize America, or reindustrialize the North Central states, or rehabilitate New York City. One cannot rebuild abstractions, and America, the North Central states, and New York are abstractions — just as General Electric is an abstraction at the corporate level. In order to repair our technocratic institutions we have to invest, and to invest requires some slowing of current consumption. This requires political leadership willing to make both possible.

General Electric makes air conditioners in Louisville. Whether the U.S. balance of trade improves a bit and whether employment in Louisville picks up depends on how well the department in charge of that business copes with what many observers expect will be a Japanese attack on the U.S. market. As with Pittsburgh, an effective response may require a coalition of political and technocratic managers. If the department has a plan, then perhaps the corporation can fund it. If GE has a plan to invest, then perhaps our country can cooperate by pressuring the Japanese to hold back. But if there is no plan, why should our political managers invest scarce time and resources?

Even where, as in autos, the entire industry is sick, with major consequences for the economy, it makes no sense for political managers to invest if there is no plan. Today General Motors, Ford, and Chrysler have unreconciled competing interests. Intervention by the government, if it helps one, will hurt the others or help them less. Without a plan there is no legitimacy in such unequal treatment.

Who Leads?

Where does the plan come from? Given our reluctance in the United States to create central planning capability, and given the constitutional obstacles were we willing, the answer would seem to be "the idea may come from a leader, but the plan comes from below, from the technocratic institutions that have competence to make plans." Since most of the time it would appear that the problems or opportunities we face exceed the capabilities of individual institutions, we must look for plans from associations of institutions. Since these often lack accountability and legitimacy, we must look to political managers who recognize the value of these new forums for cooperation to provide the legitimacy. It just does not make sense to suggest, as some are now doing, that what we need is a central institution for making industrial policy. It can't be done from the center of the U.S. government.

The answer, then, is the same that one gets when studying decision making in large organizations. When you ask "Who decides?" you find out that someone — high or low — has asked a good question. The question was embraced by the leaders. The specialists studied and proposed, the generalists reviewed and approved. Individuals are very important, but the organization "decides."

Who leads? If by that question we mean "Who does the real planning?" we must mean our technocratically managed institutions. A substantive question is best studied and managed by the mix of specialists and generalists those institutions provide. The plan for a better steel industry can come only from the steel companies working as a coalition. Jobs in the auto industry can be recovered economically only by successful design, manufacturing, and marketing. If instead we mean "Who provides direction by shaping the issues?" we must mean our politically managed institutions. It is the role of central leadership to encourage coherence in subunit action by clarifying goals. On a case-by-case basis, the political leadership must seek out and respond to industry initiative. A positive face must be put on the cooperative efforts we now require. If, in fact, we mean "Who initiates?" then it doesn't matter, for we need both kinds of institutions to make progress.

On the other hand, if we mean "Who controls?" we have a very difficult problem. "Logical" efforts to build a system that gives technocratic control to the central government destroy democracy. Legislative effort to provide control through the courts can paralyze our technocratic systems. And reliance on self-control yields what appears to be an illogical, inequitable mix of good and bad performance. Yet self-control and cooperation by individuals and organizations is the best hope we have for maintaining high technocratic performance and political freedom. Our worst problems develop when some company or group pushes its power to the limits, exploiting its freedom to capture for itself benefits that ought to be shared, and imposing costs on others without consideration.

The specification that emerges from this analysis is for a mix of political and technocratic management. Whatever the issue, as long as it exceeds the boundaries of existing institutions that have the ability to influence its resolution there is a need to call attention to the problem in a way that permits those involved in action to see that common interest may be gained by discussion.

Inevitably there follows a series of meetings among the leaders of the various institutions that might be involved in the problem. Formally or not, intermediate-level organizations get created. Choice of the participants is vital — those who must lose in any imaginable attractive solution must be left out to be dealt with later. For example, an industry faced with great overcapacity will have to deal with the problem of the inefficient units, but the president of a company with only inefficient units is almost certainly a poor member of the core group.

Two kinds of work then must follow. The substantive content of the issue under consideration must be studied — either by the staffs of the cooperating institutions or by a new institution, such as the Allegheny Conference, put together to provide new data and analysis. But the distribution of costs and benefits of proposed action needs to be negotiated. It is here that we can tell the difference between benign and malign forums. In malign associations the strong exploit their position to take advantage of the weak, rather than impose a solution that makes sense for all. But in any situation, participants in a resolution of a problem are likely to be less than satisfied with their share of the redivided pie. It is human to compare and typical to see another as the winner of a cooperative effort.

It follows directly that responsible technocratic management must include the notion of "political followership." Given the relative autonomy of our corporations and public agencies, we cannot survive in our decentralized political format if technocratic managers subvert all political leaders of whom they disapprove or all negotiations that they fail to win. Once an adequate process of study and debate has produced a consensus in some intermediate forum, an unhappy participant institution must not veto by withdrawal. The only alternative is a centrally formulated mandate.

Back to Earth

At the Harvard Business School we often turn during class from the sort of cosmic questions considered above and ask, "What difference does it make tomorrow morning?" In the present instance the answers to that question are unsettling but challenging and potentially encouraging. They have the quality of Pogo's famous dictum — "We have met the enemy, and it is us." If one believes in self-improvement, that is not a depressing diagnosis. The unsettling implications of this book are:

1. Most of what is written about the work of business and government is next to useless for interpreting what is actually happening if read or viewed on a piece-by-piece basis.
2. Partly as a consequence, but also because large organizations are complex, a diagnosis that provides an adequate basis for action is hard to carry out. For one thing, you have to find out about people and organization, not just technical and economic substance.
3. Finally, knowing "what needs to be done" is the beginning rather than the end of constructing a plan of action. Action involves a sequence of steps that must be carried out effectively — usually by others.
4. The comforting finding is that we have in our technocratically and politically managed institutions the variety and strength to achieve a high level of material progress in a uniquely free, if somewhat chaotic, society.

Information: It's Hard to Get

Most of us like to be informed, to have a sense of what is going on in the world. We are especially interested in knowing about the things that affect our lives.

The argument of this book suggests that becoming informed is a very demanding task. The problem we have seen is that the media report events, and they do this in a way that is likely to exaggerate the adversarial aspects of the story. The real difficulty, however, is that most "events" are outcomes of the interaction among several organizations. Some may be managed with technocratic managerial systems, some with political managerial systems. In any case, we need to know a good deal about the history of the organizations and their members to make sense of what is going on.

For both technocratic and political managers, events have a context that is past, present, and future. They cannot ignore how they act in terms of past commitments, because that will be read by others as a clear signal as to how they might behave in the future. The present always is only a move. It is not the game.

Diagnosis: It's Usually Complex

This being said, there are differences in the web of past and future for technocrats and politicians. To understand political managers it is important to seek out the sources of their support, both in electoral circumstances and in work roles. A member of Congress, for example, needs and gives help both in order to get elected and in order to achieve legislative objectives. He or she is thus constrained and made effective by both sorts of commitments. As we have seen in the border management case, the political linkage among substantively disconnected issues can be extensive. Consequently, the putting together of pieces of the puzzle to get a sense for the shape of the whole takes time and effort. One has to track both the issues and the players.

In contrast to the wide range of an issue's political context, its technocratic context is likely to be *deep* — in the sense that key judgments have been and will be made by specialists at low levels in the organization. It is hard to know where these specialists are coming from unless you know their previous experience, their job, the information they have, and how they are measured and rewarded.

In other words, a good diagnosis must focus on the contract, career lines, organization, information, and strategy of the key institutions or players engaged in action. To understand what's going on, you need to know the rules of the game and the roles of the players.

This information is usually difficult to obtain. But good guesses can help, because individuals often run to stereotypes. The manager trained as an engineer is more likely to understand the operating problems of his or her business than the financial ones. For this reason he or she is more likely to know what problems a regulation will cause *but also* to be able to think of a technical way to resolve the problem. The lawyer-executive is more likely to think in terms of how to block the regulation or circumvent its intent.

I believe it is no accident that Reginald Jones, trained as a chartered accountant, made his remarkable record as a leader of General Electric with (1) a key divestiture, (2) the building of systems and development of executives, and (3) a major acquisition. In contrast, his successor, Jack Welch — trained as a Ph.D. in physics — has moved quickly to rebuild GE's high-technology capability.

Similarly, legislators can be expected to look after the interests of their constituencies. If they don't, they are likely to face defeat in the next election. One can also expect a legislator or executive to work with his party.

For example, one question of interest in the spring of 1982 was the deregulation of natural gas. As customers, business and home owners alike were interested. But there was also speculation that deregulation, coupled with a windfall profits tax, would be used to help the budget deficit. Superficial analysis would suggest that there would be strong support for this move from the explorers for and producers of natural gas. Since it was also a plank of the Reagan platform, deregulation could be expected.

A little homework, however, would have revealed that under previous legislation only "deep gas" recovered from below 15,000 feet was deregulated. The tremendous premium to be earned in the exploration and production of deep gas attracted drillers and petroleum companies, *and* the tax shelter attracted doctors, dentists, and lawyers from all over the country. Hundreds of millions of dollars were invested. If all gas were to have been deregulated, the price of deep gas would *drop* to some average for all gas. This made prediction of government policy more dicey, since these were all important supporters of Mr. Reagan and the legislators. Offhand one might have predicted "no early action," since those most immediately concerned were likely to be hurt and had the ability to express their views. More analysis might reveal still more complexity, but a first cut at careful diagnosis would have revealed a very subtle problem.

In other words, for purposes of diagnosis a crude model that at least takes into account the factors that will be at work is better than no model at all. It's like fishing; a bent pin on a string and some bacon is better than staring at the water. Over time one learns about fish and gets better equipment.

Action: If It's Important It Takes Time

Once the complexity of organizations in action is understood, a sense for how long it takes to get anything important done should follow. There are almost never quick fixes. Because policy must be spelled out in detail before it is implemented, and because implementation takes organized effort, the work of technocratic managerial systems is needed. That means that those involved must be committed to the objectives of the policy. Obtaining commitment involves education, persuasion, and endless discussion before consensus provides a basis for action.

Planning action, therefore, means planning a sequence of steps by which those involved are educated, persuaded, and eventually committed to a program that has been articulated in detail. For both the participant and the observer the key questions are: Who is doing the detail? When? Why? What are the intended consequences? What are the likely consequences? What if something goes wrong? Has there ever been a successful example of this sort of thing? What is the track record of the leaders?

If one asks these questions it is easy to despair, but pessimism is the wrong response. A realistic view of what is required for effective action ought to have precisely the effects we are seeking:

- Expectations will be lowered.
- It should be natural to avoid the federal arena, since its record is so weak.
- Respect for managers in either system who have accomplished anything should be enhanced.

Informed skeptical respect for political and technocratic managers is a proper basis for progress in a democratic society.

Two Faces of Management

The startling, optimistic finding here is that we have in the United States the means to move forward, if we are willing both to face up to the difficulty of the task and to behave somewhat more cooperatively. We are not blocked by ideology, a police state, or poverty of resources from dealing with the questions that face us. The institutional fragmentation that protects our freedom is an impediment to coherent action only if the managers play their roles badly. Both political and technocratic types of systems must be handled well.

Competent managerial performance certainly means dealing effectively with one's own institution. But given that the issues that plague us cross the lines of individual or local institutions, much time has to be spent working at intermediate levels in one forum or another. In these fluid settings both faces of management must interact. Businessmen and bureaucrats must be sensitive to the nuances of constituent pressure bearing on the political representatives with whom they are negotiating. Politicians must recognize the limits of economic, technical, and administrative feasibility that constrain the technocratic managers who must implement whatever is agreed. Narrow diagnosis of the stakes involved, just as well as excessive build-up of aspiration, can doom any undertaking. And there must be faith in the eventual success of the negotiating process.

The implication for practicing managers ought to be clear. Regardless of the setting one must be relatively skilled at both sorts of management. Or, put somewhat differently, all institutions require the ability to manage the political and technocratic aspects of their systems. That may sound as if politicization is unavoidable, but it merely acknowledges in a different way the phenomenon with which Mason was concerned when he sought an apologetic for managerialism. Management work always involves some redistribution of costs and benefits to individuals and institutions not directly linked to the manager by a technocratic contract. Acknowledging that there is political content to one's actions is the beginning of managerial responsibility. After taking that large step it is only a small step to develop the necessary skill for taking part in the political process at intermediate levels. At that point due process protects society rather effectively.

The reverse side of this coin is a responsibility that managers of political systems must acknowledge. The wealth they would redistribute must be created. The institutions that generate wealth are also difficult to manage. Asking them to use their resources to achieve social objectives that are too expensive to pay for with taxes is inexcusable. It is irresponsible to use the legitimacy provided by political position to demand similar accountability of those facing a different type of management task. It is also irresponsible as well as unhelpful to criticize publicly those with whom one is negotiating. Intermediate-level forums can work only if the members abide by the norms of cooperative behavior.

If they do, if we can find numerous institutions to work on the problems of cities, regions, and industries, then without an East Asian consensus or a European social democracy we can still have an effective federal government under our existing Constitution. By recognizing and accepting the tensions that exist as we strive for efficiency and legitimacy, effectiveness and accountability, we can continue with the uniquely American approach to management of a free society.

Notes
Index

Notes

1. The Wisdom of Difference

1. *Employment and Earnings* (Washington, D.C.: U.S. Bureau of Labor Statistics, March 1982), Table B-2, p. 56.

2. Milton Friedman, *Essays in Positive Economics* (Chicago: University of Chicago Press, 1953).

3. Thomas McCraw, "Rethinking the Trust Question," in *Regulation in Perspective,* ed. Thomas McCraw (Cambridge: Harvard Graduate School of Business Administration, 1981).

2. Technocratic Management versus Political Management

1. Chester Barnard, *The Functions of the Executive* (Cambridge: Harvard University Press, 1939).

2. David Halberstam, *The Best and the Brightest* (New York: Random House, 1969), p. 436.

3. James Thomson, "How Could Vietnam Happen?" *Atlantic Monthly,* April 1968, p. 49 and passim.

4. Kenneth R. Andrews, *The Concept of Corporate Strategy* (Homewood, Ill.: Dow Jones–Irwin, 1971), pp. 26–41.

5. Alfred Sloan, Jr., *My Years with General Motors* (New York: Doubleday, 1964).

6. Joseph Bower and Peggy Wiehl, "William D. Ruckelshaus and the Environmental Protection Agency" (Cambridge: Harvard Graduate School of Business Administration, 1974), p. 14.

7. For an example of the problems that can arise, see "The Individual and the Corporation" (Cambridge: Harvard Graduate School of Business Administration, 1967).

8. Jules Jacob Schwartz, "The Decision to Innovate" (D.B.A. diss., Harvard University, 1973).

9. See, for example, John Dean, *Blind Ambition: The White House Years* (New York: Simon & Schuster, 1976), and Rowland Evans and Robert Novak, *Lyndon B. Johnson: The Exercise of Power* (New York: New American Library, 1966).

10. Richard E. Neustadt, *Presidential Power: The Politics of Leadership from F.D.R. to Carter* (New York: John Wiley & Sons, 1980), pp. 64–79.

11. Michael Blumenthal, "Candid Reflections of a Businessman in Washington," *Fortune,* January 29, 1979, pp. 36–40.

12. Stephen B. Hitchner, "The Federal Trade Commission (B)" (Cambridge: Harvard Graduate School of Business Administration, 1976).

13. See, for example, John P. Kotter, *The General Managers* (New York: The Free Press, 1982).

14. Hugh Heclo, *A Government of Strangers: Executive Politics in Washington* (Washington, D.C.: Brookings Institution, 1977).

15. David Halberstam, "The Very Expensive Education of McGeorge Bundy," *Harper's,* July 1969, pp. 21–41.

16. Carl Kaysen, review of *My Years with General Motors* by Alfred Sloan, Jr., *The New Republic,* February 29, 1964.

17. Blanche Bernstein, "Why Did We Mess Up the Food Stamp Program for So Long?" *City Almanac,* February 1981, p. 1.

3. Technocratic Management Systems at Work

1. Thomas A. Wise, "The 5 Billion Dollar Decision," *Fortune* (September 1966), p. 118. The summary here is based on Wise's two-part account, "IBM's $5,000,000,000 Gamble" (reprinted for the Harvard Graduate School of Business Administration).

2. These excerpts are from the IBM booklet *About Your Company.*

3. This account is drawn from Joseph L. Bower, David Condliffe, and Martine Y. Van der Poel, "New York State Department of Correctional Services (A), (B), and (C)" (Cambridge: Harvard Graduate School of Business Administration, 1979).

4. Exhibits in the trial of Memorex versus IBM.

5. Ibid.

6. Certainly the extended family and the tribe were among the earliest forms of stable, "technocratic" organizations, although the contract, career system structure, information, rewards, and strategy were implicit.

7. One could argue that school systems are not managed with technocratic systems as defined in chapter 2 because their budgets are voted annually. On the other hand, in many states the local community whose taxes support the school could not vote less money than the school committee had budgeted. In the "good old 1950s and 1960s" discussed here, the committee was seldom a brake in spending; hence schools might well be regarded as technocracies.

8. Carnegie Council on Policy Studies in Higher Education, *Three Thousand Futures: The Next Twenty Years for Higher Education* (San Francisco: Jossey-Bass, 1980).

4. Political Management Systems at Work

1. This account is drawn from Joseph L. Bower, Mark H. Moore, and Martine Y. Van der Poel, "Border Management" (Cambridge: Harvard Graduate School of Business Administration, 1979).

2. *New York Times,* November 19, 1978.

3. Peter J. Schuylen, "Chrysler Goes for Broke," *Fortune,* June 19, 1978, pp. 54–58.

4. In 1978, Chrysler was the nation's thirteenth largest defense contractor, with $743 million in military business.

5. Ironically, but quite consistent with this analysis, it would be the government's antitrust case against IBM that would make the company's plans for the future open to public scrutiny.

5. The President: Top Manager of a Political System

1. W. Ross Ashby, *Design for a Brain: The Origin of Adaptive Behavior,* 2d ed., rev. (London: John Wiley & Sons, 1960), p. 7.

2. See, for example, Lester Thurow, *The Zero-Sum Society: Distribution and the Possibilities for Economic Change* (New York: Basic Books, 1980).

3. A graphic example of the point was provided by a Third World participant in my class at Harvard's Advanced Management Program. He noted that while the United States and Europe might have trouble with wage or price controls, income policy in his country tended to elicit cooperation from all firms. "The government has a very cold, damp room for people who want to debate the policy."

4. Sir Edmund Dell, *Political Responsibility and Industry* (London: George Allen & Unwin, 1973), p. 29.

5. This description and the quotations are drawn from Richard Vancil, "Texas Instruments Incorporated Management Systems: 1972" (Cambridge: Harvard Graduate School of Business Administration, 1972).

6. In fact, during the spring of 1982, Texas Instruments gave up parts of this system, reportedly in order to cope with problems of management succession and a desire to increase emphasis on

decentrally managed marketing versus centrally driven technology. See *Business Week,* July 5, 1982, p. 77.

7. A. Lee Fritchler and Bernard H. Ross, *Business Regulation and Government Decision Making* (Cambridge: Winthrop Publishers, 1980).

8. William Greider, "The Education of David Stockman," *Atlantic Monthly,* December 1981, pp. 27–40.

9. Francis J. Aguilar and Richard Hamermesh, "General Electric: Strategic Position 1981" (Cambridge: Harvard Graduate School of Business Administration, 1981), p. 12.

10. Ibid., p. 14.

11. Philip B. Heymann and Randy I. Bellows, "A Failing Agency: The Federal Trade Commission" (Cambridge: John F. Kennedy School of Government, 1976), pp. 22–23.

12. Bower and Wiehl, "William D. Ruckelshaus," p. 14.

13. Ibid.

14. Quoted in *New York Times,* March 13, 1970.

6. Contact Sport: When Political and Technocratic Managers Meet

1. Often the problems are most acute with very new agencies. The worst "horror stories" of the last decade were from the *early* years of the Occupational Safety and Health Administration and the Environmental Protection Agency.

2. Heclo, *A Government of Strangers,* pp. 104–105.

3. The chemical company whose epidemiological research first revealed the carcinogenic properties of vinyl chloride was attacked as a killer of workers soon after it reported its findings to the government.

4. Obviously they fail often. Certainly the U.S. automobile company managements did not all use their resources effectively in the 1970s.

5. It happens in the private sector, but as with the San Jose laboratory at IBM that was punished for its freewheeling behavior, it can be worked on and is illegitimate.

6. Philip Selznick, *Leadership in Administration: A Sociological Interpretation* (New York: Harper & Row, 1957), p. 63.

7. This account is drawn entirely from George C. Lodge and Joseph L. Badaracco, "The Barnwell Nuclear Fuel Plant (A) & (B)" (Cambridge: Harvard Graduate School of Business Administration, 1979).

8. From the author's notes.

9. This material is based substantially on George C. Lodge and Efrem Sigel, "Consolidated Edison (A)" (Cambridge: Harvard Graduate School of Business Administration, 1972), and George C. Lodge and Clifford E. Darden, "Consolidated Edison Company of New York (B)" (Cambridge: Harvard Graduate School of Business Administration, 1968).

10. George C. Lodge, *The New American Ideology* (New York: Alfred A. Knopf, 1975), pp. 212–213.

11. The independent agency authorized to regulate public utilities. Its powers include approving rate schedules for gas, steam, and electricity, and approving utility stock and bond offerings.

12. Irving Kristol, "The Mugging of Con Ed," *Wall Street Journal,* May 17, 1974.

13. "Elliott Levitas — The Man Behind the Legislative Veto," *National Journal,* July 8, 1978, p. 1090.

14. "Reining in the Regulators," *Dun's Review,* February 1980, p. 80.

15. J. Ronald Fox and Lynne O. Cabot, "The Work of a Regulatory Agency: The EPA and Toxic Substances" (Cambridge: Harvard Graduate School of Business Administration), p. 1.

16. Ibid.

17. "Legal Affairs," *Business Week,* November 5, 1979, p. 165.

18. Robert A. Caro, *The Power Broker: Robert Moses and the Fall of New York* (New York: Alfred A. Knopf, 1974).

19. Daniel Bell, *The Coming of Post-Industrial Society: A Venture in Social Planning* (New York: Basic Books, 1973), pp. 365–366.

7. Managers and Wizards

1. Donald T. Regan, "Peas, People and the Economy" in *Toward a New U.S. Industrial Policy?* ed. Michael L. Wachter and Susan M. Wachter (Philadelphia: University of Pennsylvania Press, 1981), p. 18.

2. Lane Kirkland, "Labor's View of Reindustrializing America," in *Toward a New U.S. Industrial Policy?* p. 34.

3. George C. Eads, "The Political Experience in Allocating Investment: Lessons from the United States and Elsewhere," in *Toward a New U.S. Industrial Policy?* p. 454.

4. Thornton Bradshaw.

5. Raymond A. Bauer, Ithiel de Sola Pool, and Lewis Anthony Dexter, *American Business and Public Policy: The Politics of Foreign Trade* (New York: Atherton Press, 1963).

6. The Business Roundtable is an association of the chief executive officers of major corporations. See, for example, Thomas K. McCraw, "The Business Roundtable" (Cambridge: Harvard Graduate School of Business Administration, 1979).

7. This is a "planning system" argument worthy of Galbraith's attention, but it is not yet effectively articulated in the public debate.

8. Bernstein, "The Food Stamp Program," p. 11.

9. David C. Dufour et al., "Management Study of the Rural Electric Cooperatives" (M.B.A. diss., Harvard University, 1967), p. 210.

10. One of Ronald Reagan's triumphs is to have made his "program" locally significant. Individual voters appear to view Reagan's efforts as worth their personal support even at personal economic cost.

11. Daniel M. Kasper and Kathryn Harrigan, "Senator Kennedy and the CAB" (Cambridge: Harvard Graduate School of Business Administration, 1977), p. 11.

12. Ibid.

13. Some economists are concerned with the problem. Richard Caves has used the *Journal of Economic Literature* to chastise his colleagues for ignoring just the sort of empirical work noted above. And Harvey Liebenstein has been harsh in his criticism. For example, in his "Microeconomics and X-efficiency Theory" published in the November 1980 issue of *The Public Interest,* he commented that "if there is no general erosion of confidence in conventional microeconomics, there ought to be. We do not know the extent of our knowledge. We have a theory that appears to apply to everything."

14. Michael Hunt, "Competitive Performance in Major Home Appliance Industry" (Ph.D. diss., Harvard University, 1972).

15. Michael E. Porter, *Competitive Strategy: Techniques for Analyzing Industries and Competitors* (New York: The Free Press, 1980).

16. John Whitehead, managing partner, Goldman Sachs, interview with the author in the spring of 1980.

8. The United States Isn't a Company, It's Not Even Japan

1. Jack Friedman, "A Planned U.S. Economy in the U.S.?" *New York Times,* May 18, 1975.

2. Thornton Bradshaw, "My Case for National Planning," *Fortune,* February 1977, p. 100.

3. "Text of President's Message Seeking Reorganization of Executive Office," *New York Times,* March 13, 1970.

4. *New York Times,* March 13, 1970.

5. "Shultz to Head New Budget Unit," *New York Times,* June 11, 1970.

6. "U.S. Agencies Get Order: Join McNamara's Band," *Business Week,* November 13, 1965, p. 185.

7. Robert S. McNamara, *The Essence of Security: Reflections in the Office* (New York: Harper & Row, 1968), pp. 109–110.

8. Alexander Hamilton, "The Federalist No. 1," in *The People Shall Judge: Readings in the Formulation of American Policy,* vol. 1 (Chicago: University of Chicago Press, 1949), p. 288.

9. James Madison, "The Federalist No. 10," in *The People Shall Judge,* pp. 292–293.

10. Ibid.

11. Ibid.

12. James Madison, "The Federalist No. 51," in *The People Shall Judge,* p. 312.

13. The summary of Japanese history through 1946 that follows draws extensively on Bruce Scott, John W. Rosenblum, and Audrey T. Sproat, *Case Studies in Political Economy: Japan 1854–1977* (Cambridge: Harvard Business School Division of Research, 1980).

14. George C. Lodge and Masatake Ushiro, "Note on Japanese Ideology" (Cambridge: Harvard Graduate School of Business Administration, 1973).

15. Ibid.

16. Ezra Vogel, *Japan as No. 1* (Cambridge: Harvard University Press, 1979), p. 27.

17. Lodge and Ushiro, "Note on Japanese Ideology," p. 4.

18. Ibid., p. 5.

19. Vogel, *Japan as No. 1,* pp. 238–244.

20. "How Japan Does It," *Time,* March 30, 1981, p. 58.

21. John T. Dunlop, ed., *Business and Public Policy* (Cambridge: Harvard Graduate School of Business Administration, 1980).

9. Small May Be Beautiful, but Local Works

1. Madison, "The Federalist No. 10," in *The People Shall Judge,* p. 293.

2. A high White House official interviewed by author, November 12, 1980.

3. The quotation is from Joseph A. Califano, Jr., *Governing America: An Insider's Report from the White House and the Cabinet* (New York: Simon & Schuster, 1981). The phrases at the end of the sentence are a close paraphrase of material in the same chapter.

4. See, for example, John T. Dunlop, "The Negotiation Alternative to Markets and Regulation," an unpublished working paper (1979).

5. Warren Christopher, "Diplomacy: The Neglected Imperative," in a folio of Christopher's speeches published in 1981 by O'Melveny & Myers, Los Angeles, p. 38.

6. Robert Reich, "Regulation by Confrontation or Negotiation," *Harvard Business Review,* May–June 1981.

7. "A Conversation with Fred Friendly," *Nieman Reports,* Summer 1981, pp. 3–5.

8. George C. Lodge, speech to the Program for Senior Managers in Government at the Harvard Business School, Summer 1979.

9. August 17, 1981. The August 1982 papers were similarly narrow in coverage.

10. Dunlop, *Business and Public Policy,* p. 105.

11. Ellis W. Hawley, "Herbert Hoover, the Commerce Secretariat, and the Vision of an 'Associative State' 1921–1928," *Journal of American History,* vol. 61, no. 1, June 1974.

12. Thomas McCraw, "With Consent of the Governed: SEC's Formative Years," *Journal of Policy Analysis and Management,* vol. 1, no. 3, 1982.

13. Note that multibusiness firms are really forums of basic units joined together to enjoy a variety of benefits. Those antitrusters who oppose conglomerates see them as malign (exploita-

tive) rather than benign (generating positive results internally) forums.

14. Remarks by F. J. Borch, May 1970 (recorded by one of the officers).

15. Annamarie Hawck Walsh, *The Public's Business* (Cambridge: MIT Press, 1978), pp. 97–98.

16. See, for example, John E. Vance, *Inside the Minnesota Experiment: A Personal Recollection of Planning and Development in the Twin Cities Metropolitan Area* (Minneapolis: University of Minnesota Press, 1977), and John J. Harrigan and William C. Johnson, *Governing the Twin Cities Region: The Metropolitan Council in Comparative Perspective* (Ontario: Burns & MacEachern, 1978).

17. Michael Watson, "A Comparative Evaluation of Planning Practice in the Liberal Democratic State," in *Planning, Politics, and Public Policy: The British, French and Italian Experience,* ed. Michael Watson and Jack Hayward (Cambridge: Cambridge University Press, 1975), pp. 460–461.

18. Francis X. Murray, *Where We Agree: Report of the National Coal Policy Project* (Boulder, Colo.: Westview Press, 1978), pp. 1–2.

19. Tom Alexander, "A Promising Try at Environmental Détente for Coal," *Fortune,* February 13, 1978, p. 100.

20. Robert Miles, *Coffin Nails and Corporate Strategies* (Englewood Cliffs, N.J.: Prentice-Hall, 1982), pp. 62–64.

21. Ibid., p. 65.

22. Richard H. K. Vietor, "NIPCC: The Advisory Council Approach" (Cambridge: Harvard Graduate School of Business Administration, 1979), p. 57. Reprinted from University of Washington, Graduate School of Business Administration, from *Journal of Contemporary Business,* Spring 1979.

23. Ibid., pp. 66–67.

24. Ibid., p. 68.

25. "Robert Moses, Builder of Road, Beach, Bridge and Housing Projects, Is Dead," *New York Times,* July 30, 1981.

26. Dunlop, "The Negotiations Alternative," August 29, 1979, draft of chapter 1, p. 10.

27. "Irving Shapiro," *Industry Week,* October 27, 1980, p. 5.

28. Felix Rohatyn, "America in the 1980s," *The Economist,* September 19, 1981, p. 38.

29. The act frees the special trade representative from sections of the Freedom of Information Act, but enables Congress to directly oversee the negotiating process. In turn, the act denies Congress the right to amend pieces of the negotiation after the agreement is concluded.

30. The Senior Executive Service is the cohort of high-level civil servants created by Jimmy Carter's Civil Service Reform Act of 1978.

10. Who Leads?

1. Edward Mason, "The Apologetics of Managerialism," *Journal of Business,* vol. 41, no. 1, January 1958.

2. Ezra Vogel, "Politicized Bureaucracy: Communist China," in *Frontiers of Development Administration,* ed. Fred W. Riggs (Durham, N.C.: Duke University Press, 1970).

3. Francis Steckmust, *Corporate Performance: The Key to Public Trust* (New York: McGraw-Hill, 1982), pp. 15–16.

4. See, for example, Richard Bolling and John Bowles, *America's Competitive Edge: How to Get Our Country Moving Again* (New York: McGraw-Hill, 1981).

Index

accountability: in political management, 44–45, 274; sunshine, 244–45; vs. effectiveness, 245–49; of technocratic management, 256–57
Adams, Charles Francis, 244
administrative skills, 23
administrative tools, 24–25
advisory commissions, accountability vs. effectiveness in, 246
advisory councils, 241–42; see also overlay organizations
Air Force, 123
airline industry, 185
air pollution, 154, 263–64
air traffic controllers' union, 101, 222
Allegheny Conference, 263, 268
Allied Chemical Corporation, 128–34
Allied-Gulf Nuclear Services (AGNS), 129
American Federation of Government Employees (AFGE), 73–74
American Motors, 137
Amtrak, 120
Andrews, Kenneth, 20
Animal and Plant Inspection Service, 69
antitrust legislation, 7, 8, 163, 182, 254
Arledge, Roone, 226
Ash, Roy, 199–200
Ashby, W. Ross, 86–87, 91
Ash Council, 127
Atomic Energy Commission, 128–33
Attica uprising, 54

automobile industry, 74–82, 136, 204; technocratic management in, 65–66; problems in, 117–18; and energy crisis, 136, 174; safety regulations, 186; and free trade, 189; see also Chrysler Corporation
autonomy, loss of, 163–64
AWACs sale, 101

balance of trade, Japanese vs. U.S., 195
Balog, James, 197
banking industry, 118–20; and Chrysler crisis, 135–36
Barnard, Chester, 15, 173
Barnwell, S.C., Allied Chemical plant, 129–34
Bell, Daniel, 164–65
Bernstein, Blanche, 43, 173
Blum, Barbara, 79
Bolling, Richard, 155
border management, 67–74, 82–85, 221, 247
Border Management Agency, 71
Boston Consulting Group, 183, 187
Boston Symphony Orchestra, 20
Bradshaw, Thornton, 197–98
Brazil, 118
Breyer, Stephen, 179
Brooks, Fred, 47, 48, 49, 53
Brooks, Jack, 74
budget, federal, 41–42; 264–65

Bureau of Alcohol, Tobacco and Firearms, 72
business: government and, 1–3; political attacks on, 6–9; use of technocratic and political management, 44–45; need for cooperation with government, 118–21; multidimensional organization in, 230–32; *see also* organizations; technocratic management
Business Roundtable, 252, 258
Business Week, 200

cabinet, 105–6; staff of, 108; independent authority of, 109–10; and industrial policy, 118
Cabot, Lynne O., 156
Califano, Joseph, 223
camera industry, 204
Camp David Mideast agreement, 222
capital, cost of, 192
careers in management, 33–35, 42
Carey, Hugh, 54, 58
Caro, Robert, 162–63
Carter, Jimmy, 31, 68, 70, 71, 73, 74, 80, 91, 101, 103, 105, 131–32, 133, 193, 222, 223
Castillo, Lionel, 74
Center for Disease Control, 69
Center for Strategic and International Studies, Georgetown University, 239
central planning, 235, 237–38, 266–68; *see also* Japan
Chandler, Alfred, Jr., 13–14, 90, 182
Chemical Industry Institute of Toxicology (CIIT), 231, 236–38, 253, 254
China, 257–58
Christensen, Roland, 198
Christopher, Warren, 224
Chrysler Corporation, 67, 74–82, 117–18, 120, 135–38, 143, 266
Citroën, 136
Civil Rights Acts, 163
civil service, 27, 32, 110, 125; reform of, 71, 73–74
Claybrook, Joan, 79, 127
Clean Air Act Amendments of 1970, 154
coal industry, 6, 238–39

collective bargaining, 224
Common Cause, 45
communication, negotiation and, 224–34
compensation in technocratic management, 27–28
competition, 192, 224–25; *see also* free market system
compromise, 18
computer industry, 47–53, 185
concentration, industry, 183
Congress, 13–14; in the federal process, 31–32, 97, 218; budget and, 41; political management, 81–83, 159; and cabinet, 106; technocratic management, 107–8, 159; and Chrysler crisis, 135; steel industry and, 142; legislative veto, 153–59; constituent representation, 175–79; local interests vs. national, 176–78; purchase of public goods, 185–86; reducing influence of, 220; accountability vs. effectiveness in, 246; *see also* federal government
Conrail, 120
consensus, local basis for, 228–32
Consolidated Edison of New York, 143–52
Constitution (U.S.), 198, 203, 258, 259, 274; and conflict between technocratic and political management, 113, 120–21, 166, 201–3, 218–20; and legislative veto, 154–55
consumer: cost to, 182–84; market defined by needs of, 184–85; purchase of public goods by, 185–86
consumption, need to reduce, 265
contract: models of, 27–33, 42; patronage and, 31–32; cronyism and, 31; duration of, 32; IBM, 51–53
Cook, Donald C., 149
cooperation, need for, 172; *see also* overlay organizations
corporate managers, careers of, 33–34; *see also* executives; technocratic management
corporations: ownership vs. management of, 243–44; accountability vs. effectiveness in, 247

Costle, Douglas, 158
Council of Economic Advisers, 140
courts, accountability vs. effectiveness in, 246
cronyism, 31
currency control, 194

Dean, John, 31
decentralized planning, 235–36; *see also* overlay organizations
Decker, Gerry, 239
defense spending, 5
deficit, federal, 4, 5, 160
Dell, Sir Edmund, 91
Democratic Party, 45
Democratic Study Group, 45
Department of Agriculture, 69
Department of Commerce, 139
Department of Defense, 123
Department of Education, 71
Department of Energy, 71
Department of Health, Education and Welfare, 69
Department of the Interior, 69, 119, 239
Department of Justice, 28–29, 72, 73, 80, 139
Department of Labor, 139
Department of Natural Resources, 71
Department of State, 69, 119, 139
Department of Transportation, 69, 77–79
Department of the Treasury, 72, 139
Digital Equipment Corporation, 21
Disaster Relief Agency, 71
disclosure rules, 39, 244–45, 255
Domestic Council, 199
Domestic Policy Staff, 140
Douglas, William O., 229
Drucker, Peter, 33
Drug Enforcement Administration, 68, 70
drug industry, 188
drug smuggling, 68
due process, 172, 242–43, 274
Dunlop, John T., 168, 216–17, 227–28, 245

Eads, George, 167–68
Eagleton, Thomas, 78–79
economic growth, slowdown of, 88, 160–61
economic models, 180–81, 190–91
economic policy: determining, 10–11, 15; presidency and, 88, 90–91; need for co-operation between government and business, 118–21; dangers of politicizing, 160–65; technocratic management view of, 169–75; political management view of, 175–79; economists' view of, 180–82; domestic, and international trade, 186–96; intervention vs. free trade, 189–91; redefining basis of, 194–96; technocratic criticism of U.S., 197–98; constitutional basis of U.S., 201–3; U.S. model vs. Japanese, 204–17; tripartite negotiations for, 216–17
economic problems in 1980s, 4, 88
economics: economic policy vs., 10–11; study of, 10–11, 15–16; language of, 168, 180–82, 191
economic theory, 180–82; cost to consumer, 182–84; consumer needs define the market, 184–85; purchase of public goods, 185–86; international markets in, 186–96; libertarian vs. liberal, 188–91; of investment, 191–93; revising classic terms of, 194
education system, 6, 13–14; technocratic management for, 63–65; shortcomings of U.S., 226–27
efficiency/effectiveness: in technocratic management, 44–45, 257–58, 273–74; vs. accountability, 245–49
ego-intensive goods, 184
Egypt, 222
Ehrlichman, John, 127
Eisenhower, Dwight, 31
Eizenstat, Stuart, 80
electricity industry, 143–53
energy conservation programs, 6, 101, 146–47, 151, 164, 193
Energy Research and Development Administration, 131, 133
entitlement programs, 160

Environmental Policy Center, 242
environmental protection, 236–39, 241–42; technocratic vs. political management of, 129–33; toxic waste, 156–58; *see also* pollution
Environmental Protection Agency (EPA), 24–25, 128–34, 236; and steel industry, 140–42; air pollution, 154; toxic wastes, 156–58
European Economic Community, 138–39
Evans, Robert, 47–49, 53
executive(s): work of, 17–25; executive core, 18–19; choosing a goal, 19–22; choosing executive core, 22–24; personal skills, 23, 24; choosing administrative tools, 24–25; careers of, 33–35
executive agencies, accountability vs. effectiveness in, 246, 247
Executive Office of the President, 70–71
Export-Import Bank, 134

fair division: focus vs., 121, 122; consequence of, 134–59; Chrysler crisis, 135–38; steel industry, 138–43; Con Edison, 143–53; concern for, 160–65
false expectations, vicious circle of, 261–62, 264–66
FBI, 28–29, 72
Federal Aviation Administration, 69
federal budget, 41–42, 264–65
Federal Constitutional Convention (1787), 190
Federal Energy Regulatory Commission, 239
federal government: policymaking and management, 97–104; political management in, 97–98; need for technocratic management, 99, 100, 102; the White House, 104–13; the cabinet, 105–6; state government and, 108; cooperation with business, 118–21; multiple roles of, 199; reviewed by technocratic management, 199–200; constitutional basis of, 218–20; growth of bureaucracy, 219–20; laws of forums, 220–24; as enabler or facilita-

tor, 229; and overlay forums, 253; *see also* Congress; government; presidency
Federalism, 218–20
Federalist (Hamilton/Madison), 201–2
Federal Power Commission, 144
Federal Trade Commission, 106–7, 183
Feighan, Michael, 29
Fiat, 136
Fish and Wildlife Service, 69, 234
focus, 121; incentives and, 124; *see also* strategy planning
food stamp program, 98–99, 173
Ford, Gerald, 105, 131, 157
Ford, Henry, II, 25
Ford Motor Co., 75, 81, 137, 235, 266
forums: laws of, 220–24; negotiation through local, 224–34; overlay, 253–254; *see also* overlay organizations
Fox, J. Ronald, 156
France, 235, 237–38
Fraser, Douglas, 80, 135
Freedom of Information Act, 39
free market system, 90–91; and steel industry; and international trade, 186–96
Friedman, Milton, 11
Friendly, Fred, 225–26, 227
Fritchler, Lee, 97

General Agreement on Tariffs and Trade, 251
General Electric, 184, 230, 265–66, 271
General Motors, 6, 22, 50, 65–66, 75, 80, 137, 235, 266
Germany, 134, 141, 235, 236, 253
Gilmartin, Roger, 149
goals: choosing, 19–22; strategy planning and resource allocation, 39–41, 43–44; purpose, focus, and incentives, 123–25; *see also* strategy planning
government: defining, 1–2; and business, 1–3, 7–9; careers in, 34; use of technocratic and political management, 44–45, 114–15; need for cooperation with business, 118–21; as banker, 119–20; as regulatory agency, 120; intervention vs.

free trade, 189–91; role for, in economic policy, 194–96; advisory councils, 241–42; *see also* federal government; presidency

Great Society, 160, 190, 249–50

Greider, William, 97

group interests, 4–5

Gulf Oil Company, 129

Haanstra, John, 48–49, 122

Haggerty, Pat, 92

Haldeman, H. R., 127

Hamilton, Alexander, 201, 203, 218

Hartke, Vance, 106–7

Hawley, Ellis, 229

Hays, Wayne, 177

Head, Howard, 21–22

Heclo, Hugh, 34, 111

Helms, Jesse, 177–78

heroin smuggling, 68

Hess, Stephen, 111

Heymann, Philip, 28–30, 38

hierarchical system, 30, 122–23

home appliances industry, 188

Honda, 187

Hong Kong, 5

Hoover, Herbert, 229

Hoover, J. Edgar, 18, 28, 29

House Agriculture, Rural Development and Related Agencies Subcommittee, 98

House Committee on Banking, Currency and Housing, 77

House Judiciary Committee, 73

House of Representatives, 218; *see also* Congress

Humphrey, George, 31

Hunt, Michael, 183, 184

Iacocca, Lee, 79, 118

IBM, 21, 22, 121, 122–23, 221; system/360 project, 46–53; technocratic management of, 46–53, 83–84; SPREAD, 48–49; self-description to employees, 51–53; Memorex vs., 59–60, 62

illegal aliens, number of, 68, 84

illegal immigration, 67–74, 84

Immigration and Naturalization Service (INS), 28–29, 68, 69–70, 73–74, 85

imports, 5–6; *see also* international trade

incentives, managed vs. bargained, 123–25

income distribution, 160–61

independent agencies, accountability vs. effectiveness in, 246

independent institutes, accountability vs. effectiveness in, 246

industrial policy, 2; control of, 7–8; dilemmas for, 118; need for cooperation between business and government, 118–21; politicization of, 125–53

industrial production, Japanese vs. U.S., 195

industry advisory councils, 241–42; *see also* overlay organizations

industry concentration, 183

inflation, 4, 160

information, technocratic vs. political model of, 37–39, 42–43, 269–70

innovation, role of, 195

interdepartmental task force, 70

interest rates, 4, 192

intermediate overlays. *See* overlay organizations

International Business Machines. *See* IBM

International Communication Agency, 71

international markets, 186–96

international trade, 90–91; steel industry and, 138–43; Japanese policies, 186–88

Interstate Commerce Commission, 261

investment: economic theories of, 191–93; to repair technocratic institutions, 265

irrigation projects, 120

Israel, 222

James, E. Pendleton, 31

Japan, 4, 5, 7, 20–21, 134, 235, 236, 253; industrial policy of, 118; automobile industry, 136–37; steel industry, 138–39, 141, 142; citrus-growing industry, 153; international trade policies of, 186–88;

Japan (*continued*)
TV dumping by, 186–87; motorcycle industry, 187; growth per annum, compared with U.S., 195; appeal of economic model of, 196–97; Ministry of International Trade and Industry (MITI), 196, 205, 212–13, 214; economic model of, 204–17; hierarchical society, 205; modernization in, 205–6; in 1950s, 207; in 1960s, 208; lifestyle in, 208–11; cooperation in, 211–13; role of government, 212, 213–14; Bank of Japan, 213–14; Ministry of Finance, 213, 214; 1973 austerity program, 214; dependent state of individuals in, 214–15; "costs and dangers" of system (Vogel), 215
Johnson, Lyndon B., 18, 31, 102, 104, 160, 200, 208
Jones, Reginald, 100, 143, 255, 271

Kahn, Alfred, Jr., 244
Kaysen, Carl, 39–40
Kelly, Cynthia, 157
Kennedy, John F., 104
Kirkland, Lane, 167
Knight, Frances, 28
Korea, 5, 118
Kristol, Irving, 150–51

La Guardia, Fiorello, 144
Landis, James, 229
Lawrence, David, 262–64
lawyers: in industrial policy, 7–8; as government managers, 34; exacerbating policymaking problems, 168, 175
leadership, 266–68
Learson, T. Vincent, 47, 48, 49, 58–59, 83, 122
legislation, as constraint to management, 172–73; *see also* antitrust legislation; regulations
legislative veto, 153–59
Levin, Carl, 80
Levitas, Elliott, 155
liberal approach to economics, 190–91

libertarian approach to economics, 188–91
Lindsay, John, 54
litigation, 225
local consensus, 228–32, 248
Lodge, George Cabot, 143–44, 171, 227, 249
loyalty in management, 27, 29–31
Luce, Charles F., 145, 147, 148, 149

MacArthur, Douglas, 207
McCraw, Thomas, 11, 182, 229
McDonald, Alonzo, 251
McGovern, George, 5
McIntyre, James, 72
McNamara, Robert, 123, 199, 200–201
Madison, James, 201–2, 218, 219
management: education in, 33, 252–53; ownership vs., 254; *see also* political management; technocratic management
managerial rights, 171–72
Mason, Edward S., 256
Meissner, Doris, 72
Mellon, Richard K., 262–64
Memorex, 59–63
Memorex v. International Business Machines Corporation, 7
merchant marine subsidy, 153
Mexico, 118; illegal emigration from, 67–74, 82–83, 84
Mezines, Basil, 32
Miles, Robert, 240
military policy, 91
mismanagement, politicization and, 162–65
Moses, Robert, 162–63, 243
motorcycle industry, 187
multidimensional organizations, 230–32
Multinational Trade Mechanism, 253, 254
municipal government, 108
Muskie, Edmund, 24, 79

National Coal Policy Project (NCPP), 231, 238–39, 242

National Conservative Political Action Committee (NCPAC), 176
National Economic Development Office (U.K.), 217
national economic policy. *See* economic policy
National Environmental Policy Act of 1970, 130
National Highway Traffic Safety Administration, 77, 79
National Industrial Pollution Control Council, 241–42
national interest, 137
National Oceanic and Atmospheric Administration, 2
National Treasury Employees Union, 73
natural gas deregulation, 271–72
Navy, 123
negotiation: through local forums, 224–34; disclosure of, 245; *see also* overlay organizations
Neustadt, Richard, 31, 50, 111, 115
New Economic Program, 178
New England River Basins Commission, 231, 233–34
news media, 168–69, 226–27, 253
New York City, 144, 145, 148–50, 262
New York State Department of Correctional Services, 53–59, 221
Nixon, Richard M., 24, 102, 104–5, 110, 127, 160, 199–200, 208, 241
nuclear power industry, 128–34, 145
Nuclear Regulatory Commission, 130, 133

obstructionism, 239–41
Occupational Safety and Health Administration (OSHA), 158, 236
Office of Drug Abuse Policy, 70–72
Office of Management and Budget, 67, 70, 72, 140, 199
Office of Strip Mining, 239
Office of Toxic Substances, 157
Office of the U.S. Trade Representative, 118, 139

Office of Water and Hazardous Materials, 157
oil industry, 5–6, 119
OPEC, 5
organizations: need for, 13–25; origins of, 14–15; theories of, 15; careers in, 16–17; foundations of, 16–17; work of executives in, 17–25; choosing a goal, 19–22; choosing core executives, 22–23; choosing administrative tools, 24–25; the contract, 27–33; structure of, 35–37, 42; information systems, 37–39; strategy formulation and resource allocation, 39–41, 43–44; disclosures, 244–45; accountability vs. effectiveness in, 245–49; *see also* overlay organizations
overlay organizations, 229–32, 248–49; examples of, 232–34; general principles of, 234–45; in CIIT, 236–38, 239; in National Coal Policy Project, 238–39, 242; obstructionism vs., 239–42; National Industrial Pollution Control Council, 241–42; self-financing, 243; global answers, 249–52; national problems and, 249; need for, 251–52; education in, 252–53; overlay forums, 253–54; ownership vs. management of companies, 254; accountability of, 255; delegation of tasks, 255; combining technocratic and political management, 268
ownership vs. management, 254

Panama Canal Treaty, 73–74
Pareto optimality, 180, 181
patronage system, 31–32
Patton, Boggs and Blow, 79
performance measures, 37–39; *see also* efficiency/effectiveness
personal skills, 23–24
Peterson, Robert, 179–80
Peugeot, 136
Piori, Emanuel, 49
Pittsburgh, 262–64
planning. *See* central planning; decentralized planning; strategy planning

Poland, 118
policymaking, federal, 97–104
political appointees, 115
political careers, 34–35, 92
political management: definition of, 3, 26; compared with technocratic management, 8–12, 25–45; need for organizations, 13–25; the contract in, 27–33, 42; cronyism, 31; patronage, 31–32; careers in, 33–35, 42; organizational structure in, 35–37, 42; information system in, 37–39, 42–43; resource allocation and strategy formulation, 39–41, 43–44; accountability as test of, 44–45, 274; at work, 67–85; U.S.-Mexican border management, 67–74; Chrysler crisis, 74–80, 135–38; general considerations of system, 81–84; in federal process, 97–104, 115; constitutional root of conflict with technocratic management, 113, 120–21; entrepreneurial solutions, 117, 122–123; winners vs. losers approach, 124–25; civil service and, 125; criticism of technocratic management, 126–27, 129–34; Allied Chemical case, 128–34; in steel industry crisis, 138–43; Con Edison case, 143–53; and legislative veto, 153–59; danger to economic policy, 160–65; slower economic growth and, 160–61; mismanagement and, 162–65; loss of autonomy and, 163–64; view of economic policy, 175–79; investment theory, 193; basis for cooperation with technocratic management, 194; constitutional foundation of, 201–3; laws of forums, 220–24; advisory councils, 241–42; sunshine, 244–45; protectionism and, 258–59; merits of difference from technocratic management, 259–60; virtues of, 263–66; vicious circle of false expectations, 264–66; shaping of issues by, 267; diagnosis of issues in, 270–71; proper blend with technocratic management, 273–74
political system (U.S.), 86–88; see also Congress; federal government; presidency

pollution: air, 154, 263–64; toxic waste, 156–57, 236–38
Port Authority of New York and New Jersey, 231, 232
Porter, Michael, 183
presidency, 70, 71; executive control in, 30–31; electoral campaigns, 37; demands of office, 86; as top management of political system, 86–113; responsibilities of office, 87–89; world situation and, 87–88; domestic economy and, 88–89; military policy, 91; managerial view of, 91–92; inability to manage federal system, 99–101; managerial responsibilities of, 101–2; delegation of responsibilities, 102–4; organizing the White House, 104–13; the cabinet, 105–11; technocratic management model of, 110; separation of powers, 110; conflict between technocratic and political needs, 111–12; comprehensive plans, lack of, 112–13; see also federal government
President's Advisory Committee on Executive Organization, 199
President's Reorganization Project, 70–72, 81, 84
Price, Don K., 10
prisons, technocratic management of, 53–59
product division organization, 230
profits in strategy formulation, 39–41
protectionism, 4, 90, 137–38, 142–43, 188–89, 206, 258–59
Proxmire, William, 81
public authority, accountability vs. effectiveness in, 247
public goods, purchase of, 185–86
Public Health Service, 69
public policy, 3
public school system, technocratic management of, 63–65
Public Service Commission of New York, 144, 146–47
punishments in organizations, 27–28
purpose: focus and, 121; incentives and, 123–25; see also goals; strategy planning

railroad industry, 261
Reagan, Ronald, 2, 5, 31, 91, 101, 105, 118, 125, 126, 134, 178, 193–94, 222, 223, 264–65
recession, 4, 6
Regan, Donald T., 166–67
regionalism (U.S.), 4
regulations, 129–33
Rehabilitation Act of 1974, 38
Reischauer, Edwin O., 213
Renault, 137
resource allocation, 7; in technocratic vs. political management, 39–41, 43–44; focus vs. fair division, 121; national interest and, 137
rewards in organizations, 27–28
Riccardo, John, 75–76, 79–80, 81, 117–18
Riegle, Donald, Jr., 80
risk: technocratic management and, 174–75; investment and, 192–93
Rockefeller, Nelson, 54
Rodino, Peter, 73
Romney, George, 20
Roosevelt, Franklin D., 112–13
Ruckelshaus, William, 24–25, 109
Rural Electrification Administration, 174–75
Russo-Japanese War, 206

Saab, 136
Schultze, Charles L., 200
Schwartz, Abba, 28
Schweitzer, Glenn, 157
science policy, 10
Sears, Roebuck and Company, 184
selectivity in strategy formulation, 39–40
Selznick, Philip, 124
Senate, 218; see also Congress
Senior Executive Service, 253
separation of powers, 110, 203, 218–19
Shapiro, Irving S., 248–49
Shepard, Mark, 92
Shonfield, Andrew, 237–38
Shultz, George P., 200
Singapore, 5
Sino-Japanese War, 206

Skinner, B. F., 175
Sloan, Alfred, Jr., 22, 40
Sneath, William, 23
Social Security system, 193–94
South Korea, 5, 118
special-interest groups, 161
specialization, need for, 172
state government, 108, 119
steel industry, 189, 235–36; crisis in, 89–90, 118; fair division in, 138–43
Stigler, George, 183
Stockman, David, 97–98
strategic business units, 229–31
strategy planning: technocratic vs. political 39–41, 43–44; focus vs. fair division, 121; leadership and, 266–68; lengthy process of, 272–73
Strauss, Robert, 251
structure, hierarchy as solution to problem of, 122–23
sunshine, 244–45, 255
surpluses, distribution of, 27
Switzerland, 90, 184, 188

Taiwan, 5
tax cuts, 15
technocratic management: definition of, 3, 26; compared with political management, 8–12, 25–45; need for organizations, 13–25; the contract in, 27–37, 42; compensation system in, 27–28; careers in, 33–35, 42; organizational structure, 35–37, 42; information system in, 37–39, 42–43; resource allocation and strategy formulation, 39–41, 43–44, 266–68; efficiency test of, 44–45, 257–58; at work, 46–66; IBM case, 46–53; NY state prison case, 53–59; Memorex case, 59–63; general considerations of system, 63–66; applied to public school system, 63–66; applied to automobile industry, 65–66; view of problems to be handled by presidency, 91–92; Texas Instruments case, 92–97; lack of, in federal process, 97–104; need for, in federal process, 99–100, 102; hierarchy and loy-

technocratic management (*continued*)
alty in, 108–9; constitutional root of conflict with political management, 113, 120–21; working with politicians, 115–17, 125–28; focus vs. fair division, 121; hierarchical solution to structure problem, 122–23; managed incentives, 123–25; politicization of, 125–65; criticism of political management, 126–27, 129–34; and legislative veto, 153–59; dangers of politicization of economic policy, 160–65; view of economic policy, 169–75; struggle for effective administration, 171–74; argument for managerial rights, 171–72; risk and, 174–75; investment theory and, 192–93; basis for cooperation with political management, 194; criticism of U.S. economic system, 197–98; to review functioning of government, 199–200; desire for continuity in government management, 200–201; constitutional constraints on, 201–3; laws of forums, 220–24; sunshine, 244–45; accountability of, 256–57; merits of difference from political management, 259–60; virtues of, 260–62; vicious circle of false expectations, 261–62; diagnosis of issues in, 270–71; proper blend with political management, 273–74
television industry, 186–87, 204
Texas Instruments (TI), 27–28, 97, 104, 174, 230; technocratic management of, 92–97; OST system, 93–96; TAP, 94
Thatcher, Margaret, 189
Thomson, James, 19
Thurow, Lester, 160, 178
Timex, 184, 188
tobacco industry, 177, 239–41
Tobacco Research Council, 240–41
Townsend, Lynn, 74–75, 82
toxic pollution, 156–58, 236–38
Toxic Substances Control Act of 1976, 156–58, 231
Toyota, 137
Trade Act of 1979, 251
Trade Policy Committee, 118
trade wars, 6

tripartite negotiations, 216–17, 235–36
Tsongas, Paul, 34
Twin Cities Metropolitan Council (Minneapolis/St. Paul), 231, 234, 250–51

Underwood Typewriter Company, 22
unemployment, 4, 223; Japanese vs. U.S., 195
unions, 80, 135, 137; federal employee, 73–74
United Auto Workers (UAW), 80, 135, 137
United Kingdom: motorcycle industry, 187; deindustrialization of, 189
United States: in the world economy, 5–6; political system of, 86–88; growth per annum, compared with Japan, 195; economic model, compared with Japan, 204–17; *see also* Congress; economic policy; federal government; government; presidency
U.S. Border Management Service, 72
U.S. Coast Guard, 69
U.S. Constitution. *See* Constitution
U.S. Customs Service, 68, 69, 70, 85
U.S. International Trade Commission, 140
U.S. Postal Service, 262
U.S. Steel, 140
universities, future of private, 65
University of Pennsylvania, Wharton School of Finance and Commerce, conference (1981), 168
urban decay, 262
urban renewal, 120
Ushiro, Masatake, 208–9, 212
utilities, 151

Vanderslice, Thomas A., 108–9
veto, legislative, 153–59
Vietnam War, 104, 160, 204, 208
Vietor, Richard, 241
visa policy (U.S.), 28–29, 38
Vogel, Ezra, 211, 215, 216, 249, 257
Volkswagen, 136

voluntary confederation, 235–36; *see also* overlay organizations
Voluntary Restraint Agreement, 141
Volvo, 136

Wage Index/Consumer Price Index, U.S. vs. Japanese, 195
Ward, Benjamin, 53–59, 83, 221–22
watch industry, 184, 188, 204
Watson, Arthur, 47–48, 49, 122, 123
Watson, Thomas J., Jr., 23, 47, 49–50, 83, 203
Waxman, Henry, 79
Weinberger, Caspar, 106–7

Welch, Jack, 271
welfare reform, 98
Wellford, Harrison, 71, 73
West Germany, 134, 141, 235, 236, 253
Whitehead, Alfred N., 49
White House, organizing the, 104–13
Whitten, Jamie, 24
Williams, Albert L., 50
Williams, Richard, 70
Wise, Thomas, 46
Wolfe, Alan, 251

Zenith, 186–87

DATE DUE

DEC 15 1987